Guerrilla Publicity

Hundreds of sure-fire tactics to
get maximum sales for minimum dollars

by Jay Conrad Levinson, Rick Frishman,
and Jill Lublin
with Mark Steisel

Adams Media Corporation
Avon, Massachusetts

Praise for *Guerrilla Publicity*

"*Guerrilla Publicity* is loaded with easily implemented, practical ideas. They work! I know, because I've successfully tried several of them with my books."

—Dr. Tony Alessandra, author, *The Platinum Rule* and *Charisma*

"Seldom in life do you get a chance to learn from a real guru. Consider this book such an opportunity. Rick doesn't know book publicity—he INVENTED it!"

—Bill Catlette, speaker and coauthor, *Contented Cows Give Better Milk*

"Do Rick's 'Guerrilla' strategies work? He helped me, an unknown at the time, become a *Times* bestselling author. You can take this book to the bank!"

—Denis Waitley, author, *Seeds of Greatness*

"Publicity today—the battle for minds—is warfare with new rules. Jay Conrad Levinson has written THE must-read rule book for winning and surviving the publicity war."

—Shad Helmstetter, Ph.D., million-copy-selling author of eleven books, including *What to Say When You Talk to Your Self*

"This book teaches the publicity and marketing tools every business person needs to know today."

—Dr. John Gray, author of *Men Are from Mars, Women Are from Venus*

"This book is packed with publicity instructions, checklists, clever ideas and inspiration. It explodes with the authors' energy, enthusiasm, tenacity and brilliance. Whatever your product or service, these authors show you how to give it what it deserves: media coverage and money."

—Dan Poynter, author, *The Self-Publishing Manual*

"Rick Frishman's advice has been pure gold to my career. In *Guerrilla Publicity*, Rick draws from his many years of advising some of the most well-known names in the business. If selling your product is import to you, read this book!"

—Max Davis, author, *It's Only a Flat Tire in the Rain* and *Never Stick Your Tongue Out At Mama*

"Rick Frishman brings his wealth of knowledge and experience to his latest book, *Guerrilla Publicity: Hundreds of Sure-Fire Tactics to Get Maximum Sales for Minimum Dollars*. It's an indispensable source of information from one of the great public relations masters."

—Kenneth L. Browning, Entertainment Attorney, Browning, Jacobson & Klein, LLP, Beverly Hills, California

Praise for *Guerrilla Publicity*

"This dynamic book will help authors and everyone else to get attention in today's competitive marketplace."

—Sheree Bykofsky, literary agent and author

"Smart businesspeople disagree about many things—but they all agree that Jay Levinson is brilliant. If Jay says it, you should try it. *Guerrilla Publicity* is yet another example of his insight—cheap at any price."

—Seth Godin, author, *Survival Is Not Enough*

"In our personal development seminars at The Option Institute, one of the key principles we teach is being a 'force of nature'—knowing exactly what you want and taking thorough and persistent action to get it. *Guerrilla Publicity* is the entrepreneur's guide to being a promotional 'force of nature.' It explains exactly what to do and why to do it, plus it contains valuable resources to help you get there. What more could you want?"

—Barry Neil Kaufman, author, *Happiness Is a Choice*;
Director, The Option Institute

"This book is a clear, simple road map that shows you how to get publicity and do it on budget."

—Guy Kawasaki, CEO, Garage Technology Ventures

"Rick Frishman is one of the most expert PR people I know in gaining publicity for clients, particularly broadcast publicity. His new book shares decades of experience and is must reading for all PR pros."

—Jack O'Dwyer, Editor-in-Chief, O'Dwyer PR Publications

"Rick Frishman is, quite simply, one of the best of the best in the PR business. *Guerilla Publicity* is the perfect companion for any author or publisher who is dedicated to creating a major bestseller. You cannot afford *not* to read this book."

—Robin Sharma, author, *The Monk Who Sold His Ferrari;*
one of North America's top professional speakers

"Don't even think of going out into the publicity jungle without this book. You will be eaten alive. Whether you have a small company or are the CEO of a big one . . . *Guerrilla Publicity* will give you the tools you need get the job done!"

—Jack Canfield, coauthor, *Chicken Soup for the Soul* series;
CEO, Chicken Soup for the Soul Enterprises

"Shameless self-promotion works, and no one practices it better than Frishman and Levinson. This book is the perfect ABCs of PR. It's full of common sense and sage advice, which makes it a rarity in the PR world."

—Stephen P. Burgay, Senior Vice President of Corporate Communications,
John Hancock Financial Services, Inc.

Praise for *Guerrilla Publicity*

"As bestselling author of *Chicken Soup for the Soul*, I know how powerful publicity is. *Guerrilla Publicity* is a clear, simple road map that shows you how to get publicity and do it on a budget."

—Mark Victor Hansen, cocreator, #1 *New York Times*
bestselling series *Chicken Soup for the Soul*

"With *Guerilla Publicity,* Rick Frishman and Jay Conrad Levinson offer everything you need to know to get free media exposure and use it as a goal-oriented, razor-sharp strategy for getting ahead and stranding the competition."

—William Parkhurst, author, *How to Get Publicity*

"*Guerrilla Publicity* is a great tool for anyone looking to understand—and tap into—the power of publicity."

—Jim McCann, CEO, 1-800-FLOWERS.COM

"There are very few people who understand the art of publicity as well as Rick Frishman does. In fact . . . I don't think anyone understands publicity as well as Rick!"

—Steven Schragis, Executive Director, The Learning Annex

"For a long time I've felt that generating good publicity is the last stronghold of amateurism. Not any more. In *Guerrilla Publicity* we get the zip zap, 24/7, 'this-really-works' news from the real pros. Buy it. Use it. Take it to the bank."

—Louis Patler, President, The B.I.T. Group; author, *Don't Compete . . .
TILT the Field!* and *If It Ain't Broke . . . BREAK IT!"*

"Having been in the Public Relation's profession for over twenty years, I definitely know what works. My best advice is if you want to succeed, then read this book. These seasoned authors give you a step-by-step plan. Don't wait another second if you want to sell books!"

—Robyn Freedman Spizman, co-owner of The Spizman Agency,
Atlanta, Georgia; Consumer Advocate; author of sixty-eight books,
including *When Words Matter Most* and *300 Incredible
Things on the Internet* with Ken Leebow

"Rick's charisma and innovative ideas will help any author or business person get their message across."

—Nancy-Gay Rotstein, author, *Shattering Glass*

Praise for *Guerrilla Publicity*

"In my twenty-five years of promoting my books and programs, I attribute some of my biggest successes to great publicity. This book captures the wealth of information needed to make any book, product, or program a best-seller through publicity!"

—Robert G. Allen, author of *New York Times* bestsellers
Nothing Down, Creating Wealth, Multiple Streams of Income,
Multiple Streams of Internet Income,
and coauthor of *One Minute Millionaire*

"When it comes to PR, Rick Frishman is as good as it gets. Read this book. Imbibe this book. Devour this book. It could help make you a star."

—Joel Roberts, Media Coach and Strategist;
Former Prime Time Host, KABC Radio, Los Angeles

"Rick's book contains great information for anyone who wants to promote themselves or their product."

—Amy Weintraub, Creator/Producer, BABY SONGS videos & audios

"*Guerrilla Publicity* is a great nuts-and-bolts guide with plenty of useful advice. I think it's going to be my favorite guide for publicity."

—John Kremer, author, *1001 Ways to Market Your Books*

"Rick Frishman has helped bring the story of our ministry to America."

—Rev. Robert H. Schuller, host, "The Hour of Power"

"With *Guerrilla Publicity,* the argument "but I can't afford a publicity campaign" is lost forever. This book makes achieving great exposure possible for anyone, anywhere."

—Jennifer Kushell, author, *The Young Entrepreneur's Edge*;
President, Young & Successful Media Corp.

"*Guerrilla Publicity* will rocket your career. The hundreds of strategies and secrets can help anyone in any profession acquire the success that they dream of. Buy this book immediately and get started."

—Harvey Mackay, *New York Times* bestselling author
of *Swim with the Sharks Without Being Eaten Alive*
and *Pushing the Envelope All the Way to the Top*

Published by
Adams Media Corporation
57 Littlefield Street, Avon, MA 02322 U.S.A.
www.adamsmedia.com

ISBN: 1-58062-682-3

Printed in Canada.

J I H G F E D C B A

Levinson, Jay Conrad.
　　Guerrilla publicity : hundreds of sure-fire tactics to get maximum
sales for minimum dollars / by Jay Conrad Levinson, Rick Frishman,
and Jill Lublin with Mark Steisel.
　　p. cm.
　　Includes bibliographical references and index.
　　ISBN 1-58062-682-3
　　1. Industrial publicity. 2. Advertising. 3. Marketing. I. Frishman,
Rick, 1954- II. Lublin, Jill. III. Title.
　　HD59 .L485 2002
　　659--dc21

This book is available at quantity discounts for bulk purchases.
For information, call 1-800-872-5627.

⊙ CONTENTS

Introduction xiii

1. Put Yourself on the Map 1

2. Introduce Yourself with a Sound Bite 11

3. Build Your Campaign from the Inside Out 19

4. Build Relationships to Build Empires 23

5. Eat, Sleep, and Breathe Publicity 29

6. Build Your Marketing Plan Around Publicity 33

7. Zero In on Your Market—Save Time,

    Money, and Aggravation 41

8. Come from the Heart 47

9. Press Releases: Grab 'Em Fast and Don't Let Go 51

10. Media Lists: Play the Numbers Game 57

11. Follow Up, Follow Up, Follow Up 65

12. Media Kits—Guerrilla Style 77

13. Fifteen Things the Media Hates 87

14. Fifteen Things the Media Loves 93

15. Find Your Uniqueness and Capitalize On It 99

16. Promote Early, Forcefully, and Fast 111

17. Always Be Too Prepared for an Interview 115

18. Keep Up to Date! 125

18. Think "Headlines" 129

20. Participate in Special Events 135

21. Get Others to Spread the Word 141

22 Make Friends in the Media 147

23. Design a Seminar 153

24. Get Published 161

25. Prepare for the Unpleasant 169

26. Crisis Control—Confront Disasters and
    Turn Them Around 177

27. Grow Your Business with a Web Site 181

28. Research the Information Superhighway 197

29. Join Internet Communities 203

30. Online Publicity Strategies 209

31. In Praise of E-Mail 217

32. Growing Pains—How to Hire the Right PR People . . 225

33. Summing Up 233

    Appendix A: Sample Materials 237

    Appendix B: Resource Directory 285

    Index 293

⊙ DEDICATIONS

To God, who makes my life and light possible. May I always spread great messages to make a difference in the world. I am grateful for all your blessings.

—Jill Lublin

To my wife Robbi, with love and thanks.

—Rick Frishman

⊙ ACKNOWLEDGMENTS

I so appreciate my coauthors—Rick Frishman, a wonderful colleague, and Jay Levinson, always a kind and loyal supporter. I acknowledge with deep appreciation the efforts and superb work of Mark Steisel, who stood by this project no matter what obstacles we encountered.

Thanks to the super people at Adams Media—Jill Alexander, our patient and terrific editor; Gary Krebs; and Bob Adams. Thank you for making this happen! Carrie McGraw, thank you for publicizing the publicists. Thanks also to Michael Larsen and Elizabeth Pomada, whose friendship and literary services have been invaluable on my career path.

I appreciate, love, and acknowledge my parents, Rose Wolfenson and Seymour Lublin. Thank you for birthing and loving me into the person I am.

Steve Lillo—a partner beyond my dreams—your continuous, unending, unconditional love and support provide a rock solid foundation for my life.

I also want to acknowledge the varied contributions of so many colleagues, mentors, and friends. Thank you one and all:

- Patricia and Vern McDade, the creators of the Entrepreneurial Edge who taught me possibility with a capital P. I thank you and bless you for your teaching. I also want to acknowledge your outrageously committed staff and incredible coaches: Susan James, Mike Altman, K. Marie Lim, Lauretta Hayes, Kim Altman, Caryn Condon, Susan Harmon, Barbara Loebel, Robert Oppenheimer, Bill Rogers, Yvonne Teruya, Ralph White, Michele-Joy DelRe, and the whole family of community and colleagues who have enriched my life for many years.

- Income Builders International—the circle of angels, friends, and colleagues—particularly, Lynn Dohrmann, president, and Berny Dohrmann, founder, two visionaries committed to growing dreams and businesses. Also, Eliot Kahn, whose great service provides so much value to so many.
- Mark LeBlanc, whose unwavering brilliant advice and sweet heart has contributed greatly to my life and success.
- To the staff at Promising Promotion, past and present, who have contributed their support, dedication, and commitment
- Michelle Rochwarger—a dear friend whose profound business advice and friendship has meant the world.
- My amazing friends and family who bring such support, heart, joy, direction, advice, spirit, and sweetness into my life: Randy Peyser, Carol Kramer, Jeff Herzbach, Roseanne Roda, Hollis Polk, Marjorie Stark, Vince Delgado, Carol Heller Frank, Jessica Heller Frank, Steve Lublin and family, Jack Lublin, Lynn Fox and family, Caterina Rando, Francine Ward, Dr. Susan Van De Bittner, Ted Wunderlich, Victoria Schwarz, Shaari Kamil, Roe Regan, Gloria Wilcox, Tina Varela, Rabbi Chaim Ohel, Hannah Seelig, Camille Kurtz, and all my other angels, both visible and invisible.

—Jill Lublin

The first thank-you goes to my wonderful coauthors, Jay and Jill. Mark Steisel, your help and wisdom have been invaluable. Working with all of you has been a joy.

Thank you to our super editor at Adams Media, Jill Alexander, and to Gary Krebs and, of course, the man who made this happen—Bob Adams. Thank you, Carrie McGraw, publicity guru at Adams, and Brian Feinblum of Planned Television Arts for all their hard work. And to my friends and agents Michael Larsen and Elizabeth Pomada—thank you for all of your help.

I especially want to acknowledge Mike (Manny) Levine, who founded Planned Television Arts in 1962 and was my mentor and partner for over eighteen years. Mike taught me that work has to be fun and meaningful and then the profits will follow.

Thank you also to the many friends and colleagues:

- To my exceptional management team at PTA Hillary Rivman, David Hahn, David Thalberg, and Margaret McAllister, your professionalism, loyalty, and friendship means more to me than you will ever know. To the staff of PTA—you are the best in the business.
- To David and Peter Finn, Tony Esposito, Richard Funess, and all of my colleagues at Ruder Finn, it is an honor to be part of this amazing company.
- To my friends Mark Victor Hansen and Jack Canfield— making the journey with the two of you has been incredible, and your friendship and advice has been invaluable.
- To Harvey Mackay, for the lessons about networking and for your amazing support; you are in a class of your own.
- To my mother and father—for keeping me out of the fur business and helping me discover my own destiny. And to my brother Scott, for being such a great golf buddy— because he sometimes lets me win.
- To my children Adam, Rachel, and Stephanie: Watching you grow into fine young individuals is the highlight of my life. And to my wife Robbi—you are my strength.

—Rick Frishman

Introduction

MANY PEOPLE HAVE GREAT IDEAS, but never take the next step to turn those ideas into viable businesses. Perhaps they don't know what the next step is or discovered that the next step was more of a hurdle than a step. Well, this book will help you identify the next step and surmount the hurdles you encounter. It will teach you about publicity and give you concrete ways to publicize your product or service.

Publicity is the most overlooked marketing tool, but it can be the least expensive, least risky, and most effective and easiest to use—when you understand it and how to use it.

Most people don't know the value of publicity to their businesses or how to implement it. *Guerrilla Publicity* will show you the light!

What do we mean by guerrillas? In a nutshell, guerrillas are business operators who substitute time, energy, and imagination for money. Unlike traditional marketing, which is geared to big businesses, guerrilla marketing is targeted to operators of small businesses who have big dreams rather than big bankrolls. Guerrillas measure their performance on profits, not sales; they place primary importance on how many relationships they build, not on how many dollars they take in. Guerrilla entrepreneurs know that the journey is the goal and they are not in a hurry.

Publicity is perfect for guerrillas because:

- Publicity provides the widest exposure for the fewest bucks—far less than advertising.
- Publicity lets guerrillas tell their story in greater depth, which is crucial for new and unique enterprises.
- Publicity gives guerrillas credibility sooner because, unlike advertising, people believe information reported as news.
- Publicity is ideal for the Internet, which feeds on original content.

Most guerrillas don't use publicity because they think it's too expensive, too complicated, too time consuming, and that it requires special expertise, staff, and resources. However, they fail to realize that the media is a voracious giant that constantly devours information. Information is the media's lifeblood. It needs information to survive, tons of information! The media craves original items and is as eager to tell guerrillas' stories as guerrillas are to get the publicity.

For example, every issue of magazines as diverse as *Food and Wine, New York,* and *Wired*, to name a few, need items on new and innovative products and services for their "Best Bets" sections. A "Best Bet" listing can assure a product or service's success, but most guerrillas have no inkling of how to get this coverage.

Publicity, Public Relations, and Advertising

For the purposes of this book, publicity is getting free media exposure for your product or service.

Publicity is the art of building favorable interest in your product or service. It's creating a buzz, an identity, name recognition, and getting your message across. Publicity is a part of public relations.

Public relations (PR) is the overall planning, approach, and strategy for dealing with the media. While PR encompasses publicity, it goes beyond merely publicizing your product or service. It includes such disciplines as crisis control. For example, you would use PR to minimize the negative impact of a business disaster, such as the *Exxon Valdez* oil spill or the unintentional distribution of defective products.

Advertising is paying to promote your product or service. "With advertising, you pay for it; with publicity your pray for it," according to an old adage. Advertising can also get you publicity.

Public relations is human relations. It's how you interact with and represent yourself to the world. PR begins as soon as you meet or are seen by others. It's virtually a full-time job that starts the moment you walk out your door each morning and continues until you say your last "good nights."

PR isn't merely getting your name in the paper or appearing on radio or TV. It's about how you're perceived by others—how they see and react to you. It's about how you treat your clients, employees, and suppliers. It's how your receptionist answers the phone and how your staff represents you.

There is no such thing as private relations!

The Internet

Recently, publicity has changed dramatically. The Internet has become the publicist's major tool and is vital in promoting your product or service. Therefore, in writing this book, we consulted with leading Internet experts and devoted several chapters to the Internet and e-mail and the role they can play in getting publicity.

Let Us Know

Publicity can change your life; it certainly can change your business. So, sit back and enjoy this book. When you've completed it, please feel free to contact us at our Web site *www. guerrillapublicity.com* with your comments, suggestions, and personal experiences.

Thanks and enjoy this book!

1
Put Yourself on the Map

Master showman PT Barnum put it best:

"A terrible thing happens without publicity . . . NOTHING!"

PUBLICITY IS THE ART OF STIRRING UP INTEREST to promote your product or service. It's convincing others to sing your praises, to blare from the rooftops:

Who you are
What you do
Why it's important

Publicity . . .

- Builds your identity
- Increases your visibility
- Creates name recognition
- Gets your message across
- Compels people to buy, invest, and do business with you

Publicity is the art of putting yourself in the spotlight. As you know, spotlights are narrowly focused, they don't shine on everyone. Spotlights illuminate only those who work their way onto center stage. To capture the spotlight you must place yourself in the proper position.

Positioning is an intricate process that takes time, trial, error, endless patience, and persistence. It's more than a one- or two-shot effort that produces wonders overnight. Positioning is a coordinated series of actions that requires explicit planning, devotion to detail, and endless follow up. That's why they are called publicity *campaigns*.

 **GUERRILLA TACTICS**

In publicity, rule number one is *honk your own horn!*

- If you don't tell the world how great you are, no one else will.
- If you don't blow your horn, others will beat you over the head with it.
- If you don't assert yourself, the more aggressive people will cut in front of you and block your path, and you'll end up stuck in line, and you'll never get ahead.

So toot, toot, toot to everyone you speak with, write to, or meet. Become a one-man/woman self-advertising agency; promote yourself. Tell them all who you are, exactly what you have to offer, and how it can benefit them.

If the public doesn't hear about you or your product or service, as Barnum pointed out, *nothing* will happen.

You Are the Product

Guerrillas know that regardless of what product you produce or service you provide, you are the product. You are always selling yourself! And selling yourself is a full-time job. When you repeatedly sell yourself, you build name recognition, which will increase your business because consumers are drawn to names they know. So, your object is to make yourself known, build your name recognition, and increase your profits.

The importance of name recognition is best illustrated by celebrities. "The celebrity is a person who is known for his well-knownness," said Daniel J. Boorstein, social historian and author. Today, the world is celebrity-obsessed. Consumers insist on wearing clothing designed by celebrities, reading books written by celebrities, and eating in restaurants owned by and/or frequented by celebrities. The public eagerly spends lavishly on articles used, endorsed, or signed by their heroes.

Being a celebrity puts you on the map. It gives you a big edge in business because name recognition translates into hard currency, greenbacks, moolah, lots of money. Publicity is a time-tested method of making you a star.

People trust the familiar, even when they're not sure why it feels familiar or even exactly what it is. They find the comfort of familiarity safer than the discomfort of the unknown. People yearn to be associated with what seems familiar. The feeling of familiarity somehow elevates them, gives them status and makes them feel better about themselves. When your name first appears in the papers, on TV, or on the Internet, the public starts to take notice and becomes aware of you. In the beginning it's the I've-heard-of-her-somewhere syndrome. They become curious. "Who is she? What does she do? Why do I always hear her name?" As they get answers, you gain name recognition.

Name recognition isn't simply people's knowing who you are; it's also their knowing what you do. They associate your name with your product or service. When you gain name recognition, the public thinks of you when they want your product or service. They will stand in line to do business with you.

 **GUERRILLA TACTICS**

To get on the map, start modestly. Don't think hemispheres, think townships, unincorporated villages, or little country lanes.

- Begin by working your street and when it's saturated, branch out to your neighborhood, town, county, state, country, and continent. Spread the word. Tell everyone you know and everyone you come in contact with who you are, what you do, and how you can benefit them.
- Don't overlook anyone. You never know who might help. Start with the people you know best, your immediate family and then friends, neighbors, clergy, and your dentist. Speak with the folks who run the pharmacy, the tailor shop, and the car wash. If they can't use your product or service, ask them who they know who could.
- To expand your contacts, join clubs and organizations. Increase your visibility by volunteering, teaching, coaching, and serving on committees. Write articles or submit items about your business or interests to local publications such as free weekly newspapers, advertisers, newsletters, or Web sites. Write and publish a newsletter or organize and lead a workshop. Discover what the media is covering and cultivate journalists, editors, and radio and TV producers.

Position Yourself as an Expert

You're an expert, even though you may not think you are. If you operate a business, you're probably an expert in your field.

Professional expertise simply means that you know what you're doing. It doesn't necessarily mean that you're the world's foremost authority, although you may be. It also doesn't mean that you know absolutely everything about your field. No one does!

Besides your professional expertise, you're also an expert in a number of other facets of your life. For example, you may be a single mother, in business as a married couple, a soccer coach, or a

den mother; you may be skilled in growing roses, operatir
based office, canoeing, or living gracefully; or you may
bling in yodeling, taking photographs, or canning peache
activities are examples of what we call "personal expertise."

GUERRILLA INTELLIGENCE

Expertise has a way of sneaking up on us. We start with
little and before long, we've acquired a storehouse of
knowledge and know-how. Mastery of our chosen path
is one of life's immense pleasures. Think for a moment
about how much you know about what you do, how
long it has taken you to learn it, and how helpful it is to
others. It's a significant accomplishment. Let's call this
"professional expertise."

In most cases, professional expertise is what we sell, it's our
basic product. You may have developed innovative approaches,
breakthrough techniques, or simplified complex methods that
opened up broader markets.

Although professional expertise is usually our primary expertise, personal expertise enhances professional expertise by adding
special flavors that make it unique. Personal expertise places our
special stamp on our work and filters how we see it. The combina-
tion of your professional and personal expertise creates the perspective that makes your approaches special, original, and insightful.

 ## GUERRILLA TACTICS

Proclaim that you're an expert. Declare that you have knowledge
that others can use and tell them why it's special. Establish your
expertise by giving it away.

- Write articles.
- Give talks.
- Give demonstrations.
- Start a Web site.

- Participate in conferences and panel discussions.
- Volunteer your services to show your expertise.

Write or talk about tasks that you've performed a thousand times, for example, how to bid at auctions, bet on professional football, or buy a healthy puppy. Teach others, step by step, how to do it.

Write articles—prepare two written versions, one 1,500 words and the other 800 words. Be ready to recite them at all times. Always have copies of both articles on hand to distribute.

Keep your articles simple; don't try to state everything you know. Include no more than seven points and no less than three. Make your articles practical, not theoretical, such as, "How to Write the Perfect One-page Resume," "Five Steps to Larger Insurance Settlements," "Gorgeous Wedding Photographs at Lower Costs."

Send your articles to publications, organizations, and Web sites in your field or related fields. Send them to writers and reporters and follow them up with e-mails or phone calls. Offer your availability as an expert. Recite your article aloud as a speech. Prepare visual aids such as slides, illustrations, and charts. Practice them on your family and pals.

 **GUERRILLA TALE**

When your professional expertise is in a specialized niche, inform the media. A therapist who specialized in issues with people over forty became a media darling after he submitted an article on midlife crises to a local TV station. The station aired a feature on him and began consulting him when it needed information on the over-forty generation. Soon major TV news organizations came calling. He became a frequently interviewed and quoted national authority.

When you write articles, include a biographical sketch at the end that states who you are, what you do, what makes you special, and how you can be reached. Prepare a more extensive biographical statement to distribute at speaking engagements.

Testimonials

 **GUERRILLA TALE**

After hearing a new artist's recording, a consumer wrote the record company, "This is what my heart would sound like if it was a symphony." Viola! The company pounced on the phrase and plastered it on all its materials for a promotional campaign that helped the recording go platinum.

Testimonials help build your credibility, so gather them diligently. Leave no stone unturned. Use the following guidelines for securing testimonials:

- Get in the habit of asking every client or customer for letters of praise.
- Ask them to state how great your work was and how much they enjoyed working with you. You'll be surprised how highly they extol you and how wonderfully they express it.
- Ask for endorsements during the first thirty to sixty days or as soon as short-term projects are complete.
- Ask your clients or customers to write the testimonials on their stationery and limit them to one or two paragraphs.
- Accumulate endorsements. Build your own personal collection; they're invaluable for getting business.
- Explain to clients or customers that you plan to post the testimonials on your newsletter, Web site, and in promotional materials.
- Point out to your clients or customers that the testimonials could help them increase their own visibility.

If clients hesitate, offer to prepare drafts for their approval.

Update Web sites regularly to add recent testimonials and delete dated ones. However, you may want to continue to run a few dated testimonials because they attest that you have a long track record of customer satisfaction.

Switching Gears

"Sacred cows make the best hamburger."
—MARK TWAIN

When it comes to publicity, the fact that the media is interested is more important that the reason for their interest. So, don't get lofty or feel that a reporter's approach is beneath you. Make the most of it, as much as it may hurt; grin and bear it. Publicity can be humbling, but it's still publicity that can work to your advantage.

When the media seizes upon angles that you're not pushing, it's usually better to adjust and be their resource than to fight for your own agenda. Many roads can lead to your destination. So, get whatever publicity you can or else you may find yourself alienating the press and ending up with nothing.

 **GUERRILLA TALE**

A cancer survivor's press releases promoted her new clothing line. The media that picked up her story concentrated on her medical triumph rather than her designs. Instead of throwing in the towel when her clothing line wasn't featured, the designer adjusted. To remain in the limelight, she kept in contact with the media as a cancer survival expert. She kept them posted on developments, sent them information, and when questions arose, she quickly responded. She also actively promoted her clothing line. She always mentioned it when she spoke to the media. Within a few months, the press began referring to her as the cancer-surviving clothing designer and soon ran separate features on her design business.

If the media isn't interested in covering your business-writing service, switch gears to get their attention. Pitch them on the fact that you build replicas of famous buildings using toothpicks, that you can simultaneously play three string instruments, or that you were a Navy SEAL.

GUERRILLA TACTICS

Successful sales people lug around a bushel full of products in their sample cases. If one item doesn't sell, they move on to the next. When you approach the media, have backups and if they don't bite on your first pitch, pitch them your backup. If they show any interest in your backup, go with it; give them what they want. Then pitch your initial item after you've built a more solid media relationship, or when they owe you a favor.

Be Persistent

To succeed, guerrillas must be persistent. They must learn to over-come rejections, lack of interest, and fierce competition. In the face of rudeness, guerrillas must plaster an enormous smile across their faces and keep politely plugging, plugging, plugging. They must remain in the game until the very end, until the last salvo is fired. To make it work, the quest for publicity must be more than a campaign; it must be a personal crusade.

Publicity is a cumulative process built on repeated efforts. When you contact radio or TV producers, chances are they won't bite. Persistence is the key—staying in the game—because you never know when they might need you. A media contact may not respond to your first contact, but may phone you back after your sixth, tenth, or twentieth call.

Remember

Position yourself for promotional opportunities. You're the product, so honk your own horn. Build name recognition and pro-claim that you're an expert. Tell people that you have knowledge that they can use and explain why it's special. Obtain testimonials from your customers or clients. Be persistent and always keep the door open!

2
Introduce Yourself with a Sound Bite

"The short words are best, and the old words are the best of all."
—WINSTON CHURCHILL

LIKE IT OR NOT, WE LIVE IN A WORLD OF SOUND BITES. These days, no one has time to listen to the full story. People want a synopsis, a digest, a capsule of information delivered in a few seconds that is easy to swallow and switches on their mental light bulb. So if you get an opening, you better make good! You better be ready to say what you mean quickly, clearly, and compellingly.

You must be able to deliver your sound bite—your message that tells people who you are, what you do, and how your product or service can help them—in less than thirty seconds. For television or radio cut it down to ten or fifteen seconds. Radio news segments come in ten-second increments. "If you can't express what you want and why it's newsworthy in ten seconds, you're off the phone," advised a news director for a major NBC affiliate.

The more succinct you make your statement, the better your sound bite will be, and the more likely that it will make an impression on your listeners.

GUERRILLA TACTICS

ose of a sound bite is to catch your listeners' attention. It's a verbal business card to deliver when you're introduced to new people. Your sound bite is your "elevator speech," a snappy self-description that you can rattle off in the time it takes an elevator to rise from the lobby to the fifth floor.

As theatrical impresario David Belasco said, "If you can't write your idea on the back of my calling card, you don't have a clear idea." A sound bite is the foundation on which to build a forceful and memorable public persona. It's the first impression you make, an attention-grabbing device that will get you and your message noticed and remembered. Think of it as money because every time you use it, someone considers paying you.

ABCs of Sound Bites

Your sound bite must be a grabber, a memorable message that makes listeners want to buy your products, champion your causes, and fight your wars. If it's short and gets their attention, it buys you more time to sell. Your sound bite must be interesting enough to attract immediate attention, powerful enough to be remembered, and convincing enough to stir overloaded listeners into action.

In thirty seconds or less, your sound bite must explain: (1) who you are, (2) what you represent, and (3) why you make a difference.

The following are examples of a variety of effective sound bites:

- "I used to weigh over 300 pounds. Now, I'm a size 8. I can teach you how to lose weight and keep it off."

  —diet book author
- "I teach people to look rich, even if they aren't."

  —fashion advisor

- "I'm the James Bond for the new millennium. I make computers secure, detect break-ins, and restore lost data."

  —computer security expert

- "I'm a recovering parent of teenage children. I repair lives with ten-minute phone counseling consultations."

  —psychological counselor

- "My name is _____. My free tips on *www._____.com* make investors rich from Internet stocks."

  —investment broker

- "I'm a ghost writer. I'll turn your experiences, adventures, and ideas into books."—freelance writer

- "I train your brain and set your imagination free."

  —biofeedback instructor

- "My name is _____. I free folks from financial worry. Give me a call and I'll do the same for you."

  —financial consultant

Most people aren't accustomed to promoting themselves. So when it's time to blow their own horns, they don't know what to say, and what they do say is either understated and ineffective or overstated and offensive. However, in business, with so many competitive businesses vying for the same dollars, you must distinguish yourself from the crowd. The best way to start is with a carefully crafted sound bite.

How to Conduct Research for Your Sound Bite Checklist

Be creative. Determine which of your unique qualities can make you a star or what features of your product or service are novel or groundbreaking. In our celebrity-obsessed society, the media desperately seeks new faces. It loves to splash their names in headlines, tell the world their stories, and ride their coattails to fortune and fame. Write a sound bite that will captivate the media, show them your star potential, and make them want to move mountains to advance your career.

 ## GUERRILLA TACTICS

Research recent publicity phenomena to determine what types of information intrigue the media. Ask yourself what drew the media to Darva Conger, Elian Gonzalez, and Richard Hatch? What elements conspired to transform people we never heard of into household names? Isolate what these stories had in common and why they captured and held the publics' attention. Then examine which of the common threads you can weave into your sound bite.

Before creating your sound bite, take time to answer the following questions:

- What's most interesting or unusual about you and your work? What makes it memorable?
- How did you get into this career?
- What excites you most about your career?
- What are your strengths?
- What do you provide your clients or customers?
- How do you satisfy your clients or customers?
- What motivates you?
- What's on your drawing board?
- How do people first respond when you tell them about yourself? What interests them most? What questions do they ask?
- What makes people stop, listen, or especially say "wow"?

In drafting your sound bite, write down the reasons why what you do is unique and/or unusual and why your target audience can't do without it. Identify what's special about your work and find the most colorful words to describe it.

Since your sound bite serves as your verbal calling card, it must be an attention-grabbing introduction. Incorporate your sound bite into letters, mailers, announcements, brochures, ads, Internet chat rooms, forms, questionnaires, and applications.

How to Write Your Sound Bite

First, write whatever comes to mind without worrying how long it runs or how much space it occupies. Be honest and truthful, but approach it from the rosy side. Take your time, this isn't a race. When you finish, circle every descriptive word that you've written. Then list each circled word on a separate sheet of paper. Next, place the words you've listed in the order of their importance. Review each word. Ask whether the words you selected are the most descriptive and colorful words available. If not, add or substitute more hard-hitting words.

Draft a sound bite consisting of one or two sentences. Begin with, and give prominence to, the most important words on your list. Although your sound bite should clearly and cleverly communicate your message, clarity is paramount. Don't sacrifice clarity for cleverness.

Read the completed sound bite aloud several times and change whatever sounds awkward. Trust your ear. Read your sound bite to others to get their input. Consider making changes they suggest.

Recite the sound bite out loud until you believe it and feel comfortable delivering it. When you believe your sound bite, others will also. You'll also sound more confident and convincing.

Time how long your sound bite runs. If it's more than thirty seconds, cut it so that it is thirty seconds or less. After you've whittled it to less than thirty seconds, try to cut another ten to fifteen seconds without weakening the message. Don't memorize your sound bite, instead picture keywords and reel them off in order as if you're descending a ladder.

Practice your sound bite in front of the mirror, in your car, and in the shower. Audiotape and videotape yourself. Concentrate on looking sincere, enthusiastic, and confident, but don't overdo it. Don't act, emote, or be dramatic. Speak conversationally, with sincerity. Don't be a ham or a clown. Do be professional.

Practice, practice, practice—on your family, friends, pets, plants, and appliances. Leave strangers alone, they might have you arrested. When you deliver your sound bite, imagine that you are meeting the president, the pope, Steve Jobs, or Oprah. Practice with the notion that your business depends on your being booked on Oprah's show.

Delivering Your Message

When you give your sound bite, maintain eye contact and smile softly. Not some big, silly grin, but a warm smile that conveys confidence, assurance, and conviction. Show listeners that you're happy to deliver your message and that you believe in yourself and your message. Project your expert status by speaking with authority, excitement, and passion.

Excitement and passion are contagious. Your audiences will sense your conviction, feed off it, and want to share their feelings with others. Football immortal Vince Lombardi reportedly said, "If you're not fired with enthusiasm, you'll be fired with enthusiasm!"

 **GUERRILLA TACTICS**

Your sound bite needs to be appropriate in a wide variety of settings and situations, so plan ahead:

- Customize your sound bite for specific audiences and situations. For example, if you're speaking, exhibiting, or attending an auto dealers' meeting, sprinkle in terms relating to that industry like "on all cylinders," "out of gas," or "cruise control." Using their language breaks down barriers, lightens the mood, and makes groups feel that you're speaking directly to them. In doing so, you become one of them, at least for the time you're together.
- Prepare a backup sound bite. Be ready to ditch your standard spiel if it's inappropriate, if someone else in the group has a strikingly similar pitch, or if your sound bite doesn't seem to be going over.
- Prepare a list of ad-lib comments that you can throw in to

sound spontaneous. Remember, your main objective is to get your message across, so if altering your sound bite improves your chances, be sure to go for it.

• Trust your instincts. You'll quickly learn how and when to alter your sound bite and become adept at making changes based upon your instincts and observations. Work in references to hot news items, scandals, or events that will make your sound bite more relevant and up to date.

Repeat your sound bite at every opportunity. Always have a ton of business cards on hand to distribute with your pitch. If you have brochures or other business materials, hand them out liberally. Think of them as emissaries that will spread your message. Repetition reinforces name recognition, brand identity, and it builds confidence.

Remember

Create a memorable sound bite that will make people sit up and take immediate notice. Practice your sound bite until you can recite it naturally and with confidence. Always deliver your message with authority, excitement, and passion. Customize your sound bite for special occasions, and vary your pitch so that it seems to be spontaneous.

3
Build Your Campaign from the Inside Out

*"It takes a person who is wide awake
to make his dreams come true."*
—ROGER BABSON, INVESTMENT BANKER,
AUTHOR, AND EDUCATOR

GUERRILLA INTELLIGENCE

In business, results are the bottom line. Glamorous, exciting figures may initially get ink, but even the most high-profile personalities won't succeed in business if they can't get the job done. If the word gets out that you can't deliver, doors will slam in your face and it will become increasingly difficult, if not impossible, to sell yourself. At that point, people will no longer trust you. They won't listen to you, and if you hope to get back on top, you will have a long, steep, rocky hill to climb.

So, if you're not an expert, stop here and polish your skills before you go any further. Become an expert or you'll simply be wasting everyone's time!

PUBLICITY STARTS FROM WITHIN; it must emanate from you. You must be motivated, set your own course, and stick with it. To launch a successful publicity campaign, you must identify your objectives, plan how to achieve them, and have the ability to accomplish them. Never promise what you can't deliver! When you claim that you're an expert, you can't bluff! You must be able to deliver. You must know what it takes and be able to get the job done expertly.

Sing Your Own Praises

That being said, you're probably an expert already. The most obvious signs of expertise are that your customers or clients keep coming back, pay what you charge, recommend you to others, and that your peers consult you for advice and assistance. When you're an expert, capitalize on your achievements by:

- Positioning yourself as an expert.
- Explaining how your expertise can benefit target audiences.
- Delivering what you promise.

How you go about singing your own praises is tricky; it can be the difference between success and failure. Self-promotion, when done well, is a public service, but when done poorly, is offensive. No one wants to listen to obnoxious, self-serving boasting—it scares folks away.

It's not enough to tell others that you're an expert, you have to specifically explain how your product or service can benefit them. For example, "Hi, I'm Computer Cal and I can save you hundreds of dollars on the ideal system custom-built just for you."

 **GUERRILLA TACTICS**

Train yourself to spot opportunities, and when you see openings, pounce. Consider the following ways to turn regular situations into occasions to give your message:

- Opportunities won't just come knocking on your door; you have to make them happen! Have you ever wondered why some people are always so witty? It's because of their outlook and their focus. Humorous people are on a perpetual vigil, they're continually looking for the humor in every situation. They constantly search for openings for witty comments, observations, and jibes. They know how to lighten most situations with a joke. Top salespeople and politicians possess a similar talent. They excel at weaving information about their products and positions into the most remote, unrelated subjects.
- Ask all your friends for the names of people they know who might help you deliver your message. When you make new contacts ask them for the names of others who might help.
- Position yourself for opportunities by joining clubs, groups, and organizations where you can meet people and tell them who you are, what you do, and how it can help them. Go to bars, cafes, and restaurants where people in your industry or the media hang out.

Unexpected opportunities can occur any time and at any place, so be prepared to capitalize on them. You might be walking your dog, riding on the bus, or at a restaurant when you run into a reporter, a writer, or a producer. You never know when opportunity might strike. It's your job to be prepared to deliver your message, to sprinkle your seeds everywhere. Plan to go the distance. A publicity campaign is an ongoing process that never stops. Co-author Jill Lublin tells clients that, "V8 publicity—I should have done my publicity today" won't work. You can't be half-hearted. A successful publicity campaign builds on volume. It takes repeated efforts, over the long haul, to spread your message and tell the world who you are.

 **GUERRILLA TACTICS**

The call letters for radio station WIMF, "What's in it for me?" is the key concept to understanding what the media needs. When you're trying to sell writers, editors, and producers, they will want to know how your product or service will benefit them and their audience and how it's different, unique, or special. They want scoops and exclusives on stories with wide appeal.

Feed the media what they want. Explain precisely why your product or service is special and how it will interest their audience. Target your pitches. For example, if you're a CPA, approach business editors with your article on tips on how to hang onto money that the IRS usually gobbles up. If you're a landscaper, tell the garden show producer about your water-saving sprinkler system.

Your Staff

Use your staff to deliver your message. Set up an internal program to:

- Teach your sound bite to each staff member.
- Drill your staff until they know your sound bite cold.
- Create scripts for them to follow when they answer phones; greet clients, customers, or suppliers; attend trade shows; and otherwise interact with the public and the media.

Leave nothing to chance. Hold training sessions if you must. Distribute your sound bite to every staff member from your sales manager to your custodian. Provide incentives for successful efforts. Remember: your staff can be your best word-of-mouth!

Remember

Make sure that you are an expert on the product or service you're promoting. Never bluff! Continually tell the world that you're an expert and how you can help them. Learn to spot opportunities to toot your own horn and always be prepared to seize upon them. Enlist your friends and train your staff to deliver your message.

4
Build Relationships to Build Empires

"If I have seen farther than others, it is because
I was standing on the shoulders of giants."
—Isaac Newton

GUERRILLA INTELLIGENCE

When talking about building and maintaining long-term, ongoing relationships, think in terms of:

- Campaigns, not ads
- Careers, instead of jobs
- Decades, rather than days, months, or years

Remember that you're in business for the duration, not simply for a one-shot quickie. Develop media contacts that you can grow with, contacts that will evolve into invaluable sources in the future.

THE TERM "PUBLIC RELATIONS" consists of two words, "public" and "relations." Relationships are publicists' inventory, their stock in trade. Relationships are the most valuable assets in publicists' portfolios. Relationships are what publicists trade on.

From the moment you first contact the media, you're building new relationships. Generally, these relationships won't provide instant results, you must nurture them. They probably won't launch your career or even get your name in print, but building relationships is where you start.

Of course, building solid, long-term relationships takes time and effort. It's a slow, deliberate process, similar to erecting a brick wall. To build such a wall you must firmly and precisely place, align, adjust, and mortar one brick at a time, row after row, until the wall is completed. Unlike building a brick wall, however, the work on long-term relationships is never completed.

Every contact with the media is important, even calls that are intercepted by voice mail and aren't returned. Repeatedly leaving your message builds name recognition, it places you on their radar screen. After a few messages, strangers, who never knew that you existed, know who you are and why you're calling. And later, when they need what you have, they may call you.

Position Yourself

The media feeds on information. It devours massive amounts of content that must continually be replenished. It's a never-ending cycle. However, the media can't possibly generate all that content itself; so it relies on outside sources to supply material.

Become a resource by furnishing information to the media. Don't wait to be asked. Volunteer to become a member of their team. By offering your help, you can ease their burden, earn their gratitude, and, before long, they'll rely on you, be obligated to you, and help you out.

 **GUERRILLA TACTICS**

Take the "concierge approach" to building relationships with the media by offering them information, services, and access to your contacts. Become a full-service resource for the media:

- Ask people in the media for a list of the projects on their editorial calendars for the next thirty, sixty, or ninety days. Then offer to introduce them to sources who could help them and link them with those contacts. For example, if a journalist or a producer is working on a story about nursing homes, find out what information is needed to round it out. Give him or her the name of the former nursing home director you met at a seminar and offer to set up an interview.
- Call or e-mail media people when you read their stories or see or hear their features. Tell them how much you enjoyed their pieces and give them additional information and insights that could help with a follow-up story.

Always remember that the best way to get the media to write more about you or to invite you back on their programs is to help them reach their goals.

Extend Yourself

Take the extra step. Give the media more than they expect. Provide three sources, not just one. When faxing articles, research to uncover similar articles that they could use. Check out Web sites before you recommend them and visit related Web sites. Become the media's researcher, investigator, contact person, and colleague.

When speaking with media contacts, listen. Be sure that you understand exactly what they want. Ask directly what they need to complete their story. Then try to get it for them. Make an indelible impression by exceeding their expectations, by going beyond what's required and beyond what others will do.

For example, give the media statistics, sources, leads, and Web sites. Suggest story angles or approaches and be supportive. If a media contact is working on a story about nursing homes, call three or four people associated with nursing homes, find out what they can contribute, and ask if they would be willing to speak with your contact. By helping the media you'll be helped in return.

Personal Acts

Few things are appreciated more than personal acts—considerate gestures that aren't required or even expected. These acts can be as basic as a thank-you telephone call, e-mail, note, postcard, or even a small gift. Remember, it actually is the thought that counts, so keep it simple.

After making a new contact, send a handwritten nice-to-meet-you note. Always send thank-you notes for business referrals, and consider making a date to take these contacts to lunch or to an event of mutual interest. Act promptly, otherwise the full impact of your gesture might be lost.

In our world of busy schedules and brief e-mails, the fact that you've gone to the trouble to write a handwritten note will distinguish you. Don't be elaborate or go overboard. Simple notes or even postcards are usually enough. To make a grander statement, send flowers, a box of candy, a book, or a bottle of wine to show appreciation. If you're marketing an inexpensive product, send the product with a short handwritten note. Small efforts usually pay big dividends by:

- Keeping you and/or your product in your contact's mind.
- Portraying you as pleasant, considerate, and smart.
- Producing more referrals.
- Drawing you closer, which in turn allows you to identify and satisfy more of your contact's needs.

Rejections are inevitable, so make the most of them. What you're offering may not interest your target or it may not be special. You may be trying to sell flounder to a chef who needs turnips. Or, as Sigmund Freud said, "Sometimes a cigar is just a cigar."

Rejections can be opportunities. They can form the basis for future successes and can be building blocks for long-term relationships. After rejections, media contacts may remember your name, your courtesy and consideration, your professionalism, and your willingness to help. They may even remember where to turn if they need flounder.

 **GUERRILLA TALE**

A few years ago, coauthor Jill Lublin pitched an idea to a producer for a nationally syndicated cooking show that the producer didn't buy. After the rejection, Jill continued to call the producer each week, even though she didn't have anything to offer. She simply called to say hello and find out what the producer was working on. Most of the time, Jill got the producer's voice mail and just said, "Hi, this is Jill Lublin of Promising Promotion. I'm just calling to say hello. Hope all is well."

About a year and a half later, a client hired Jill to promote a video called "Cooking for Busy People." Jill immediately contacted the producer who loved the idea and booked Jill's client on the spot. After Jill's client appeared on the show, the orders for her video poured in. Sales went through the roof and her single appearance launched a thriving business—all because of Jill's persistence and her repeated calls to develop an invaluable media contact.

Remember

The media constantly needs information, so become a media supplier and a media resource. Feed the media information and hook them up with your sources. Become a part of their team—a media asset. Create and maintain favorable relations by sending follow-up notes after all media contacts. Try to turn rejections into solid relationships.

5
Eat, Sleep, and Breathe Publicity

"In this business, you can never wash the dinner dishes and say they are done. You have to keep doing them constantly."
—MARY WELLS LAWRENCE,
ADVERTISING LEGEND

GUERRILLA INTELLIGENCE

Publicity never sleeps, it's an ongoing, 24/7 process that never stops. Since you're the product, you're also your own best marketing tool. Publicity accompanies you everywhere. It extends well beyond the usual business settings. Even when you hire marketing or promotion professionals, you're still responsible for your own publicity.

Self-promotion is essential; you must become your own PR firm. You can't be shy or embarrassed, or rely on others to champion your cause. Look at the successful people you know. They quickly let everyone know who they are, what they do, and how important it is. Follow their lead. With practice, extolling your own virtues will become easier. And before you know it, it will be fun.

SELF-PROMOTION CONVEYS ENTHUSIASM; it shows your conviction and passion for your work. Enthusiasm is contagious. It inspires, excites, energizes, and makes people want to help you out. So give them the chance!

Increasing visibility and building name recognition requires repetition. Repetition makes the unfamiliar familiar. It breaks down barriers and opens doors. When your name and message become familiar, you gain credibility and you become a known commodity.

Opportunities

Learn to spot promotional opportunities and how to capitalize on them. Always be alert for openings that you can spin to your advantage, opportunities for you to sell yourself. At first, it may feel strained, uncomfortable, awkward, pushy, or overly aggressive. But before long, you'll develop a knack for when to jump in and when to back off.

 **GUERRILLA TACTICS**

When you meet people, take the opportunity to sell yourself:

- Tell them who you are.
- Tell them what you do.
- Tell them how your product or service can help them.
- Answer their questions.
- Ask if they know who could use your product or service.
- Ask if they know writers and people in the media who might cover your product, service, or industry.

Carry It with You

If you deal in a product, carry it with you. Take it everywhere, not simply obvious places, such as trade shows, conferences, and business meetings. Take it when you go to the store, to concerts, even to church. If it's too big to lug around, carry pictures that you can show easily.

 **GUERRILLA TALE**

On a flight from New York to Washington, D.C., coauthor Rick Frishman's client, Kurt Eichenwald, was holding in plain sight a copy of his book Serpent of the Rock: Crime, Betrayal, and the Terrible Secrets of Prudential-Bache. *Seated next to Kurt was a producer from* 60 Minutes. *They quickly struck up a conversation. The producer asked about Kurt's book and bingo, that's all it took—*60 Minutes *ran a full segment on Kurt and his book.*

So, even if it's a nuisance or inconvenience, always carry your products, brochures, and business cards with you. Make it a habit. Stuff them in your pockets, purses, or brief cases. Never pass up a chance to show them, explain them, and respond to all questions and comments.

 **GUERRILLA TACTICS**

Become a walking advertisement by wearing T-shirts, sweatshirts, or other apparel that advertises your product or service. Place your logo or pictures of your product on your computer case, attaché case, book bag, or portfolio. Hand out pens, calendars, flashlights, and other novelty items imprinted with your name or logo that get your name out to the public.

To attract customers, a Northern California real estate firm painted a vintage 1950s panel truck a distinctive yellow and parked it just off a well-traveled intersection near its office. The firm name, logo, address, and phone number are elegantly painted on the truck's sides over an arrow that points the public to the firm's office. It has become a landmark and a topic of conversation that has brought the firm loads of business.

Remember

Publicity is a full-time, 24/7, job. It never stops! Good self-promotion can inspire, excite, and energize prospective customers or clients. Become a walking self-advertisement. Always carry your product, brochures, and business cards with you. Put your logo and company name on anything that people might see.

6
Build Your Marketing Plan Around Publicity

"I am putting real plums into an imaginary cake."
—MARY MCCARTHY, AUTHOR

WHEN PUTTING TOGETHER A BUSINESS or marketing plan, include a publicity component. Investors know the value of publicity and expect a blueprint of the tactics you intend to pursue.

Besides satisfying investors, a publicity plan helps sharpen your focus. A publicity plan:

- Serves as a checklist for justifying every element and expenditure in your publicity proposal
- Helps you come up with a realistic budget
- Forces you to confine yourself to approaches that fit both your needs and bankroll
- Allows you to schedule sufficient time to develop, conduct, and finance an effective publicity campaign

 **GUERRILLA TACTICS**

Start your publicity efforts at least nine months before you product comes out or your business is scheduled to be up and running.

During the process of writing your publicity plan, be sure to include the following activities:

- Identify your target audience.
- Identify your strategy for reaching them.
- Identify the publications, programs, and Web sites you plan to use.
- Budget for consultations with PR/publicity professionals to help you keep on track, make mid-steam changes, and position yourself for the future.

Publicity Budget

The central question in any publicity campaign is always "How much are you going to spend on publicity?" Start your budget by including identifiable, fixed expenditures. For example, a guerrilla whose service was designing Web sites budgeted for:

- A three-quarter-page ad in *Radio/TV Interview Report*.
- Listing in the *Yearbook Experts*.
- Subscriptions to *ProfNet* and the *PR Newswire Media Campaign*.

GUERRILLA INTELLIGENCE

Richard A. Cortese once said, "Whatever you think it's going to take, double it. That applies to money, time, and stress. It's going to be harder than you think and take longer than you think." At the very least, your marketing expenses should be 10 percent of your annual budget, and a good chunk of it should go to publicity. In preparing your budget, be sure to include the cost of implementing a media plan.

Media Campaign

Outline the specific steps that you intend to take to publicize your product or service. Each publicity campaign requires an individual plan that is specifically tailored for that campaign. The plan below is provided as a guide for reference purposes only; it is not to be followed verbatim. It's intended to illustrate the scope and depth a media plan requires. The specific details of your media campaign will include many of the elements mentioned and others that are not.

In preparation for your media campaign you may also want to make arrangements for a toll-free telephone number for customers or clients and to start soliciting customer endorsements.

The implementation plan for a media campaign that follows outlines the types of tasks you should accomplish at different time intervals, starting with nine months before the formal introduction of your product or service and continuing through the time after the introduction has been made. Remember, this outline is only a suggested guideline. You will prepare your plan to meet the specific needs of your product or service. Not all suggested activities are appropriate for every media plan.

Nine Months Before Introduction

Activities for nine months prior to the introduction of your product or service focus on writing articles, designing brochures, newsletters, and promotional displays, and scheduling and preparing for speaking engagements.

Before you write any articles, you will need to research which newsletters, Web sites, and other print media would be good venues for your product or service. Once you know the audiences you will be targeting, you can write for them specifically. Send your resulting articles to your selected list in this time period, so that they will be published close to the time your product or service is introduced.

The same approach is true for designing point-of-purchase graphic displays for retail outlets. Spend some time determining which markets are appropriate for you. Know who your potential customers are so that the design of your display can speak directly to their wants or needs. Once you have completed the text and design of your point-of-purchase display for retail outlets, you can send it to be reproduced so that it will be ready when you need it.

This advance time is also good for producing articles and handouts for future speaking engagements, product or service order forms, and business cards. Schedule fifteen talks and workshops. Solicit pre-orders. The commitment to use the product or service builds interest and can help with financing.

Six Months Before Introduction

The six months before introduction of your product or services will be dedicated to getting the word out. You may choose to:

- Distribute camera-ready articles to national and major city business, lifestyle, and women's news editors at the top forty newspapers and key magazines, including *Inc.*, *Entrepreneur,* and *Income Opportunities,* as appropriate.
- Send 100 press releases to generate articles and coverage by media that focus on business (e.g., *CNN Financial News*, *Wall Street Journal*, *Fast Company*, *Business 2.0,* and *Wired*).
- Send 100 press releases to syndicated radio and TV shows that focus on business.
- Send your press release via the PR Newswire, which reaches over 25,000 media outlets.
- Place articles and news releases in newsletters, e-zines, and Web sites, such as Action Plan Marketing, Get Clients Now, American Express Business Advisory Network, MizBiz.com, Small Business Administration, Small Business Development Centers, and both the national and local chambers of commerce.
- Prepare flyers for pre-introduction orders.
- Prepare 1,000 pre-order postcards for distribution to national organizations such as the National Speakers Association, the National Association of Women Business Owners, and the United States Chamber of Commerce.

Three Months Before Introduction

A key activity in the final three months will be writing and distributing your media (press) kit. The contents of a media kit are discussed in detail in Chapter 12. Customize your media kits for your different audiences, such as business groups, artists, educational institutions, and nonprofit organizations.

For each publicity campaign, create a media kit that contains:

- Your logo on the kit package
- A news release about your product or service
- A list of interview questions
- A photo of the product
- Your photo
- Reviews and articles about you and/or your product or service
- Your contact information, including toll-free telephone number and Web site address
- A product sample, if feasible

Other activities that you should accomplish in the final three months of the pre-introduction campaign are listed below:

- Place thirty telephone calls daily to secure media interviews with the aim of having daily media interviews run before, during, and after introduction of your product or service.
- Place articles in newsletters and periodicals to get even more timely coverage (e.g., National Association of Women Business Owners, *Working Woman*, Bull Dog Reporter, *Bottom Line*).
- Mail 100 initial press release packets with testimonials, flyers, and reply postcards.
- Update and maintain Web sites to include current information on publicity, speaking engagements, pre-orders, and events.

Thirty Days Before Introduction

In the final thirty days prior to introducing your product or service, you should complete your plans for the actual introduction.

Perhaps you will prepare a national contest soliciting ideas for the wackiest publicity ideas for your product or service. This time would also be well spent forging alliances with other speakers on similar or related topics to promote the product or service.

Print three-fold brochures (that you designed nine months before introduction) containing ten tips, your toll-free telephone number, and Web site address. Mail brochures to your customers, clients, and those on your media list, and distribute them at speaking engagements and in response to telephone and Web site inquiries. E-mail the first issue of your newsletter just before your introduction.

Upon Introduction

The flurry of activity leading up to your introduction continues with the possible activities listed below:

- Launch publicity contest.
- Do a Morning Drive Radio Tour interview, which consists of twenty individual interviews that reach twenty radio stations nationwide.
- Give a one-hour Teleprint Press Conference with fifteen print reporters.
- Send samples of the product to 300 chambers of commerce throughout the United States to support your speaking engagements, 300 people/groups who might invite you to present a workshop, 200 members of the national media, and 100 business-course professors at colleges, entrepreneurial, and graduate schools.
- Collect comments, personal anecdotes, and endorsement from customers or clients.

Ongoing, Postintroduction

Your job is not over once the product or service is introduced. You will need to continue to keep its name in the public eye. So you will want to continue your publicity. The following activities are just a few ideas of how to do this:

- Publish a monthly e-mail newsletter.
- Place stories monthly in other newsletters including those listed above.
- Collect comments, personal anecdotes, and endorsements from customers/clients.
- Update and distribute brochures containing excerpts to media, organizations, schools, and libraries.
- Maintain your toll-free telephone number.
- Update your Web site continually.
- Identify and exploit market niches with an eye toward new niches including women, alternative—non-traditional, non-establishment businesses, such as artists, organic food, home schooling, and alternative health (acupuncture, yoga, meditation) groups—and service businesses.
- Write and distribute articles that link your product or service to news developments and trends.

Remember

Your publicity campaign will cost more than you expect—they always do. Allocate at least 10 percent of your annual budget to marketing and earmark a good portion of it to publicity. Outline the specific steps you plan to take to publicize your product or service and write a detailed publicity plan.

7

Zero In on Your Market— Save Time, Money, and Aggravation

"All distances are the same for those who don't meet."
—PENELOPE FITZGERALD, AUTHOR

GUERRILLA INTELLIGENCE

When a publicity campaign veers off in the wrong direction it's usually fatal; the campaign is finished. You may not detect your mistake until it's too late. And, by the time you do catch it, you may not have the resources to get back on track or begin again. You may have spent all your capital and have nothing to show for it.

Every publicity campaign needs a direction; it needs a target. The hardest job in marketing is seeing your target and staying focused on it. In other words, know where you're going before deciding how to get there. Identify your destination. Then map your route. When you know the destination, the route often is clear.

HOW OFTEN HAVE YOU GOTTEN LOST because you didn't really know where you were going? You end up stuck some place you don't want to be, and in order to begin again, you still have to get back to where you started. Frequently, you don't know how to get back, which route to take, and in the process you risk getting even more lost. If you do get back, you may be too exhausted to start again.

Two Audiences

Publicity is a unique marketing tool because it forces you to identify and reach two separate audiences:

1. The buying audience—individuals who purchase your product or service.
2. The media audience—members of the press and electronic media who will publicize your product or service.

The Buying Audience

All marketing tools require you to identify the ultimate consumer. In publicity, first identify your potential customers. Ask who will buy what you sell? Your buying audience could be either universal or smaller specialty groups such as farmers, fire fighters, pet owners, left-handed people, overweight people, or combinations of these groups.

Define your buying audience as narrowly as possible in order to link it with the most effective media outlets. Also identify various segments of your buying audience because you may find that different promotional efforts work better with particular segments.

The Media Audience

When you've identified your buying audience, try to determine which specific media outlets would best reach them. It's nice to think that the world is your buying audience, but remember it's expensive to market to the world, so try to narrow it down.

When you've broken down your buying audience, it's easier to match it with your media audience. PR professionals excel at knowing which media outlets will most effectively reach which markets. For example, if the buying audience is senior citizens, they could target *Modern Maturity*, the magazine of AARP. For clients hoping to sell apparel to new mothers, they would pitch *Parenting* magazine.

Sources to find the best media outlets include:

- Bacon's Media Directories—*www.bacons.com/direcories/maindirectories.asp*
- Bacon's MediaList Online—*www.medialistsonline.com*
- Broadcasting & Cable Yearbook—*www.bowker.com*
- Burrelle's Media Directory—*www.burrelles.com/indexmd.html*
- MediaMap Online—*www.mediamaponline.com*
- Media Finder—*www.mediafinder.com*
- Standard Periodical Directory—*www.mediafinder.com/secure/product1.cfm*
- National Directory of Magazines—*www.mediafinder.com/secure/product1.cfm*
- Online Public Relations—*www.online-pr.com*

Setting Your Target
Be Realistic

Set achievable goals. If your dream is to conquer the world, don't try to do it in one swoop. It's like trying to devour an entire pie in one gulp. You'll make a mess, choke, get sick, and probably lose your taste for pies, and you'll never get the whole thing down.

Set modest, achievable goals; meet them; and then take on bigger, more ambitious targets. If you miss modest goals, it's relatively easy to regroup and begin again. However, if you fail to meet large, unrealistic goals, getting back on track can seem like an insurmountable chore.

Be Specific

Quantify your goals. Instead of merely trying to increase your sales, set dollar targets, for example, gross sales of $100,000 in three months, $300,000 in six months, and $750,000 for the first year.

GUERRILLA TACTICS

Research your target. Before you approach an editor or a producer, know their work. Don't pitch Oprah stories related to cooking or cookbooks, which she avoids. Instead, focus on the self-betterment, human redemption features she prefers. No matter how fascinating your pals, dinner companions, and coworkers may find your story, it may not interest certain editors or producers. So, find out what they want before approaching them. You have several ways of finding out this information:

- Listen to their programs, read their articles, and check out their Web sites.
- Note what kinds of features they run, the slants they take, and the type of audience they attract.
- Contact and ask them what would interest them.

Once you've completed your research, you are ready to shape your presentation and pitch stories that fit. Don't try to force a square peg into a round hole.

The bottom line for editors and producers is what your story can do for them and their audience. If you want to be their resource, prove to them that you know what they want, understand their needs, and can deliver stories that fill those needs. Once they see that you understand their needs and can deliver, they'll shoot your name right to the top of their list of reliable resources.

Be Prepared

When your story is bumped, and it will be, roll with the punches. At this point, your main job is to remain on your media contacts' radar screens. Invite producers and editors to call you at the last minute if they run into problems, if features fall apart, or guests cancel. Show producers that you're a professional, that you know how to play the game. Once editors and producers accept you as a professional, they'll call you to fill in or when news breaks in your area of expertise.

GUERRILLA INTELLIGENCE

Things in the media always change and major decisions often are made at the last moment.

Features scheduled months ago frequently are postponed, canceled, or put on hold for a story about something newer, trendier, flashier, funnier, or sexier. Features are routinely canceled for late breaking news, when guests become sick or test poorly, and when features don't successfully materialize. Magazine covers and stories are frequently replaced at the eleventh hour when editors decide that replacements will sell more magazines.

 ## GUERRILLA TALE

The producers of The Oprah Winfrey Show *were interested in Dr. C. P. Chambers, the author of* Are Bald Men Sexier?*, but never got around to booking him. One Wednesday morning, nearly one year after the show first contacted Dr. Chambers, a producer called coauthor Rick Frishman to book the author for a feature on bald men that was scheduled for the coming Friday, just two days later! Of course, Dr. Chambers dropped everything and immediately flew to Chicago.*

The following day, Oprah's staff again called Rick and explained that while interviewing Dr. Chambers they mentioned that the second half of the show was a segment on short men, for which they needed more guests. Dr. Chambers recommended Rick and, voila, both Rick and Dr. Chambers appeared on Oprah's Friday program, suddenly, at the last minute and when they least expected it.

The moral of this tale is be prepared. Practice your act and get it down pat. Be ready to promote your product or service on short notice. Producers, editors, and writers have "fall-back lists," sources who will show up at the very last moment. Get yourself on that list. Inform producers and editors that you'll be available on short notice. Make yourself their resource.

Remember

Identify your market and don't forget that you have two audiences: consumers and the media. Set realistic and specific monetary goals. Research your target media by listening to their programs, reading their articles, and visiting their Web sites. Be prepared for change because everything always changes.

8
Come from the Heart

"Happiness is when what you think, what you say,
and what you do are in harmony."
— MOHANDAS GANDHI

THE STANISLAVSKY METHOD OF ACTING teaches that to be convincing everything actors express must come from the heart. In other words, actors can't fake it, because when they're on stage or screen they project their true convictions. The same theory applies to publicity. To be successful you must honestly believe in what you are promoting. You can't fake it.

GUERRILLA INTELLIGENCE

Audiences sense whether you really mean what you're saying. That's why actors make such great spokespersons. They understand that their performances must emanate from their hearts, that their lines must be delivered from the inside out.

Rick, who puts all his clients through media training, points out that, "It's nearly impossible to teach people to convincingly convey what they don't honestly feel."

When you appear on TV or radio or when you talk to an editor, express your true beliefs. Never bluff. People who work for the media are savvy. They're besieged with a gazillion requests for publicity and have developed the knack to quickly smell a rat. Any claim or proposal that they feel is bogus, phony, or hype will be rejected immediately. And, once you've turned the media off, it's nearly impossible to get back in their good graces.

The public reacts similarly. After years of being bombarded by a relentless stream of pitchmen promising, promising, promising, the public has become selective. They want to believe, but they've been burned too many times. They now insist on results. Today's audiences may sit through, be entertained, or even amused by hucksters whom they don't believe, but they'll seldom buy what doesn't ring true. And if they buy it, and it doesn't work, they'll remember who sold it to them.

If you don't believe what you're promoting, the public won't believe it either, and they certainly won't buy what you're selling.

True Believers

Conviction and enthusiasm are contagious. People buy because of your excitement. Your passion and belief becomes their cause. Consumers who believe will become your sales force, they'll preach your gospel, and follow you into war. True belief creates legends and fuels success. Impassioned advocates soar up the corporate ladder and build empires. People listen to them, emulate them, and invest in them. True believers are pied pipers and apostles, and they make remarkably effective spokespersons.

Jim McCann, a client of Rick's, has had extraordinary success as the TV spokesman for his company, 1-800-FLOWERS. Although not blessed with matinee-idol looks, a booming voice, or even a polished delivery, audiences sense that McCann believes, from his core, that 1-800-FLOWERS will deliver all he promises. They believe that he's more than just a petal pusher, that he's a true believer. Consumers are all the more likely to listen to true believers and to buy what they're selling.

More than the Product

Not all promotions are immediately successful. Campaigns for great products may suffer from poor packaging, poor delivery, or poor timing. But these flaws can be fixed. If the message makes sense and the product or service works, people will eventually sit up and listen. If you hope to persuade others to buy what you're selling, it must be more than just a company or a product. You must believe that:

- What you're promoting will change the world.
- Your promoting it will make a difference.
- You know more about it than virtually anyone else.

 **GUERRILLA TALE**

Attorney Richard Essen, who specialized in defending clients charged with driving while intoxicated, never lost a case. Resentment against him ran high because the public believed that he profited by keeping dangers to our safety on the roads. However, Essen passionately wanted to use his success to bring about a long-overdue legal change. Features in the Wall Street Journal *and on* 60 Minutes *were initially hostile to him, but turned favorable when Essen cited his undefeated record as proof that our system of dealing with intoxicated drivers was critically flawed and needed repair. Audiences responded to Essen's knowledge, experience, logic, and belief in his position by demanding change—and legislators got the message. As a direct result of Essen's crusade, a number of states adopted the changes that he championed.*

Remember

You truly must believe in whatever you publicize. If you don't, others will sense your misgivings and won't trust you or your message. You can't fake it! To convince others, you must believe that what you're promoting will change the world, that the fact that your promoting it will make a difference, and that you know more about it than virtually anyone else.

9
Press Releases: Grab 'Em Fast and Don't Let Go

"Many attempts to communicate are nullified by saying too much."
—ROBERT GREENLEAF, DIRECTOR OF MANAGEMENT RESEARCH, AT&T

PRESS RELEASES ARE A PARADOX. Sending them to the media can be like supplying blood to vampires. Vampires, like the media, prefer to go out and get their own sustenance, but they'll use what you send if they think it's special or when they're desperate.

Generally, mass mailings don't work. Every day, the media is flooded with press releases. They come in faster than commuters shooting through FasTrak lanes. Most radio and TV producers don't read press releases. At best, they glance at them, set aside the few that look interesting, and toss out the rest. Producers rarely receive a press release, read it, jump on it, and begin developing it as a feature. Nevertheless, don't be selective—send press releases everywhere because some may draw responses.

When compared to radio and TV, print journalists generally pay more attention to press releases. However, they also have enormous demands on their time and short attention spans. So, grab them and grab them fast!

Why Send Press Releases?

Good question. Press releases are necessary because there's a chance they'll catch someone's eye. When you send a press release, you hope that recipients will phone and say, "Hey, what you sent is really cool. Tell me more about it." Press releases are intended to stir up interest and generate follow-up calls.

GUERRILLA INTELLIGENCE

Ironically, the media expects and wants press releases, even though they probably won't read them. Editors, writers, and producers are addicted to information. They can't get enough of it and live in mortal fear that they might miss something that's newsworthy. They also are adept at sniffing out stories and finding needles in haystacks. So, sending press releases is a cost of playing the game; it's the ticket for admission.

Press releases sent to the print media should differ from those directed to electronic communicators, but both must convey news. All releases should provide information—the who, what, where, why, and how of your story—quickly and concisely. Try to limit all releases to a single page.

Print Media

The print media can publish a press release, or parts of it, with little or no change, and their job is done. Since journalists work under tight deadlines, they often run the press releases they receive with no changes. On other occasions, they augment press releases with quotes and information from their own sources or they extract key points from your release to use as the basis for their own pieces. But in the crunch of pressing deadlines, journalists will run well-written press releases verbatim.

 GUERRILLA TACTICS

For the print media, the first paragraph of your press release is vital. The first paragraph is intended to alert the media, to inform them what you're promoting. It should run no more than three or four sentences and set forth all the main points covered in the release. Don't muddy your opening paragraph with too much detail. Writers and editors don't care about every trivial point and will gloss right over them. Plus, extraneous details can deaden the impact of your more important main points. If you insist on including details, put them at the end of your release or place them in a separate, more comprehensive, article that you send as a part of you media kit.

Use subsequent paragraphs to further explain your story, including background, more specific information, and even include quotes or endorsements. But keep the entire release to one page.

After you've drafted the body of the press release, tie it together with a catchy headline that will make the reader want additional information. Headlines are short, one-line summaries that identify what you're promoting. Use bold caps and select colorful words with strong impact. Study newspapers, magazines, and Web sites for examples of great headlines and place them in a file for future reference. Make a list of words with strong impact.

Always include your contact information at both the top and bottom of each page.

Warning: Avoid repeatedly sending the same press release to the same contacts. A single, well-written press release for each contact is fine; it's all you need. Don't send out the same press release every thirty days or so; it's a waste of paper, postage, and effort. Getting the same stuff over and over again can turn off media sources that you hope to cultivate. Also, send your press release to only one online distribution service. Most services send releases to the same list of recipients.

Radio and TV

Radio and TV producers react to press releases differently than their counterparts in the print media. They seldom read press releases, but when they do, they usually just scan the headlines and bullets. Unlike print journalists, radio and TV producers can't simply run your press release in the exact form that it was sent. If they're interested in your story, their work is just beginning. They need to find an angle and then line up guests, prepare questions, and produce the segment.

Producers' lives are blurs. Everything is an emergency or a crisis, and they simultaneously juggle a million things on their desks and in their minds. So make press releases for producers shorter than those you send to journalists. In releases to producers, the headline and first sentence must grab them and convince them to read further.

GUERRILLA INTELLIGENCE

Approach producers as if they have ADD (attention deficit disorder). Get their attention fast. If your press release doesn't capture the producers' attention within the first ten seconds, you're dead; they'll be off on something else.

Headlines

Headlines are critical. Think of headlines as nuggets, small but valuable jewels that exist to catch peoples' eyes. Headlines are the first, and often the only, thing people read. Headlines must immediately grab the readers attention or your release will go straight in the dumpster.

The media is obsessed with three topics that it thinks audiences crave: money, sex, and health. So, whenever possible, tie your headlines to those subjects.

 **GUERRILLA TACTICS**

Compose lively, one-line headlines that will make editors or producers continue reading. For example:

"How to Have Ten Orgasms a Day"

"Get Immunity from Mad Cow Disease"

"Five Ways to a Free College Education"
"How to Buy Illegal Drugs Legally"

Headlines should be no more than one line, take only seconds to read, and focus on value and benefit.

If a headline grabs the reader's attention, it will buy you another twenty seconds to explain yourself. Remember the ADD analogy. Producers won't read too many words so practice writing concise, lively headlines; short, clear first paragraphs; and bulleted main points.

Bulleted subheadings are also headlines that are intended to attract attention and quickly provide information. When writing your bulleted items keep the following tips in mind:

- List bullets in the order of their importance because most readers don't usually make it through the entire list.
- Include no more than five to seven bullets. Five are better.
- Hold each bullet to no more than two concise sentences. One sentence is preferable.
- Write bullets as if they were shot from a gun: bang, bang, bang—short, clear, and hard hitting. Aim for maximum impact.

Editing Headlines

Editing is an acquired skill that comes with lots of practice. Read newspapers and magazines and make a list of headlines that attract your interest. Note what those stories were about, how the headlines were worded, and why they caught your eye. Then try your hand at writing your own headlines for the same stories. As you're writing, try to develop a feel for the rhythm, the use of language, and the impact the words create.

Visit Web sites. Entries on the first screens are headlines, so study them in an effort to get a feel for the techniques used. When you read news items on Yahoo!, AOL, etc., you're reading headlines. Print out those screens and circle the headlines that you like.

Then write your headlines and bullets using the same techniques.

Ask yourself what's newsworthy about the piece. Is the author or spokesperson well known—a celebrity or an accomplished researcher? Identify what's new in the article and draft your headline accordingly. Probe for interesting, unusual slants.

Establish a "Who Gives a Damn" meter. Determine if anyone would care about the information presented. If so, identify specifically who would care. Then determine why they would care. Once done, practice writing headlines and bullets targeted to those who would care.

One Sheets

Cut away all the fat and even trim some meat. Condense each press release to a single page called a "one sheet." Producers and journalists don't have much time to read, so they want the facts only. They want to know why they should carry your story and why it will interest their audience. The media always asks, "What's in it for us?" Will your press release give them an interesting story, a dynamic interview, or produce a stimulating guest?

In every press release, try to include three things that your product or service will do to change the audience's life. Spell them out in the bullets. For example, *Your new automobile will:*

- Make you feel like a million bucks.
- Impress your friends, neighbors, and business associates.
- Save you money by providing years of warranted service.

Remember

Media people are information junkies who want to receive press releases. Write tight, one-page press releases with compelling headlines that will grab a reader's attention within ten seconds. Convey your information in a clear first paragraph and then bullet the important information. Capitalize on the media's obsession with money, sex, and health.

10
Media Lists:
Play the Numbers Game

*"Publicity is easy to get. Make yourself so successful
you don't need it and then you'll get it."*
—ANONYMOUS

MEDIA LISTS ARE DATABASES containing the names and information about people and organizations that can help promote your product or service. They're your Rolodex, PalmPilot, and address book. They're the roster of your network.

When it comes to media lists, collect as many names as possible. The more names included on your media list, the greater your chances of getting your story told. It's simple mathematics. If you send a press release to 200 media contacts, it's more likely that your story will be picked up than if you send it to only twenty contacts. It's the old theory of throwing lots of mud on the wall and hoping that some of it sticks. You never know just where it will stick and which contact will be interested in your story.

GUERRILLA INTELLIGENCE

Direct mailings usually yield a 1 to 2 percent response. Although some respondents may agree to air your story immediately, the majority usually just want more information. Since the percentage of those who ultimately end up publicizing your story is so low, sending larger mailings increases your chances for success.

Media List Checklist

Start compiling a media list by including the names of all contacts who might conceivably publicize or help promote your product or service. Don't be overly selective. Sometimes, the person who seems to be the most unlikely contact will fall in love with your story and go to great lengths to promote it. Or that contact may refer you to others who can help.

Your media list should contain the contact's:

- Name
- Employer
- Street address
- E-mail address
- Telephone
- Backup telephone numbers
- Specialty area
- Source information, such as how you got his or her name, how and where you met, and friends or associates in common
- Miscellaneous historical and personal information, such as projects pitched to the contact, projects bought, dates you last spoke and the results, and notes on the contact's hobbies, families, or other interests. Knowing a bit of personal information about your contact will allow you to add the personal touch to your conversations when appropriate.

Compiling a Media List

It's never too soon to start a media list. A media list is always a work in progress because it's never a finished product. It's something you'll always be adding to, updating and revising.

 **GUERRILLA TACTICS**

Creating and maintaining your contact list of media and other individuals who may help you publicize your product or service is one of the most important things you can do for your business. The suggestions below will help you get started:

- Begin creating a media/contact list now, even though you may not even have the idea for a business. Jot down the names of members of the media and interesting people and how they might help.
- Form the habit of making notes and collecting names. Carry a small notebook or a personal digital assistant, such as a PalmPilot or Visor Handspring at all times. Keep notebooks in your car, briefcase, and purse. Always carry a pen, even if you're out jogging.
- List the names of every person you know who might remotely help: writers, reporters, editors, radio and TV producers, and publicists. Study the media to discover who's covering your field and add them to your list.
- Ask your friends, family, and business associates for names to add to your list.
- Call local newspapers, magazines, radio and TV stations; e-mail online publications for the names of editors, reporters, and producers who cover areas that could help you.
- Ask everybody you meet for his or her business card.
- Toss all your notebook entries and business cards into a bowl, a shoebox, or a file drawer. Set aside a specific time each week (for example, every Monday at 9:00 A.M.) to organize, add new entries, and revise your list. Insert comments on how you met, mutual friends or contacts, and any other information that might break the ice when you contact them.

Services

Subscribe to Internet services that give the names and contact information for media people. Some good sources are listed below:

- Bacon's MediaList Online—*www.medialistsonline.com*
- MediaMap Online—*www.mediamaponline.com*
- Media Finder—*www.mediafinder.com*
- Online Public Relations—*www.online-pr.com*
- Burrelle's Media Directory—*www.burrelles.com /indexmd.html*

Online services are updated regularly and are usually more reliable than print directories. Still, verify all information before making a contact.

Books of media lists can be out of date the moment they're published because media people are nomads who move around incessantly. Sure, the main listing for the *Chicago Tribune* will be the same and even the managing editor may remain unchanged, but editors and producers won't be because they're constantly changing jobs. If you simply send blanket mailings to names listed in directories, you'll end up sending press releases to people who left their positions or died months ago.

CASH—Clean Up, Ask, Send, and Handle

Update your list on an ongoing basis. Every three months, at the least, review the entire list from top to bottom. Most media jobs pay poorly, so the turnover is huge. Unless you keep your list current, you'll end up wasting time and energy trying to contact people who are no longer in a position to help you.

Clean up constantly. Whenever you hear of a change, note it and update your list. Staying current is time consuming, but it's essential and it keeps you up on changes in the industry that you depend upon.

A quick and inexpensive way to update your media list is to mail a postcard to everyone on your list. Be sure to include a return address. When cards are returned undelivered, update the information or delete those entries from your list. Although these mailings will help remove dead wood, they're not always accurate. Nor will they provide information about current editors and producers. You'll have to do that yourself.

GUERRILLA TECHNIQUES

Use the CASH Method to keep your contact and media list up to date.

- *Clean your list constantly.* The best approach for cleaning up your media list is labor intensive. It entails calling each newspaper, radio, and TV station and asking, "Is Harry Schwartz still the Lifestyles editor?" If he isn't, find out who is, and ask to speak with Harry's replacement. Also, get the replacement's direct phone number and e-mail address. Find out where Harry went and try to get his new phone number, mailing, or e-mail address, because he still could be a valuable contact. If Harry is still with the paper ask to speak with him.
- *Ask for the information you need.* If either Harry or his replacement pick up the phone, introduce yourself and say "I only want to take thirty seconds of your time. Is it okay if I send you a _____? Please take a fast look at it. I think it's great and I'm sure you'll like it, but I just wanted to let you know that it's coming." If you get voice mail, recite the same short pitch. Keep it brief! Always clearly convey that you understand and respect how pressed your contacts are for time.
- *Send your materials to your contact.* As soon as you get off the phone, send the package to Harry or his replacement *by next day delivery.* Addressing your package to a specific person by name, in this case Harry or his replacement, rather than an unknown editor gives you a clear advantage. They know who you are, that you're sending a

package and generally what it contains. Advanced warning increases the chances that your package will be opened. If nothing else, this approach shows that you're courteous and considerate, which people remember.

- *Handle the situation to build your relationship with your contact.* The day after you package is scheduled to arrive call Harry or his replacement. Don't wait more than a day because if you do your package will probably be buried in his in-basket, lost forever to the world. Tell Harry, his replacement, or the answering machine, "I'm calling to make sure that you got the material I sent about _____. I know it probably just arrived and that you have 10,000 things on your desk, but I just wanted to make sure that it got into your hands. Thanks." Call again every week or ten days thereafter. Say that you're just checking in. Ask if anything is happening with your package and whether there is anything that he/she needs from you. Don't pester or push, instead gently nudge.

Categorizing

If you compile a beefy media list, you won't always want to contact everyone on the list. So categorize and prioritize your list. Divide the entries on your list into three groups, ranked according to their usefulness for your product or service. Here we call them A, B, and C. But you can designate them in any way that makes sense to you.

The A List

Place media that provide the biggest bang for your bucks on your A List. Usually, these contacts work for the national media or national trade industry media. Your A List will include your most important media targets, the ones you want to land and to hold on to. Examples of A List media include *The Oprah Winfrey Show*, *Entertainment Tonight*, the *New York Times*, the *Today Show*, *USA Today*, the *Wall Street Journal,* and national trade industry publications in your field.

B List

A notch below the A List, but still important, your B List includes less popular national media and dominant media in large metropolitan areas that can put you on the map. Although the contacts on your B List may lack the size and clout of those on your A List, frequent coverage by media in this group can be the equivalent of A List coverage. Try to turn B List contacts into As and treat them like As. B List media include large-city newspapers, such as the *Atlanta Journal-Constitution, Chicago Tribune, San Francisco Chronicle,* and *Orlando Sentinel*; *Rosie O'Donnell Show, Live with Regis and Kelly, Jenny Jones,* and big-city morning shows.

C List

Local media in both urban and rural areas will comprise your C List. These media are often ideal for local promotions. To have a broad reach, you have to send more mailings to local media because each outlet covers less territory. Sending more mailings will require you to make more follow-up calls. However, it may be easier to get C List coverage, and those stories could be picked up by the larger media. C List media include local newspapers, such as the *Yakima News, Marin Independent Journal,* and the *Jersey Journal*, and local radio and cable television stations. Remember, C list media could be the easiest and best approach for you.

Remember

Media lists are the roster for your network. Create a large list filled with names and contact information. Since the media is in constant flux, update your list on an ongoing basis, at least every three months. Categorize your media list by subject and prioritize each subject area by the effectiveness of the publicity it can provide.

11
Follow Up, Follow Up, Follow Up

"The key to promotion is follow-up . . . when you don't follow up, you lose the pro and wind up with just the motion"
                                        —RICK FRISHMAN

GUERRILLA TALE

Georgia, a financial planner, took all the right steps to get her publicity campaign off to a flying start. She wrote a snappy sound bite that usually elicited eager responses; she identified thirty radio, TV, and newspaper contacts and sent a photo and professional-looking press kit to each. When she was done, she sat back, concentrated on her planning business, and waited. Three weeks later, her mailings produced just one response, and that response was a dead end.

A few weeks before the publication date for his book, Stan sent query letters to magazines asking if they were interested in publishing excerpts of his book. A few days later, before he received any responses, Stan telephoned each magazine. He asked editors if they had received his letters and if they were interested in his excerpts. After a steady stream of rejections, Stan finally got through to an editor who said that the magazine was on deadline and was short one story. Stan immediately faxed an excerpt and sent by overnight delivery a copy of his book, biographical information, and photo to the editor. The excerpt from Stan's book ran two weeks later.

Guerrillas take the initiative! After they get things rolling, guerrillas strike quickly and often. They don't take the attitude "My work's done," because they know it isn't. They know much of their work has just begun. Guerrillas don't sit around and wait for things to happen. Guerrillas make things happen.

The only magic formula for getting publicity is the Three Fs—follow-up, follow-up, follow-up. As we've previously said—and can't stress enough—people in the media are swamped with work and have to juggle more publicity requests than a tank of octopuses could handle. Plus, they surround themselves with electronic fences, so they're hard to reach. Securing a booking or getting an article about your product or service published can take ages because journalists and producers frequently drop what they are working on when hot stories break. It's simply how the business operates.

Keep the Door Open

Lack of response isn't the worst thing that can happen, rejection is. If your pitch is rejected, that means your media contact isn't interested. So, try to avoid outright rejections. Your job is to keep the door open and nurse the media until your story is told, which usually takes time. Be patient and understanding, but be persistent and keep gently nudging your media contacts, reminding them about your story.

 **GUERRILLA TACTICS**

Whenever your get an outright rejection, ask, "Whom else can I call?" Then use the name of the person who rejected your idea to gain access to the new contact. For example, if Mike Smith gave you

Betty Greene's name, tell or leave a message with Ms. Greene that Mike Smith of the *Washington Post* suggested that you contact her.

After you make the initial contact, you can't wait for the media to respond and you can't leave anything to chance. If you do, all your hard work, all those endless hours and mounting expenses, can wash straight down the drain. At every stage of the game, you must be persistent, tenacious, and determined. You cannot assume that good things will just happen. You must make them happen.

Expect rejection, but do your best to avoid it. Nevertheless, you will be rejected. Count on it; but you can't let it stop you. Think of a publicity campaign as a marathon, not as a dash. It requires more than one short burst of speed. In a marathon, the primary objective is to cross the finish line. So, you must stay in the race and continue to run doggedly, determinedly, step-by-step, and mile-by-mile until you reach your goal.

Had Stan given up, or just sat back and waited for editors to respond to his queries, the magazine probably would have published another story, one from their slush pile. Sure, luck was with Stan. He happened to hit the magazine when it needed just what Stan was offering, but guerrillas make their own luck. They understand that diligent follow-up improves their odds. The bottom line is that if Stan had not followed up and ignored the rejections, his excerpt wouldn't have been published.

GUERRILLA INTELLIGENCE

Following up is not simply a short-term strategy, it's a critical element of every publicity campaign. Following up is making sure that things get done correctly and on time. It's a time-tested method for laying a foundation, building for the future, and completing the marathon. Following up broadens your contacts, sharpens your skills, and shows your professionalism, talent, and dedication. It's an essential step in building networks, which will dissolve if they're not maintained. Network maintenance also requires follow-up.

Being a Pest

Following up puts you on a slippery slope between persistence and pushiness. While you must be persistent, it's essential to stay in your contacts' good graces if you hope to sell your story. When you e-mail or call the media, be warm and friendly, not pushy. Approach your media contacts with gentle little nudges. Let them know that you understand and sympathize with their plight. Be patient, because if you're too pushy, they might give you a quick rejection to get you off their backs—which is the last thing you want.

Tell your contacts straight out to let you know when you become a pain. Say something like "Look, I know that when I'm pitching a story I can get to be a real pain in the butt, so tell me if I'm getting out of line." Ironically, when they see you as a potential pain, they tend to treat you better. Rehearse exactly what you plan to say. Write it down, because you want to get your message across without sounding threatening or obnoxious.

How to Follow Up

Initially, many people find it hard to follow up. Some are shy or feel that they're being a nuisance or groveling. Others simply don't know how to go about it. In the beginning following up may feel awkward, uncomfortable, and unpleasant, but you'll adjust to it. It won't take long, but it will take some planning and practice.

GUERRILLA INTELLIGENCE

Professional, prompt, and repeated follow-up isn't just good business, it's necessary business. Follow-up is as important as any other business task—attracting clients or customers, satisfying them, and fulfilling orders, to name just a few. But most people don't approach it systematically. They follow up only when they can steal time from other tasks that they consider more important or as a last resort to try to breathe new life into efforts that seem likely to fail.

Follow-up must be an integral part of your operation! It's essential if you hope to succeed.

Set aside a regular time each day to follow up. Make following up a part of your daily routine. Schedule it like an appointment and enter it on your calendar. Allot a set amount of time to follow up with media contacts, prospects, customers, friends, and anyone else who can help your business.

Don't worry about making a pest or a nuisance of yourself. Media people are always busy and they understand that followup is a part of the business. Usually, their failure to respond is due more to lack of time than lack of interest in you or your story. So, think of your following up as doing the media a favor, similar to a hotel wake-up call, a reminder that at first may be jarring, but that becomes well appreciated when the initial shock abates.

When you follow up, do it promptly. Media people can't wait around. Most of them are on tight schedules and have time slots or spaces they need to fill. So try to get to them early by placing follow-up calls as soon as they should have received your information. Generally, follow up no later than three days after you've mailed your package.

 **GUERRILLA TACTICS**

On your follow-up call, your first sentence should state your name. Identify who you are, and clearly, but briefly, say why you're calling. For example:

JANE: "Hi, this is Jane Doe, the human fly. I sent you information on my foolproof system to build strength and flexibility. Did you receive it?"
MEDIA: "Yes."
JANE: "What did you think of the idea? Is there anything that you didn't understand? Would you like to set up an interview?"

Put your pitch first. It will provide context for who you are, why you're calling, and give you a place to begin the conversation. Then ask your contact if he or she received your information.

On your first follow-up calls, don't merely call to confirm that your contacts received your package. Also ask if they understood everything and if they need any further information.

If your contact doesn't recall receiving the information, ask, "May I send you another package?" Then recite your sound bite and ask for and answer any questions. Offer to fax or e-mail the information for faster delivery. If your contact agrees, ask for the fax number or personal e-mail address. Use this data to update your records. Media people often have more than one telephone number or e-mail address; one may be listed for the general public while the other is private. If, however, your contact prefers receiving the information by regular mail, send it that way as soon as you hang up.

Send e-mail with a return receipt in order to verify that it has been received. Also program your e-mail to automatically give your contact information—name, business, address, telephone number, fax number, Web address, and business motto—at the end of the message. For faxes, use a fax cover sheet that includes the same information.

If you fax information or send it via e-mail, follow up by telephone no later than the next day. If you send it by regular mail, wait until you think it should have arrived and then call. If a follow-up call is answered by a machine, leave a brief message. In the message, spell your name, give your phone number, your sound bite, and repeat your phone number. Remember to speak clearly, put a smile on your telephone voice, and always be brief, considerate, and polite. Continue to call until you get a response.

It can take a dozen phone calls to secure an interview with a major-market newspaper or broadcast outlet. Fortunately, the media is used to persistent callers; it's part of their job. If they're abrupt, don't take it personally. They may be on deadline, having a bad day, or otherwise involved. The contact also may refer you to a colleague who can help, and your next call may hit the jackpot.

When journalists or producers show interest and promise to call back, try to pin them down as to when you can expect to hear from them. Find out if there's anything additional you can send or do in the meantime. If they don't call within the appointed time, which is likely, call them with a gentle reminder.

When you finally hook up, be specific about what you want—an interview, an article in a particular section or time slot, a review, or a photo placement. But also be reasonable. Don't sacrifice a tangible commitment by pushing for more, especially with new contacts. For example, if you get a listing in "Best Bets," don't demand a feature story. With closer contacts, try to up the ante, but don't get greedy.

On occasion, you may not be the right fit for your contact. So, when you're asked not to call again, don't. Try to salvage something positive from rejections by thanking contacts for their time, asking them what other stories might appeal to them, requesting names of others who might be interested in your story, and inquiring if you can contact them on future projects.

Explore all alternatives. For example, when a newspaper's features editor wasn't interested in a story on a designer's furniture, the designer contacted the paper's Sunday Magazine section editor, who gave him a three-page spread with photos. Changing the "angle" of your pitch could generate renewed interest or expand your potential markets.

Seize upon breaking news developments related to you or your business and make the most of them.

Maintain records of your follow-up efforts and place them in the project file. Refer to your records before placing follow-up calls. On your record, log in the date of each follow-up attempt, the time, whom you contacted, the method of contact (e-mail, telephone, press release, letter, face-to-face meeting, etc.), the subject of the contact, and the result. For example, "Reached answering machine." "Reached Dan James; may be interested in interview—he'll call back w/in 3 days."

 **GUERRILLA TALE**

Several years ago, a group of disabled comics successfully promoted their performances. About a year later, the Americans with Disabilities Act became law. The troupe quickly called media contacts from their earlier campaign and a radio personality invited a group member to appear on his show as an expert on the new law. Other media soon followed. By recognizing their special opportunity, the troupe enjoyed an extended period of free publicity and were able to raise their price per appearance.

Sample Follow-up Log

DATE/TIME	CONTACT	SUBJECT	TYPE	OUTCOME
1/17/01 10:40 a	Bill Brewer *NY Post*	Cats	E	Follow-up
1/17/01 11:20 a	Josh Jonas *Newsday*	Jackson CD	E	Follow up on 1/22
1/17/01 11:20 a	Sue Krebs *Jersey Journal*	Cats	T	Spoke, will think about it
1/17/01 11:50 a	Steve Lillo *Planetlink*	Web Links	E	Will appear on 2/4

Contact with Prospects and Customers

At meetings, conferences, or other networking events, do you collect business cards only to forget them or run across them months or years later piled up in the back corner of a dusty drawer? If so, you're wasting important opportunities.

Treat business cards like receipts.

When you collect business cards at an event, organize the data when you return. If you have contact-management software, enter the information and schedule a time to call. If you don't have such software, write the name of the event on the back of each card with other pertinent information about the contact.

Place the cards of those you promised to call in a separate stack, and make sure to call each within the next three days. By calling promptly, you can build on the excitement generated at the event and the time you spent together. Prompt calls also make it less likely that they'll have forgotten you.

Capitalize on news developments to follow up with prospects and clients. When you come across items related to prospects, clients or their business, contact them. Ask how they are, what they think about the development, how it impacts them and even to explain it to you from their perspective. Show interest and concern, but don't try to sell them. Simply try to plant positive thoughts about you and build for the future.

 **GUERRILLA TACTICS**

Dedicate a portion of your daily follow-up time to renew contacts with prospects and customers. They merit as much of your attention as the media.

It Gets Easier

After a while, following up becomes easier. With practice, it becomes routine and even fun. People in the media, even those who repeatedly reject you, become friends or professional associates. Before long, following up becomes a skill that you've mastered, perfected, and made your own.

Following up also enhances other parts of your life. It teaches you patience, understanding, and persistence. It teaches you to plan, position yourself, to wait your turn, to be professional, and to seize opportunities. Plus, it can help you make lots of money!

Rule of Seven

Occasionally, you'll get lucky and everyone will want to plug your product or service. Getting publicity will seem easy, it will fall into your lap. Well, that may happen when you're hot, but under normal, ordinary conditions, getting publicity is a long process that takes lots of work.

According to the Rule of Seven, it takes seven steps, calls, or e-mails, to actually get the average booking. Expect six nos before you get a yes—or, after seven calls, you may never get a yes and have to move on. Whenever media people say no to you, be gracious. A no may be no for now, but not forever. Never burn bridges!

GUERRILLA INTELLIGENCE

Create a solid plan. Believe in it and stick with it. Think positively. When you're trying to get a booking and you're stuck smack dab in the "Rule of Seven," remember that every "no" puts you that much closer to a "yes." Don't think of every roadblock or rejection as a defeat, see it as putting you closer to your goal. Be flexible. When contacts tell you, "No," pursue other options who may say, "Yes."

Most importantly, don't get discouraged or upset. Don't give up. Keep plugging! It will pay off handsomely. Getting publicity takes patience, persistence, and follow-up, follow-up, follow-up. It may seem repetitive, but it seldom gets dull.

Remember

Following up is a critical element of every publicity campaign. It's making sure that every element proceeds correctly and on time. When you follow up with your media contacts, be patient and understanding, but persistent. Gently nudge them to remind them about your story, but don't be a pest. Set aside a regularly scheduled time each day for following up.

12
Media Kits—Guerrilla Style

"If you have a great press release, you have a great press kit."
—Jill Lublin

LESS IS OFTEN MORE, and that's especially true with media kits. Traditionally, publicists blanketed the media with bulging, elaborate media kits (also called press kits) in the hope that a few members of the press might bite. The costs were great and the responses were slim, which helps explain why PR was used primarily by large corporations and exceptionally rich clients.

Well, things have changed drastically. Even if guerrillas could afford to send lavish media packages, we question whether they're worth the cost and whether they still work.

Today, the media is savvy; they've seen it all. They no longer want to be showered with reams of promotional materials, no matter how beautifully they're written, designed, or packaged. They've seen every gorgeous presentation, read all kinds of hype, and they don't have the time, or the inclination, to fight through stacks of paper to uncover possible gems.

GUERRILLA INTELLIGENCE

Forget the mustard, hold the catsup, the mayo, relish, lettuce, tomato, onions, pickle, bacon, cheese, guacamole, and even the buns. The media wants only the beef. All they want is your story—clearly and concisely told. If producers or journalists want more information, they'll ask. They're not bashful.

The beef in a media kit is a juicy, tasty press release. (See Chapter 9.) Unlike traditional media kits, a guerrilla kit should be a scaled-down package built around a killer, one-page, press release. The release can be supplemented by a few selected supporting documents including articles about you, but be cautious. Too many supporting documents can kill the impact of a great press release. Always include your business card.

The Centerpiece

A media kit needs a terrific, one-sheet press release as its centerpiece; everything else is gravy. Without a great press release, your package will usually be ignored. As the diva in your opera, the press release deserves prominence. It should be the first item seen when your package is opened. If you use a two-pocket folder or envelope, place the press release as the first item in the left hand pocket.

 **GUERRILLA TACTICS**

Press Releases

For your first mailing in most campaigns, send only a killer press release and no more than two or three of the items listed below in the Media Kit Toolbox. Select for inclusion items that will best represent your campaign and remember, don't overdo it.

Media Kits

Media Kits are no longer necessary for most initial mailings, but ideal for follow-ups. When a media contact requests more information, send everything you've got. When additional information is requested, you can't overdo it.

Media Kit Toolbox

In addition to your press release, media kits may include:

- Company history
- Personal biography
- List of suggested questions
- List of articles and appearances
- Brochures
- Copies of newspaper articles
- Your photograph
- Your business card
- Endorsements and testimonials
- An expansive article
- Quiz, trivia, and anecdotes
- Giveaways

Press Release

See Chapter 9, "Press Releases: Grab 'Em Fast and Don't Let Go," for a detailed discussion of press releases.

Company History

In three or four paragraphs that run no more than one page, tell your story. For example, how you started your company in your parents' garage, spun it off from UNICEF, or began by selling fat-free muffins door to door. Then, track your company's growth through product developments, mergers and acquisitions, and expansion. Describe your financial growth, goals, and projections for the future.

In writing your company history, build on the human interest angle, such as how you rose from rags to riches, overcame adversity, or employed the homeless. Stress ideas, vision, innovation, commitment, and long, hard, dedicated work. Write a narrative that the press can run without making any changes. Avoid technical language. Just tell your company's story, don't pat yourself on the back—let the media do that.

Sparingly weave general financial information about your company into the narrative to show growth and potential. Give general figures, not detailed numbers. If you wish to provide more in-depth information, include financial statements, annual reports, and projections on separate sheets.

Personal Biography

Your personal biography charts your background. In contrast to your company's history, your personal bio should be about you, the individual, and your accomplishments. Your bio is an opportunity to blow your own horn, to tell the media who you are, what you've done, and how you got there. Make its tone light and personable. Your personal bio is intended to document that you're an expert who merits media coverage.

Keep your personal bio succinct—limit it to one side of one page. Your bio is a place for information, not prose. Include only factual information that readers can scan for items of interest. Outline your training, experience, and achievements in chronological order. Also list your hobbies, interests, and charitable, civic, social, and athletic activities.

List of Suggested Questions

For your list of suggested questions, treat the print media differently from radio and TV. Always send radio and TV producers a list of suggested questions. But don't send suggested questions to print journalists without getting their prior consent. Print journalists often resent your questions and feel that as journalists they should ask their own questions, not yours. So ascertain their preference before you send them questions and note their responses for your media-contact list records.

Radio and TV hosts seldom read press kits or examine products or services beforehand. They read only what producers put in front of them, and they probably won't read that until moments before they're on the air.

Many producers will rely on your suggested questions. They may rewrite them or change their order, but they usually won't stray far from their basic meanings.

List and be ready to reel off the answers to a minimum of five questions on each of four topics. Review prior interviews that writers or hosts conducted, study their questioning patterns and approaches, and draft questions that fit.

List of Articles and Appearances

People in the media move cautiously. They're paid to produce lively, entertaining shows and articles. Dull or bad subjects are deadly and can cost them their jobs. Therefore, they want to see your track record. If you've been interviewed by the *New York Times, Fortune,* or *Wired* or appeared on *The Oprah Winfrey Show*, *Larry King Live,* and the *Today Show*, radio and TV producers will assume that you're good, they won't have to stick their necks out.

Writers and editors like to read pieces that others have written about you. They may take or rework material from earlier features. Prior articles may let them avoid what others have covered or help them come up with unique angles or spins.

In listing your articles, provide the publication's name and the date the piece ran. In listing appearances on radio and TV shows, list the program's name, date, and include favorable quotes about you from producers or hosts.

Brochures

If you have a brochure on your product or service, include it in your media kit. In most cases, it's not necessary to create a special brochure for your media kit, just include the brochure that you usually distribute for your business, but make sure that it looks professional.

Brochures in media kits are more than throw-ins because they convey credibility. They show that your business actually exists and provides an example of how you've decided to promote yourself to the public.

Copies of Newspaper Articles

Include two or three copies of articles about you and/or your business written by other authors. Remember, the press likes to see how others covered you and your business. Articles by other authors also support statements in your brochure and enhance your credibility—with both the public and the media—because people tend to believe what they read.

If articles about you have not been written, try to get some written and published. Contact you local paper to write about your product or service. It's not hard to convince hometown papers to run a feature on you because they like to spotlight local businesses. But it may take persistence. If you run into a brick wall, write an article yourself, or have one written for you, and submit it to a local paper.

Don't disregard older articles that were written about you, but supplement them with current pieces that tout changes or developments in your business. Older pieces show you have staying power, that you were news then and that you are still news, which may be a story within a story.

Also include reviews such as book or product reviews or mentions of your product or service in "Best Bet" sections.

Photograph

The press runs pictures to give stories a human face. People like to see what you look like. It adds to the story. In addition, after seeing your picture, an elusive producer may recognize you as someone he or she saw at a PTA meeting, the gym, or the bus and decide to help out a neighbor.

Five by seven inch black and white shots are fine for press kits. Color and larger images can get costly, especially if you're sending a lot of press kits.

Think about your pose, clothing, and setting. How do you want to be perceived? If you want to appear professorial, go for the glasses, tweed sport coat, and academic classroom setting. When you're promoting your home repair service, pose in your overalls in front of your truck.

Your Business Card

Throw a few of your business cards in your media kit. Many

envelopes and folders come precut to hold standard-sized business cards. If your card is not standard sized, attach or clip it to the left hand pocket. Members of the media will often file your card separately and hang on to it long after they've discarded your media kit.

An Expansive Article

If you feel that you must tell the press more than you can fit in a one-page press release, write a more expansive article. Use the article to tell your story fully with all the gory details. The press often picks up such articles and runs them as is or uses them as the basis for their own pieces.

Don't waste time sending more-detailed articles to radio and TV producers because they won't read them. Consider yourself lucky if they even read your press release.

Quiz, Trivia, Anecdotes

Create quizzes or games, such as anagrams and crossword puzzles, for your media kit. Audiences love them and they keep your message in the public eye. The media will use them in on-air interviews and run them as sidebars or box stories with print articles. Quiz takers invariably repeat questions to others, which helps to spread the word even further.

People are fascinated by, and usually repeat, interesting tidbits and lesser-known facts about you, your product, service, and industry. Trivia creates memorable links that the public will continue to associate with you.

Anecdotes provide context. They turn abstract ideas and theories into understandable, memorable stories. They're great for getting your point across. Verbal anecdotes are usually more effective because people generally prefer to listen rather than read, but reading can deliver a more indelible message.

Giveaways

Everyone loves freebies. It's amazing what people will take and keep when it's free. They may not need it. They may never use it, but they'll take it and hold on to it.

Small inexpensive promotional items such as calendars, tipping percentage cards, pens, pencils, flashlights, and sewing kits can be included in your media kit. Millions of items can be imprinted with your name, logo, or motto. Try to send something useful or that makes you stand out. Although people are usually flooded with these promotional items, your calendar may be the one an editor decides to hang.

Contact Information

Sending media kits is meaningless if the media doesn't know how to contact you. Expect every item in your kit to be removed from the folder and separated from everything else you sent. So be sure that your contact information is on every item.

 **GUERRILLA TACTICS**

Put your name, address, e-mail address, Web site, telephone numbers, fax number, and Web site address on your media kit cover and on both the top and bottom of every sheet you include. One surviving straggler might convince a producer to call, e-mail, or visit your site. So print all your contact information on your letterhead or make sure that each sheet lists it.

Packaging

Place all press kit materials in a two-pocket envelope or folder. Folder prices begin at around thirty cents each and increase in accordance with quality. The cheapest envelopes work, but don't look great. For about a dollar each, you can buy envelopes made of a shiny stock that looks better.

Print your logo or a photograph of your product along with your contact information on the cover of the media kit folder. For example, to promote a book, use the book cover image as the media kit cover. If you're in a financial crunch, simply paste a label with the subject, your name, and contact information on the media kit cover.

Use bright or unusually colored media kit folders. Color code and layer various sections of your kit. For example, run your press release on light blue paper, your biography on green, suggested questions on pink, etc.

Distribution

After you've gone to all the trouble of creating and sending your press kit, let's hope people open it. Your package will be competing with lots of other materials recipients receive, so take steps to make them want to read it.

 **GUERRILLA TACTICS**

The best way to get your package opened is by sending it by Federal Express. People open packages sent via FedEx, but that doesn't mean that they read them, only that they usually open them. FedEx packages carry the greatest perceived importance. United Parcel Service and Airborne come next and the rest of the overnight carriers, including the United States Postal Service, follow.

Overnight packages convey the impression that their content is important. They show that you value what you're shipping and that you incurred expense to assure that your media kit was promptly delivered. However, the proliferation of overnight delivery has removed some of the luster, and the cost runs high, especially for large mailings.

Guerrillas might find it preferable to send press kits via overnight delivery only for small, targeted distributions or in response to requests for information.

In lieu of overnight delivery, call attention to your package by using colored envelopes or by placing brightly colored stickers or labels on plain envelopes. Also consider stamping clever or provocative statements or teaser copy about the content on the envelopes. For example, a brightly colored yellow or orange sticker could state "Enclosed—Your ticket to tomorrow," "How to Beat the IRS," or "Your Prayers Are Answered Inside."

Remember

Don't overload your press kit with tons of slickly produced materials. Instead, include only the most pertinent information. Essentially, the media only wants your story—clearly and concisely told. Write a great one-page press release. Put your contact information on every page. Create an attractive, attention-getting kit that media people will want to open. Consider sending kits to the most important media via overnight delivery.

13
Fifteen Things the Media Hates

"It is an immutable law in business that words are words, explanations are explanations, promises are promises—but only performance is reality."
—HAROLD S. GENEEN, FORMER CHAIRMAN,
INTERNATIONAL TELEPHONE AND TELEGRAPH

THIS CHAPTER OUTLINES THE FIFTEEN THINGS your contacts in the media dislike most. Take heed. Avoid engaging in behaviors that have a high likelihood of alienating the very people you need to help you publicize your product or service.

1. Not Taking "No" for an Answer

Persistence is an admirable trait, but there comes a point when you must accept defeat. Media professionals won't build relationships with pig-headed pushers who call 500 times after they're told, "no." When your media contact says, "No," accept it. Don't even ask, "Why?" Walk away before you ruin a potentially valuable relationship.

2. Long News Releases

One killer page is all you need. If the media wants more, they'll ask for it. Come up with a great headline, state the major points in a strong first paragraph, and bullet everything you want to stress. Include secondary information in a background release.

3. Lying, Hype, and Misrepresentation

Be honest and reasonable. The truth always emerges, and when stories aren't based on facts, the media usually ends up holding the bag. Your media contacts won't forget who got them burned; nor will they give you the chance to do it again. As for hype, media pros know a good story when they see one, and their antennae usually cut through hype.

4. Lack of Preparation

Know exactly what you want. Don't approach the media for advice on how to proceed. Study your targets before pitching them. Identify their areas of interest, the approaches they use, and give them what they want. Pitching a story to the wrong outlet shows that you haven't done your research. It wastes everyone's time.

5. Small Talk

Get right to the point. Be clear and brief. Don't confuse chitchat with courtesy. With the media, making small talk isn't polite, it borders on rudeness. Most media people are too busy to gab. Small talk holds them hostage; it keeps them from attending to business. Small talk is thinly veiled manipulation that rarely works.

6. Overkill

Media kits that weigh as much as your Cocker Spaniel turn off the media. Less is more. When in doubt, leave it out. Most recipients resent bulging kits and won't read them. The last thing they want is more stuff. If you must send tomes, bind them securely because it's maddening to watch papers falling out and scattering in every direction when you open an envelope.

7. Cold Calls

Unsolicited phone calls are intrusions. They interrupt busy people while they're working, which may explain why you sometimes encounter a foul mood at the other end of the line. E-mail first to alert your media contacts that your press release has been sent. If your message or the press release strikes a chord, they'll get back to you. Similarly, don't send unrequested video-tapes, because media people won't watch something they didn't request. Unless you receive express permission, never call the media at home!

8. Freebies

Avoid offering free tickets and other bribes. Many media outlets prohibit gifts altogether; some bar presents over a fixed dollar amount (often $25); and others require gifts to be shared with coworkers, or donated to charity. Generally, journalists and producers want good stories, not T-shirts or coffee mugs.

GUERRILLA INTELLIGENCE

Food is often welcome. Many media people who work the late-night shift in newsrooms and stations love receiving free food, but don't expect them to publicly express their appreciation. When Jill interviewed the press, they said that they loved receiving chocolate chip cookies. Clever packaging, such as placing the picture of a publicity seeker on a pizza box or your picture on a box of donuts, can produce positive responses. Free food may build good will, but it won't guarantee you publicity.

9. Name Dropping

Nobody likes name droppers. Name dropping often indicates that the story is weak. In most cases, the connections that celebrated names are intended to conjure up are tenuous at best and unless the celebrity is directly involved, they seldom change the story's value. While name dropping may work with friends, it will hurt you with media professionals.

10. Lack of Focus

Stories that focus on the source, instead of the needs of the audience, generally do not appeal to the media. Your discovery of a foolproof method of pickling pimentos may be the biggest thing in your life, but it's probably of little or no interest to the rest of the world. If you want your story covered by the media, it must have audience appeal.

11. Confirmation Calls

Opinions on making unrequested calls to your media contact to check to see whether the faxes and packages you sent have arrived draw mixed responses. Some media pros see them as helpful reminders for keeping track of items on their plates. Others resent them as pestering. Media people often want to let the information soak in, and prefer to respond without reminders when, and if, they're interested. While follow-up calls are used to make the initial booking, confirmation calls are to find out if the agreed-upon event occurred.

12. Gimmicks

If you use a gimmick, it better be sensational, because the vast majority of gimmicks fail to gain the intended impact. And, the reason you're using the gimmick must be clear. Never assume that your contact will get the point you're trying to make. Most media people prefer conventional approaches. A reporter for a big-city newspaper told us that a woman who appeared outside his office clad in a bikini and blowing a trumpet provided a good laugh, but she didn't get the publicity she wanted because she never mentioned why she was there.

13. Not Following Up Requests

Media professionals depend on others to supply them with the information they need to do their jobs. If you send press releases, and call or fax, and then don't follow up when additional information is requested, you make it difficult for them to meet their deadlines. If you say, or even imply, that you're going to do something, do it and do it promptly. Otherwise, your contacts will consider you unreliable and unprofessional. If you don't respond promptly, it may be too late. You can't expect the media to wait for you.

14. Same Ideas

Don't repeatedly send the same idea, no matter how cleverly you repackage it. Writers and producers recognize and resent old dogs dolled up in new duds. "A lump of coal is still a lump of coal, and no matter how you package it, it's not a diamond," a producer explained.

15. Getting Upset

Grow up! This isn't Miz Mazie's nursery school. The media expects to deal with adults and won't tolerate your hissy fits. Be professional. If you can't keep your cool, find another business and see a shrink.

14
Fifteen Things the Media Loves

"Reporters are like alligators. You don't have to love them, you don't necessarily have to like them. But you do have to feed them."

—ANONYMOUS

IN DIRECT CONTRAST TO THE PREVIOUS CHAPTER, this chapter provides insights on how to gain the attention and respect of media people.

1. News

Above all else, media people want newsworthy items. The first thing they ask is, "Will our audience care about this product or service?" News is what affects people's lives and what they discuss at the dinner table and around the water cooler. For the media, news is not just about information, it's about communicating value and benefit for their audience. So, provide news rather than trying to sell your wares.

2. Brevity

Save everyone time and effort by sending short, concise messages, preferably by e-mail. Cut to the chase; be direct and avoid subterfuge. E-mail your ideas and state what you're pitching and how it will help their audience. Long missives often go unread.

> ### GUERRILLA INTELLIGENCE
>
> Warning! Faxes often are not delivered to the intended recipient. Some newsrooms, TV and radio stations, and offices have only one fax machine or one per floor. It may be operated by an intern or a clerk. In large organizations, faxes are often undelivered or delivered to the wrong person. Journalists and producers may not respond to calls inquiring into whether a fax was received because such calls are usually ruses to further the caller's agenda. If you send faxes, follow them up with e-mail.

3. Knowing Targets

Every story isn't for every media outlet. Research the audience you wish to reach and identify which outlets best target that audience. Study them: read their articles, watch and listen to their programs, and visit their Web sites before sending them your materials. Customize your pitch to stress how it will benefit each outlet's audience. Send business stories to business reporters, not to home and garden reporters, unless the story has a home and garden angle.

4. Relationships

Media people like to deal with people who build relationships rather than merely try to sell a story. Although individual stories are important, people in the media know that careers are built by forging strong relationships. To the media, professionals build relationships and they prefer to work with professionals rather than one-shot wonders.

5. Preparation

Do your homework. Have your act together and be ready to deliver what the media needs. Know your subject inside out and have written materials completed and on hand to send upon request. If you are publicizing a product, send the product to the media or arrange for them to see it. Having your act together shows your commitment and that you're a dedicated professional. It makes the media's job easier.

6. Broad Appeal

The media wants stories that reach a wide variety of individuals and features that make audiences say, "I know someone who's going through that." They look for stories that make people think, feel, and identify. Search for broad themes.

7. Ties

Stories that complement larger news events, such as breaking news or trends, are usually well received. Media people look for topics that will spawn families of stories. For example, during the Columbine High School crisis, they ran stories on raising boys, handling grief, treating trauma, gun control and violence, and the media's treatment of such stories.

8. Experience

Reporters and editors like to see how other media outlets have covered your story, so send them articles that others have written about you. Producers want to know how you came off on camera or radio so give them a list of shows you've appeared on and offer to supply tapes for their review.

9. Visualization

The media loves stories that they can picture. In your written materials, use visual terms to create graphic images, and tell stories that illustrate and give life to your main points.

10. Celebrity Tie-Ins

Explain to your media contacts how the product or service you're promoting is connected to well-known personalities. The public craves information about celebrities, and products linked to them get plenty of ink and air time.

11. Prompt Response

Since the media work under tight deadlines, time is always of the essence. Respond promptly to requests. Send requested material by the fastest route, either hand delivery or overnight express. Delays can cause postponements or cancellations. Remember, time is always of the essence. You're always in a race.

12. Courtesy

Be polite and respectful to media staff people, especially those who answer the phone. Before speaking with media contacts, learn the proper pronunciation of their names. Butchering a media contact's name will get you off to a rocky start; it will put you in a hole before you begin.

13. Visual Aids

A picture is worth 10,000 words. Send charts, graphs, photographs, illustrations, and other graphic aids that reporters can stick under editors' noses to show why your story merits telling.

14. No Road Blocks

When working with the media, smooth the way and remove all obstacles that could derail or weaken your story. Anticipate problems and help keep your story on track through the whole process, even after it runs. Make sure that it continues to provide value and benefit to listeners, readers, and viewers.

15. A Pleasant Attitude

Be pleasant, enthusiastic, and professional. See yourself as a valuable resource for journalists and producers. Be natural, positive, and make a connection. Don't whine, complain, gush, or be phony. Become a person that media professionals enjoy associating with.

15
Find Your Uniqueness and Capitalize On It

"All progress is initiated by challenging current conceptions,
and executed by supplanting existing institutions."
—GEORGE BERNARD SHAW

EACH OF US IS UNIQUE. We have different backgrounds, experiences, and accomplishments. Even those of us who do the same things go about them differently. Look at yourself and identify how you differ from the norm.

Take inventory. Find out what's unique about you and what special ingredients distinguish you and your product or service from the crowd. Then come up with clever, interesting, and unusual ways to tell the world about it.

Are you unusually tall, strong, old, young, athletic, talented or accomplished in music, art, crafts, or cooking. Are you a member of a minority or are you handicapped? Do you work in a trade or profession typically done by members of the opposite sex? Have you overcome adversity? Have you lived outside the country, in a car, in a commune, in a refugee camp, or in a leper colony? Have you climbed Mt. Everest, piloted jet bombers, or saved someone's life?

Have your experiences given you special insights, under-standings, or perspectives that makes your voice unique? If so, explain how it's unique. Who can benefit from your uniqueness and how?

GUERRILLA INTELLIGENCE

Self-appraisal is tricky. Often, we're completely unaware of qualities in ourselves that others find obvious, and what we think we are simply isn't so. If we asked our friends and neighbors to complete a questionnaire about our uniqueness, the results would be startling. To identify your unique characteristics:

- Discard all your preconceptions about who you are, they're probably invalid.
- Zero in on your uniqueness by asking yourself what about you do people find intriguing? What do they want to know? What questions do they ask?
- Then, for a more in-depth analysis, complete the following checklist. This is your personal checklist, a checklist for your business is provided later in this chapter. In completing the checklist, write full narrative answers. Include as much information as possible, whatever comes to mind, without editing yourself. In this exercise, more is better.

Personal Checklist

Your name: _____

Your age: _____

Your place of birth: _____

Your current address: _____

Your family: _____

Spouse's name and occupation:

_____

Children's names and occupations:

_____

_____

Parents' names and occupations:

_____

_____

Siblings' names and occupations:

_____

_____

Well-known or accomplished relatives:

_____

Your previous addresses (cities, states, countries only):

_____

_____

Where you were educated, and in what specialty?

_____

_____

_____

Your present occupation:

_____

Your degrees, licenses, certifications:

_____

_____

How and why you got into your current business:

_____

_____

_____

Your previous careers:

_____

_____

_____

Your accomplishments and awards:

_____

_____

_____

_____

Your well-known teachers or business associates:

_____

_____

Your interests, hobbies, and special skills:

_____

_____

_____

Examine Your Business

After you've examined yourself, turn to your business. What's special about your market? Does it involve special secrets, processes, connections, or ways of doing business? Does it require special equipment or exotic materials? Must you have expert knowledge of products or customs in other countries or cultures? Are you the only business in Southern Michigan that imports, sells, or makes your particular product? Is your service the fastest; the best value; the most inexpensive, experienced, reliable, creative, or efficient? Do you offer the best service, warranty, or references? Is yours the only licensed, certified, approved, affiliated, endorsed, or recommended product or service?

Complete the following business checklist. As you write each answer, focus on how your business benefits your customers.

Business Checklist

Your business name:

_____

Your business address:

_____

_____

_____

Years in business:

_____

Your business history:

_____

_____

_____

Explain what you do:

_____

_____

Special knowledge, training, or skills required:

_____

_____

Special formulas, processes, copyrights, or patents:

_____

_____

_____

Do you have competitors:

_____

Difference between your business and your competitors:

_____

_____

_____

Explain the reasons for your business success:

_____

_____

_____

Describe your business plans:

_____

_____

_____

 **GUERRILLA TACTICS**

Upon completing both checklists:

- Reread each answer, but make no changes.
- Circle all words or phrases you've written that denote anything unique, special, or particular to you or your business.
- On a separate sheet, list all the circled words and phrases. Then explore scenarios of how these unique items could be used to promote you and your business.
- Every six months, review and update the answers on your personal checklist as well as how you could capitalize on them to promote your business.

Capitalize on Uniqueness

After you've identified both your own and your business's uniqueness, get creative. Find a hook, a link, or a device to capitalize on that specialness, something that will capture the media's interest. Since media professionals are under severe time pressures, they may simply go with the slant in your news release. However, be prepared for them to spin it in other directions.

GUERRILLA INTELLIGENCE

Remember, reporters care only about items that will benefit their audiences. What you're promoting may be inventive. It may even be groundbreaking or earth shattering, but if it doesn't relate to business, *Forbes, Fortune,* and *Fast Company* won't give it much ink, if they cover it at all.

It's not enough to claim that your services are special. You must convince the media that your services are special in relation to their audience. Producers and journalists want stories about what's new, creative, unusual, glamorous, and the best. They want to tell their audience that you can help them because you do or have something unique and/or do it better.

After you've completed the checklists, review your answers and make a list of all possible benefits to your customers. For example, your location, low prices, business experience, satisfied customers, or special training may be just what potential customers are looking for.

List groups that you and your business could help and how they could help them. Conduct a survey, hire a research firm, call friends, family, and network contacts to solicit their input and suggestions. Their observations will provide insight.

 **GUERRILLA TACTICS**

Positioning of your product or service is essential. Use the unique characteristics of your customers' wants, needs, and perceptions to position your business in both the marketplace and the media. Follow the five steps below to get the information you need:

1. *Address customers.* Verify what your target customers want from your product or service. Ask current customers what they like best about your product or service and why they do business with you instead of your competitors. Learn exactly what prospective customers want and see if that's a viable direction for your business. Build your identity around your ability to delight your customers. Get written testimonials attesting to your customers' satisfaction.

2. *Address the competition.* Survey your competition to learn how they represent themselves in the marketplace. What do they claim? What do they promise? Do they deliver? Distinguish yourself by going a notch higher, delivering more, faster, cheaper, or more reliably. Use your competitors as a standard for improvement. Pull away from the pack.

3. *Address perceptions.* Find out how the public perceives your industry. Accept generalizations as truths, and bill

yourself as the exception to the rule. If businesses in your industry are considered unreliable, distinguish yourself by promoting yourself as being dependable and responsible. Call yourself the pain-free dentist for frightened patients, the courier that protects fragile cargo, or the dry cleaner that never breaks buttons.

4. *Address potential customers.* Prepare media materials that emphasize the benefits that your potential customers will receive. State, without hype, exactly what you will deliver. Spell out concrete benefits that potential customers will receive, such as lower tax payments, continued good health, less stress, more leisure time, or financial savings.

5. *Address your business.* Comprehensively examine your business to identify everything unique about it.

If you're a member of a minority group, be sure to send your information to the media that covers your group. Don't think of it as exploitation; it's not. It's guidance and inspiration for those who may have to cross the same mine fields you've already cleared. Take whatever is unique and different about you and use it to help others.

GUERRILLA TALE

Jill Lublin's client, Ryan, an Asian-American industrial designer, was "downsized" from his corporate job at the worst possible time, when his wife was pregnant with their third child. Within twenty-four hours of his discharge, Ryan started his own online business and recruited eight employees in seven counties. He then sent out a press release heralding himself as "The Virtual Office Warrior" who vowed never to work in an office again. Both the general press and the Asian-American press ran articles on Ryan. Calls from new clients poured in and Ryan never looked back.

The articles on Ryan mentioned that he was an industrial designer, but they concentrated on how he turned a potential disaster into an exciting, profitable business. Media professionals knew that Ryan's story would appeal to millions of young bread-winners who were vulnerable to corporate guillotines. Their coverage had little to do with Ryan's profession, it had to do with inspiration. They sought to appeal to readers by relating how some guy, who had the rug pulled out from under him, managed to not only get back on his feet, but also land squarely and be pointed in a promising new direction.

Approach the media that covers your industry. If you're a woman in business don't contact just women's publications, pitch both women's and business publications. If you're a minority woman, also contact media that covers your minority.

Puns on Names

Puns can produce agonized groans, but they also forge indelible links, which the public doesn't forget. Simple, common name links can be memorable, for example, Art by Art, Phil the Bill, Jumping Jack's, Mac the Knife. You've heard a million of them. Each identifies the business operator and couples it with the business.

 **GUERRILLA TALE**

Joan Kraft, a technical writer, wanted to promote her first one-woman exhibit as a fine-art painter. She sent out a press release with the headline "Arts and Kraft." When a major newspaper published an article on Joan, it ran the same headline she had written for her press release. Joan's exhibit quickly sold out.

Write headlines that put a unique twist on your career. For example, the media loved a juggler's article "Juggling Your Business Life," a feature on a magician called "How to Put Magic Back in Your Business," and a piece on a plumber entitled "Plugging Security Leaks."

Timing

Hallmark Cards built its empire around holidays, and there's no reason why you can't use events and holidays as opportunities to promote yourself.

During the Christmas holiday season, the public is interested in psychologists' articles, talks, and seminars on loneliness; pieces by dietitians about healthy eating; features by physical trainers on exercise; and advice by financial planners on credit card debt and investing. Other propitious publicity opportunities include the beginning of the school year, Halloween, Election Day, Thanksgiving, New Year's Day, Presidents' Day, Mother's Day, and Father's Day.

Remember

Take inventory. Complete the checklists to identify your uniqueness and the uniqueness of your business. Then find a link to capitalize on that specialness that will capture the media's interest. Focus on what consumers want, your competitors' claims, and perceptions about your business. Then distinguish yourself.

16
Promote Early, Forcefully, and Fast

"You can get much farther with a kind word and a gun than you can with a kind word alone."

—AL CAPONE

YEARS AGO, PUBLICISTS WERE CALLED "advance men." The term was coined because their job was to travel around and drum up public interest before a product or service was introduced. Although the term isn't widely used today, the basic concept remains unchanged: in order to mount an effective publicity campaign, you must begin early and lay the ground work well in advance of the product or service's introduction.

GUERRILLA TACTICS

As a general rule, if you're running an event, send the press package out six weeks prior to the scheduled date. The press, particularly TV, won't even talk to you until the week of the event. The print media will usually publicize an event a day or two before it's scheduled to take place.

If you send your press package six weeks before the event, e-mail or call your media contacts during the following week and every week thereafter. Ask if they received your package, whether they understood what it was, whether they have any questions or would they like more information, and whether they have entered your event on their calendar.

What works one time may not work later. So, if you begin early and find that an approach isn't meeting your goals, you'll still have time to implement other alternatives.

It's critical to get your events listed in the coming events or calendar sections of newspapers, newsletters, Web sites, and bulletin boards. However, some media listings are restricted to events that charge less than a set amount, usually $25 to $50. So, check ceiling amounts.

An effective way to get around price ceilings for free calendar listings is to schedule a free introductory evening the night before the event. For example, if you're charging $500 for a weekend seminar, list the free introductory evening, not the seminar itself. Then promote the seminar at the free introductory session. In the meantime, try to convince the media to run a feature promoting you as an expert and lauding the benefits of your seminar.

GUERRILLA INTELLIGENCE

Writers, editors, and producers have little time to talk with you on the phone. Usually, they're so busy that even the briefest conversation takes them away from more pressing projects. As a result, they tend to be unresponsive. If you do reach them, they may be curt and impatient. Don't take it personally, it's the nature of the business.

In the first ten seconds, seasoned news people know whether they're interested in your pitch. "It's what's up front that counts!" In the first ten seconds, you must grab their interest and make them want more.

When you pitch a busy editor or producer, it's not a social occasion like the chamber of commerce mixer. Hit the media hard and fast, or they'll turn you off.

Be the First

It also helps to be the first in your field to get the media's attention. Ideally, they'll recognize you for the sheer innovative genius of your product or service and beat down your door to do features on you. But this isn't always an ideal world and you'll probably have to generate the interest yourself.

Contact the media yourself. If you're the first local dietitian to call a reporter to comment on her exposé on weight loss programs, you could find yourself quoted in subsequent articles. After reading pieces, write or e-mail compliments, offer suggestions for follow-up features, and explain precisely how you can help. Specifically, offer to make your sources available to them.

Start Early

Begin your publicity campaign as soon as you get the idea for a new business or event or before you write your book. Authors of bestsellers plan their books' publicity long before their books are written. They put the PR wheels in motion fast.

First, plan your campaign. List all steps you plan to take, estimate the costs, and set target dates. Then send announcements, get listed in the "Business Brief" and "Movers and Shakers" sections, and write articles. Lay the groundwork early.

Forcefully and Fast

"If you think you can, you can.
And if you think you can't, you're right."
—MARY KAY ASH, CHAIRPERSON,
MARY KAY COSMETICS

Delivering your message forcefully conveys enthusiasm and passion. It's more dynamic and convincing. Enthusiasm and conviction are contagious. If others believe you or are stirred by your passion, they'll follow you and work their butts off to help you, which is what you want. If you come across as lukewarm about your product or service, expect the media to respond accordingly.

The media is impatient. They're overworked and sleep-deprived, and won't waste time promoting weak or inarticulate spokespersons or drawing out information. It's your job to communicate, to present your message clearly, concisely, and forcefully or you'll be history.

GUERRILLA INTELLIGENCE

Remember, you have only ten seconds, that's all. If you can't deliver a convincing message in ten seconds, the media won't listen. The first ten seconds will buy you another twenty seconds, so your follow-up must also be strong. If you can't interest the media after thirty seconds, they'll think your story's weak, that you don't know it well enough, or you're not prepared.

Speak plain English. Your objective is to get your message across, to be fully understood. Unless you're dealing with a special subculture and must prove that you know the lingo, say it simply, clearly, and fast. It's far more important to be understood than to try to be cool.

Remember

To mount a successful publicity campaign, you must begin early and lay the groundwork well in advance of the product's or service's introduction. Send the press package six weeks prior to the scheduled date and then call or e-mail your contacts to see if they've included your event on their schedule or have questions. Deliver your message forcefully to convey enthusiasm and passion.

17
Always Be Too Prepared for an Interview

"Luck is the residue of preparation."
—ANONYMOUS

BEING INTERVIEWED IS GIVING A PERFORMANCE. For most of us, it's not something that we are accustomed to and the very thought can make us catatonic. When the microphone approaches, even the most articulate, witty, and knowledgeable person can get butterflies and lose it all together.

GUERRILLA INTELLIGENCE

If you know your stuff, the uneasiness usually dissipates as soon as the first words are out and the answers start to flow. Interviews become opportunities, platforms to display your acumen and mastery of your subject.

Problems during interviews usually occur because interviewees don't adequately know their subject. The main reason they have difficulties is because they don't have the content down or know what they want to say.

Before you're interviewed, know exactly what you want to say. Rick Frishman insists that all his clients undergo training before they're interviewed. "No director," he points out, "would send an untrained, unrehearsed actor on stage, and in PR we're the directors and our clients are the actors. Our clients must know their lines and how to deliver them or the audience will get up and leave."

 **GUERRILLA TACTICS**

Prepare five main points to work into every interview. They should be similar, if not identical, to the main points in your press release. Also have another fifteen to twenty subpoints, or three to four under each of the five main categories, to reel off because you never know how long an interview will run.

The second step in preparing for an interview is to strengthen those points by using devices such as anecdotes, stories, jokes, and statistics that will make your points more entertaining and memorable.

The third step is to appear natural, spontaneous, and unrehearsed, which takes lots of practice.

Practice, Practice, Practice

Let's assume that you know your content, because if you don't, you're not ready to be interviewed. So before you do anything else, get your content down. For interviews, know what you're talking about and say it with authority. You must be convincing.

Once you know your content thoroughly, you are ready to plan for interviews and practice to improve your interviewing skills. Some important techniques and tips are listed below:

- Write down the five main points you wish to cover.
- List stories, facts, anecdotes, and jokes under each of the five main points.

- Anticipate the questions that interviewers will ask and prepare answers that include your main points. Study the host's
  prior interviews to determine his or her favorite questions
  and approaches. Ask yourself those same questions and
  work your main points into your answers.
- Keep your answers and explanations simple. Complex information tends to lose or bore interviewers and audiences.
- Never try to steal the limelight from the host or interviewer.
  Your job is to make them look good.
- Ask friends and family to grill you. Pretend that they're
  Larry King, Katie Couric, or Johnnie Cochran.
- When friends and family question you, videotape yourself
  or stand in front of a mirror to observe your performance.
  Be conscious of your posture, facial expressions, and ges-
  tures. Work your main points into your answers, and ask
  your interviewer to critique your performance honestly.
- When friends and family are unavailable to assist you, inter-
  view yourself aloud.

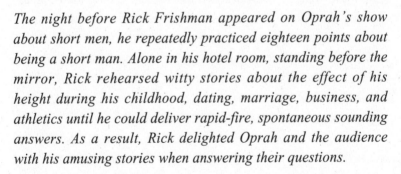

GUERRILLA TALE

*The night before Rick Frishman appeared on Oprah's show
about short men, he repeatedly practiced eighteen points about
being a short man. Alone in his hotel room, standing before the
mirror, Rick rehearsed witty stories about the effect of his
height during his childhood, dating, marriage, business, and
athletics until he could deliver rapid-fire, spontaneous sounding
answers. As a result, Rick delighted Oprah and the audience
with his amusing stories when answering their questions.*

Rehearse to make your interview responses seem unrehearsed.
Talk to the audience and interviewer, don't make speeches or lecture them. Reword canned replies so they don't sound automatic
or robotic. Give them new life.

Your goal is to connect with as big an audience as possible.
So, be down to earth. Avoid "Esoteric-land." Most people don't

live there. Big words, complex theories, and wordy answers may seem impressive, but they put most people to sleep.

Don't act too smart or too dumb; find a happy medium. Remember the purpose of your appearance is to communicate your message and to build public interest. Speak so that people can understand you and want to hear and respond to your message.

Take Control

In interviews, take command. Tell yourself it's your interview, your performance, and your only opportunity to sell yourself. Don't wait for the perfect question, it may never come. Be ready to smoothly swing any question to your main points.

Always answer the interviewer's question. If it doesn't involve your main points, just touch on it and then slip into your main points. Move into your main points by saying, "That reminds me of a story." or "When I was _____."

Never alienate an interviewer. Good communicators act as if every question is brilliant or insightful even when they're changing the subject to stress their main points. It's the feeling they convey, the way they look, their smile or facial expression. Say, "What a great question." or "No one's ever asked me that before." and address it briefly before pursuing your agenda. Interviewers will give you plenty of slack when you make them look good. Similarly, when you take control, don't let interviewers feel that they've lost control. Be respectful and deferential.

Be a good, sensitive listener. Wait for the right opportunity, see if the interviewer moves to get you back on point and if so, how strongly. Use the interviewer's questions to move into your points, but always move gently. If you're abrupt, the audience, and the interviewer, will feel manipulated.

Never state anything "off the record." It usually comes back to haunt you.

Knowing how and when to slide into you main points takes practice. So be patient, practice, and conduct mock interviews.

Stay Loose

The way you act during the interview has a major effect on how your message is received. Let your knowledge and confidence shine through. You can be most effective when you:

- Act natural and avoid language, expressions, and gestures that you don't ordinarily use.
- Keep your responses simple and light.
- Avoid long, complex explanations, and never lecture or preach.
- Smile frequently, but avoid prolonged, big grins and long, loud laughs.
- Be humble.
- Never try to steal the limelight from the host or interviewer. Your job is to make the interviewer look good.

GUERRILLA INTELLIGENCE

Don't drink coffee before an interview, it dries you out. Drink water if your mouth gets dry, even if the camera is on you. If you're not dry, it's still wise to drink water during interviews to prevent dryness. Sipping some water can also give you time to pause and think before answering tough questions.

Interview Components

Interviews have three components: the questions, the answers, and the solutions.

The Questions

Although you have little control over the questions, you can anticipate them. Each interviewer usually has a distinguishable style and asks questions that follow a similar pattern. Study other interviews that the host conducted to identify the type of questioning you can expect. Then practice slipping your main points into answers to those types of questions.

The Answers

When you reply, try to give examples that the average person can relate to. Create bonds by asking audiences, "How many of you have ever had this happen?" or "Do you know anybody who _____?" Audiences will remember similar incidents and will identify with what you're saying. But most importantly, they'll keep listening to you.

The Solutions

When people identify with what your are saying, you've got them. At that point, they want solutions. They want you to tell them exactly what they should have done and to teach them how to act if they face the same dilemma again. When they want answers, they'll more than listen, they'll hang on your every word.

 **GUERRILLA TACTICS**

Never tease. When you have them hooked, give them enough hard, solid, concrete information to change their lives. You want them to say, "Wow, this person wasn't just trying to sell his or her product or service, he or she was trying to teach me, to help me." So don't engage in hype or self promotion. Instead, help, show, teach, and be a resource.

Concentrate on providing relevant responses that can help the audience understand the topic. Resist the temptation to plug your product or service continually; let the host do the hype. Most hosts are seasoned professionals who know the best times for promotions, so leave it in their hands. Both hosts and audiences respond more favorably to those who answer responsively than to those who seem to be shameless hucksters.

The Unexpected

Prepare for the unexpected. Interviewers frequently meander down dark, back alleys that don't lead where you want to go.

Some interviewers will try finding out your deepest secrets, such as you were once charged with insider trading, you've had seven wives, or you finished third on the *Gong Show*.

Obviously, you can't ignore these subjects, so prepare for them. Confront all of your ghosts and the skeletons in your closet; practice brief, responsive answers that are honest and sincere.

Since the purpose of the interview is to sell your book or to promote your sportswear, respond directly and gracefully to all questions. Work your main points into your answers. When that is impossible, don't force the issue. Respond briefly to the question and hope that subsequent questions will provide you with openings to make your points.

GUERRILLA INTELLIGENCE

If you're on *Good Morning America* and want to be invited back, take care not to break the show's cardinal rule, "Do not overpromote your product or service." For example, if your product is a book, do not say, "As stated in my book" or mention the title of the book more than once. Similarly, don't repeatedly mention the name of your product or service. Talk about the subject and situations. Help instead of selling. It will get you repeat appearances!

Media Coaches

Everyone needs media training. Few of us are accustomed to appearing before the media, which is an acquired skill. Most professional spokespersons are experienced actors. If you plan to represent yourself, invest in a media coach! Rick and Jill consider Joel Roberts (2461 Santa Monica Boulevard, Santa Monica, CA 90707, 310-286-0631) to be the best media trainer in the country.

Media coaches operate in most major cities. Check in the yellow pages under Coaches & Communications and Media Skills. PR firms also conduct media training and can give you the names of top local coaches. Media coaches are Houdinis who can turn even the most awkward and clumsy buffoons into media stars. They can teach you how make the most of interviews by helping with both content and technique. They can show you how to identify your main points, how to move into them seamlessly, and how to present them more interestingly and entertainingly. Regarding your interview techniques, media coaches can critique how you speak, smile, sit, hold your hands, position your legs, or tilt your head. They will even teach you what to wear. By videotaping scripted interviews, coaches make it easier for you to correct mistakes or poor techniques that you otherwise would miss.

Coaches can help you to turn questions to your advantages. They can also teach you how to get a feel for the audience, to question or make contact with them. They can help you deal with nervousness and its manifestations such as tics, nervous tapping, or awkward movements.

 **GUERRILLA TACTICS**

Two good alternatives to media coaches are public speaking groups such as The National Speakers Association (*www.nsas-peaker.com*), Toastmasters International (*www.toastmasters.org*), and acting classes. At these organizations, which are located in most major cities, you can get experience speaking before groups of people and receive solid evaluations. They're also great places to network and develop contacts. Most community colleges and adult education programs offer acting and drama classes, which can help you overcome fears of appearing before audiences.

Postmortems

After the interview, thank the interviewer. State that you're new to interviews and ask for tips. Many interviewers are seasoned professionals who can be enormously helpful.

To conduct your own postmortem:

- Go over each question asked in the interview and grade your answer to it.
- Ask yourself if you covered all your main points. Did you handle them effectively? How can you improve?
- Identify main points you missed or didn't answer well and prepare better responses for future interviews.
- Ask friends and colleagues to critique your performance objectively.

Remember

Before any interview, know exactly what you plan to say. If you don't know your subject, don't give an interview! Work five main points into every interview and have another fifteen to twenty sub-points that you can cover. Listen to the interviewer's questions carefully and take control of the interview. Always be prepared for the unexpected, and get help from media coaches.

18
Keep Up to Date!

"Our Age of Anxiety is, in great part, the result of trying
to do today's jobs with yesterday's tools."
—MARSHALL McLUHAN, COMMUNICATIONS
THEORIST AND EDUCATOR

AS WE'VE STATED, in media relations credibility is essential.
Media relationships are built on trust, and the media must be confident that it can rely on information you provide. If you send out-
of-date items in your press release or media kit or your Web site
isn't current, your media contacts will cross you off their lists.
They can't risk running inaccurate information.

So, if you plan to deal with the media, keep up to date!
Update everything regularly including your press release, media
kit, Web site, and your answering machine message. If you don't,
you'll fall victim to the relentless tides of change, and once they
sweep you under, you won't be able to breathe.

Continually read, watch, listen, and browse. Become a media
junkie. Constantly study the media. Categorize the hot stories
reported, the outlets covering them, and how they approach those

stories. Are they conservative, liberal, business oriented, new age, aggressive, passive, or opinionated? Examine the repercussions of their coverage and how long various stories run.

Learn the players. When you contact media people, be in a position to say, "I loved those pieces you did on _____." Talk to them about their work and then pitch them similar or related items.

Jump on developments that might relate to your business. Copy articles about innovations and trends and add them to your media kit to illustrate the potential of your business. Rewrite press releases and articles to stress how those changes will boost your sales. Spot trends and position yourself to capitalize on those trends. Link your business with items in the news.

Include Dates

Date every page of all print materials you distribute, and prominently post the current date on your Web site. Displaying the current date on Web sites each day can keep your site at the top of some search lists. These search engines sort by the most recent update dates, so daily updates will maintain your priority position. The top listed sites get the most hits, which means more people and more publicity.

When you make a point of keeping current, media people will notice it; it will became an asset, a story in itself. The media will want to deal with you because they know your information is current.

 **GUERRILLA TALE**

Although Planned Television Arts (PTA) www.plannedtvarts.com, Rick Frishman's agency, has a central switchboard with a full-time operator, company policy requires everyone in the agency who works with clients to record daily answering machine messages.

Rick's message states:
"Hi, this is Rick. It's Wednesday, November fourteenth. Hit one to skip this message and go straight to the beep. I'm here

today until six. Leave a message, and I'll get back to you. If you need to speak to someone, hit zero and the operator will help you."

Rick and his associates give clients their direct phone numbers so calls come straight to their extensions. They record a daily message and use the agency operator only as a back up. When clients call, they know that Rick, or others at PTA, are in the office that day, that their message will be heard, and that their call will be returned. In our voice-mail world, knowing that your message will be heard is at least half the battle.

Daily messages tell clients or customers that instead of hiding behind electronic fences, you're using existing technology innovatively to get and respond to your messages. Daily messages give callers a feeling of well-being because they know that they're not in voice mail hell. Clients or customers are impressed by businesses that understand their concerns.

Acknowledge E-mails

Acknowledge that you've received and read e-mail messages. Even a brief few words—"Thanks a lot," "Sounds good," or "I'll get right on it,"—can make an enormous impact. Senders appreciate knowing that you read their messages. Although most e-mail programs have a return receipt feature, it acknowledges that e-mail was received, not that it was read.

Responding is easy. All you have to do is use the e-mail "Reply" feature and type in a few words. Brevity and all lower case responses are perfectly acceptable, and if you can respond quickly, all the better!

Remember

Media relations is about credibility, so keep up to date. Read, watch, listen, and browse the media. Learn who the players are and what subjects interest them. Contact them when you have a good match. Record a daily telephone message and respond to all e-mail.

19
Think "Headlines"

*"What is written without effort is in
general read without pleasure."*
—SAMUEL JOHNSON, ENGLISH CRITIC,
ESSAYIST, AND POET

IMAGINE A WORLD WITHOUT HEADLINES. Headlines are
signals or road signs that give order to the glut of information that
pervades our world. By identifying what things are about, they let
us make choices and decide what to read. Like their cousin, the
sound bite, headlines are symbols of our times, an era when
everything must be packaged to sell quickly. Today, no one
seems to have time for the whole story; they want the quick ver-
sion, the one line that will tell them what the story is about. As a
result, we're living in a world of headlines.

Look at the Internet, where messages of maximum clarity
must be delivered in minimal space. Web pages feature words or
short statements (headlines) that you click on to link to additional
content. The purpose of headlines is to capture readers' attention
and to get them to read the material that the headline touts.

Headlines are the equivalent of book, CD, and DVD titles that inform us what lies within.

> ## GUERRILLA INTELLIGENCE
> Learn to write great headlines. Besides being a valuable publicity tool, learning to write terrific headlines will force you to:
>
> - Sharpen your focus
> - Clarify your objectives
> - Deliver messages with the greatest clarity and impact

Before you write a headline, answer these questions:

1. What is the story about?
2. Why are you telling it?
3. Whom are you communicating to?
4. How do you want them to react?

All good headlines have three characteristics in common. They are clearly written and concisely worded, and will cause the reader to seek more information.

Clarity is rule number one. If a headline doesn't clearly describe what the story is about, it won't attract its target readers, which means it will fail. Readers must be able to get the message immediately; it must jump right out at them. Few readers will spend time figuring out unclear headlines. They'll turn their attention to other items. Readers expect headlines to summarize the information in the story; they want clear information, not puzzles.

Conciseness is essential because most people won't take the trouble to read long headlines. As it is, most readers simply scan headlines for key words that alert them to matters of interest. Long headlines defeat the purpose of a headline; readers might as well read the opening sentence or paragraph.

To write concise headlines:

- Summarize your material in one sentence. Make the original sentence as long as you wish.
- Scrutinize each word in the sentence.
- Underline each word that's essential in getting the message across.
- Circle each word that isn't essential in getting the message across.
- Rewrite the sentence without the circled words.
- Examine each remaining word to determine if it is needed.
- When each word in the headline is essential, your headline is done.

Cleverness

Clever, witty headlines attract attention. However, watch out! Drafting clever, catchy headlines can have a dangerous downside by diverting writers from more important objectives. In their desire to create witty headlines, writers may fail to clearly convey the message. They also may fall victim to the sins of being too cute and cloying. Never sacrifice clarity to be clever. Cleverness can be elusive. Often, writers draw blanks and can't come up with clever headlines. When that occurs, and it will, simply compose clear and concise headlines.

Be sure to consider where your headline will appear. For narrow-column newspapers and newsletters, keep headlines to two or three lines. Since headlines are intended to attract attention, bending the rules of grammar, style, and even spelling may help. Often, an incorrect usage is just the thing that catches the readers' eyes and interests them in the text that follows. Celebrity names in headlines also catch the eye. Audiences want to know what popular figures think and how they act. They're hoping for some dirt.

 **GUERRILLA TACTICS**

Practice writing great headlines by trying the following exercises:

- Ask friends or family members to cut headlines from a newspaper and place them in an envelope. Have them seal the envelope and give the newspaper and sealed envelope to you. Read the headline-less stories and write your own headlines.
- Compare the headlines you composed with those that appeared with the stories. Decide which you prefer; note your reasons and the particular techniques that appeal to you. Continue this exercise for at least five days until you feel adept at writing headlines.
- Rewrite headlines you see in the media to improve them.
- Create a headline file. In the file, place the headlines that were cut out and placed in the envelope for exercise 1 above.
- Collect great headlines from various sources and add them to your headline file.
- Compile a list of "words with impact" for use in future headlines. Enter your list of "words with impact" in a computer file or your PalmPilot, and add to it continually.

Additional Tips

When it comes to creating headlines, writers take different approaches. Although the following suggestions are time tested and seem to work for most people, don't be afraid to strike out on your own and experiment with different ways. However, if you're just getting started, it may be advisable at first to follow these suggestions and then branch off:

- Unless you're deeply inspired, write the headline after you've completed the piece. Writing stories usually crystallizes your thoughts, which results in your ability to craft sharper headlines. If you write the headline first, you risk making the story fit the headline, which is the opposite of how it should work.

- Draft at least four or five headlines for every story and let them sit. After a while, the right one usually pops out. Sometimes they all stink and fall lifelessly to the bottom of the sea. In that case, ask someone for help, a friend, relative, or whoever happens to be around. Brainstorm, bounce your headlines off them, and see what your combined efforts produce. Everyone thinks that they can write great headlines, so give them a chance to help you out.

- When you're stuck, change gears. Often your approach to writing a headline doesn't work because the idea is limited or unsound. In that case, abandon your original approach and try something new.

Remember

Headlines provide order by informing readers what the story that follows is about. Readers are headline-oriented and routinely scan for items of interest. All headlines must be clearly and concisely written and cause the reader to want additional information. Headline writing is a learned skill that requires lots of practice.

20
Participate in Special Events

"Special events, no matter how large or how small,
are exceptional opportunities to do business under the
social umbrella. So firm up your handshake,
grow your smile from within, dust off your cocktail
chatter and go seed your benefits, benefits, benefits."
—RALEIGH PINSKEY, PR AUTHOR AND SPEAKER

GUERRILLAS SEE SPECIAL EVENTS as prime marketing opportunities. At these events, people with similar interests gather in a nurturing atmosphere and are highly approachable. Everyone attending a special event is there to make contacts, talk shop, and do business. Special events are efficient forums to promote your business because you're with droves of potential customers, clients, and contacts in a confined area and time.

Attending special events is an effective way to learn to present yourself to potential customers, referral sources, your industry, and your community. Moreover, many of these events are inexpensive. These events encourage you to meet and build relationships with peers, resources, and authorities in your field who can show you the ropes and how to get your career on the fast track.

Attend events in your area sponsored by local groups, for example, business, professional, or trade associations or civic, religious, fraternal, or social organizations. Most likely, you have family, friends, or business associates affiliated with such groups, and you may already belong to one yourself. If so, become more active; change your focus and turn it into a business activity rather than a social activity. Meet and establish relationships with contacts who might buy, support, or promote your product or service.

Get to know your peers in your community. They can be a rich vein of referrals. They can send you their overflow—clients or customers they can't serve—and introduce you to valuable resources that could take years to discover on your own.

A great way to meet peers is by attending events hosted by local trade and professional associations such as the Bar Association, the Art Directors Club, the Building Contractors' League, and the Bat Corkers Alliance. Check the calendar of events in your local paper, grab a stack of your business cards, stuff your briefcase with brochures, practice your message, and get ready to shake lots of hands.

Virtually all organizations are involved in community service and they're always looking for volunteers for community projects as well as their own programs. Volunteering and serving on and chairing committees provides you with a platform to display to others your knowledge, dedication, and ability. Devoting time and effort to others is rewarding on numerous levels. Besides helping those less fortunate, it gives you visibility as a leader, a community pillar, and a good citizen.

As your local network grows, find larger venues. Attend regional, state, national, and even international events, especially when they're held in your area. Volunteer to assist when national events are hosted locally. Offer to introduce, escort, assist, and house featured guests and dignitaries. When you become a central part of the hosting group's efforts, you are building relationships and expanding your visibility as a leader in your chosen field.

 **GUERRILLA TALE**

A part-time film critic for a free, county newspaper volunteered to assist a local film festival. She was assigned to escort the chief critic for a major city newspaper. They spent lots of time together mostly watching and discussing films. The big-city critic liked her take on films, and after the festival assigned her freelance work as an occasional reviewer and interviewer. A few years later, he decided to retire and convinced his editor to name her as his successor.

Trade Shows

Exhibit at and attend trade shows to build visibility, credibility, and community. Shows and expos run by local trade groups and chambers of commerce are bargains. Exhibitors are usually charged modest fees and elaborate booths are not required. Local shows help you build a strong network and customer or client base in your community. To exhibit at local chamber of commerce trade shows, you may have to join the chamber, which is usually a smart investment because it increases your visibility and makes you a full-fledged member of the established business community.

It's more expensive to exhibit at state, regional, national, and international trade shows, but the returns can be gigantic. Fees for the worst booths run at least a thousand dollars and you'll pay even more to design, build, and outfit a booth. While these trade shows can put you on the map, you also can get lost in them. At the larger shows, some booths can be the size of aircraft carriers. Despite the heavy traffic, you may feel like a minnow in the ocean.

 **GUERRILLA TACTICS**

Even if you don't exhibit at them, trade shows are worth attending. When you attend, make your two key objectives to work the floor and meet the press.

When you work the floor:

- Circulate, visit, and examine every booth.
- Take handouts and study what's being offered.
- Sit in on presentations, seminars, and meetings.
- Get a feel for the pulse of the industry; find out where it is and where it seems to be heading. Look for trends, developments, and new innovations, and learn what your competitors are up to.
- Talk with exhibitors, attendees, speakers, and the press.
- Introduce yourself, deliver your message, and add them to your network.
- Hand out your business cards to anyone who breathes, even faintly.

It's easy to identify reporters from their badges. They usually say "Press" or are a distinctive color. When you meet the press:

- Be bold. Stop them, introduce yourself, ask what they're working on, and give them a quick pitch. Be brief. Trade shows are not the time to push it with the press because they're working. Instead, just make contacts. Don't go into long, detailed spiels, or try to hold the press captive. If you do, you'll blow potentially important contacts.

Ask if you can send them material, take their card, give them yours, say thanks, and walk away.

When you respect the demands on their time, people in the media will usually remember you positively. Most reporters like to spice up stories with comments or quotes from trade show attendees, and tend to reward those who treat them considerately. So prepare responses. If your comments are clever, witty, or insightful, reporters may want to speak with you again. Frequent, witty quotes can launch you as force in your industry.

Be patient and persistent. Rome wasn't built in a day. Be

prepared for rejection, indifference, and curtness, even rudeness. Not everyone will be interested. However, many people will be curious, and the more contacts you make, the better your chances of success.

GUERRILLA INTELLIGENCE

Don't be bashful. Trade shows are not for shrinking violets. They're opportunities to deliver your message and expand your network and customer or client base. Be direct, assertive, and even bold. Walk up to strangers and introduce yourself, tell them who you are, what you do, and how it can help them. Most people will usually be warm and receptive. Trade shows allow you to perfect the delivery of your message, gain greater visibility, and increase your name recognition.

Distinguish yourself. At trade shows, everyone is clamoring for attention so it's important to come up with clever ways to stand out. Consider the following suggestions as possible ways to differentiate yourself from the pack:

- Go against the grain. If you're a man, affiliate with women's groups. Learn about and volunteer to support their causes.
- Create event-specific business cards for a special event, trade show, or expo.
- Hand out useful items such as pens, pads of paper, or flashlights or items specifically created for the event.
- Sponsor contests, give awards, and donate prizes.
- Become a featured speaker, panelist, host, or master of ceremonies or write articles.
- Find ways to capture the spotlight.
- Don't ask dumb, personal, or overly complex questions of speakers simply to draw attention. It will alienate both the speaker and all others in attendance.

Remember

Special events present outstanding marketing opportunities because everyone in attendance has the same interests. Conferences and conventions are solely about learning, making contacts, and doing business. They give you the opportunity to meet, learn from, and spend time with your peers and the top authorities in your field.

21
Get Others to Spread the Word

"I quote others to better express myself."
—MONTAIGNE, FRENCH WRITER
AND PHILOSOPHER

A SINGLE GUERRILLA FIGHTING ALONE can wage a heroic battle. But to win wars, guerrillas need alliances, truckloads of them—the more the merrier. Guerrillas need comrades in arms to share the load and spread the word.

Everyone is a potential ally and a possible source of business and referrals. Everyone you know, hear about, meet, and do business with is a prospect for your network. Grow your network into an army. Enlist battalions to champion your cause, extol your virtues, and recommend you. The larger and more extensive the army, the more ground it can cover and the more business it can produce. Businesses are built on referrals.

Building a Network

Building a network isn't difficult. You've been doing it all of your life without being aware of it. The major difference between building a network and what you've already been doing is that the focus should be on promoting your business.

 **GUERRILLA TACTICS**

When asking the people you know to help you publicize your product or service:

- Be direct and bold.
- Tell your contacts that you've started your own business or have expanded your existing business and are seeking referrals.
- Point out why you're soliciting their assistance. Perhaps you've moved into larger offices, put on additional staff, added new equipment or merchandise, or just wrapped up a major project.

- Explain what you have to offer and the importance of their help. Stress that you're trying to develop mutually beneficial relationships.
- Specifically ask acquaintances for names of people that you can contact; ask the acquaintances for permission to use their names.

Ask your acquaintances how you can repay or help them.

Most people will be receptive. They understand the reciprocal nature of business, and know that relationships are partnerships in which each partner benefits by helping the other. If people like you and, better yet, if they believe in you, they'll be happy to recommend you. It's simply good business.

Ask everyone you meet for three referrals. At first, people may be hesitant. After all, they may not be 100 percent sure about the quality of your work, and might be reluctant to climb too far out on a limb.

Be patient and persistent.

Ask only for the chance to prove yourself. Once you do, they'll be clamoring to recommend you.

Referral Fees

In some businesses and areas, referral fees are unethical, while in other areas they are the norm. So check out what's acceptable in your locale. If referral fees are the norm, clarify that status with all referral sources ahead of time so that you both agree on the amount of those referral fees.

When you secure clients or jobs as the result of business referrals, reward the people who made the recommendations. If they can't or won't accept a referral fee, give them something—a gift, a gift certificate, tickets to an event, a charitable contribution—or perform extra or personal work for them to show your appreciation. Even the smallest gesture will be appreciated, and it's good business. Consider it your obligation.

In Your Field

When looking for referrals in your field, approach former bosses, former coworkers, and established businesses. Former employers and coworkers are great sources because they know you and the quality of your work, and are usually eager for you to succeed. Another possible step would be to contact larger, established businesses and offer to handle their overflow or to assist with projects when they need help.

 **GUERRILLA TACTICS**

Some people in your business field may fear that you might steal their clients or customers. To ease their concerns:

- Be willing not to disclose to referred customers or clients that you operate a separate business.
- Offer to act as the referral source's employee while handling their referrals.
- Work out of the referral source's offices or use their stationery.
- If, after a referral is completed, the clients or customer wants to hire you directly, don't accept the business without first obtaining the source's consent and agreeing to pay a referral fee.

GUERRILLA INTELLIGENCE

Don't steal customers or clients. Over the long run, you'll be judged on your reputation for ethics, honesty, and loyalty, which far outweighs whatever you might receive from stealing referral source's clients or customers.

Complementary Fields

Solicit businesses in different, but complementary, fields. Create alliances to refer clients or customers to one another. For example, if you're a florist, approach wedding, party, and event planners or coordinators; caterers; wedding photographers or videographers;

and facilities where events are held. If you operate a payroll preparation service, attend events for business accountants, financial consultants, and small business operators.

If you make or sell a product, distribute samples. Let key people experience how terrific your product is. If you make floral arrangements, pastries, or illustrations, outdo yourself. Knock their socks off! Give out samples that will send them rushing out of the back room to meet you or dashing to the telephone to place orders. Personalize samples to include something unique for each person or business you pitch.

If you run a service business, print a one-page explanation of why your service is superior. Bullet each reason and place at the top of the page. Use attractive paper that reflects the level of professionalism, design, or inventiveness you want to convey. Include photographs and illustrations. List fee schedules and guarantees. Attach letters from satisfied customers attesting to the excellence of your work, your professionalism, and how much they enjoyed working with you.

When soliciting businesses in complementary fields, try to meet with those who run the business. If that's impossible, leave a handwritten note with your sample or written material. In the note, express regret that you couldn't meet face to face and explain that you're expanding your business and seeking referrals, and you would love to speak with them at their convenience. Follow up the note with subsequent visits, phone calls, or e-mails.

Remember

Businesses are built on referrals, and everyone is a potential source of new business. Use your existing contacts: friends, relatives, and those with whom you've done business. Ask each for three referrals and clarify in advance whether they expect referral fees. When sources produce referrals, show your appreciation.

22
Make Friends in the Media

"My pappy told me never to bet my bladder against a brewery or get into an argument with people who buy ink by the barrel."
—LANE KIRKLAND, FORMER
PRESIDENT OF THE AFL-CIO

THROUGHOUT THIS BOOK, we've stressed the importance of cultivating media relationships because we feel that they're the fabric from which successful publicity campaigns are sewn. So, excuse us if we seem to be rehashing well-covered ground, but we firmly believe publicity revolves around your relationships with your media contacts—and how you approach the media to build new relationships and nurture and maintain those you have already established.

Media relationships should be mutually beneficial. You look to the media to publicize your product or service and they look toward you for the stories you can provide. Let's be honest, if you didn't want publicity, you'd probably never bother with the media and vice versa. Essentially, it's a simple exchange, giving in order to receive.

GUERRILLA INTELLIGENCE

Although a media relationship may benefit both parties, it isn't an equal relationship—it isn't even close. Sometimes you do all the work and nothing happens. The relationship is unequal because the media has a monopoly over the means of distribution. While you may have raw materials, the ingredients to bake the cakes, the media controls delivery. Without the media, your cakes would languish in the bakery; they wouldn't be widely disseminated to the public.

When the media is hot on one of your stories, it's easy to misinterpret the nature of the relationship. Your contacts may phone you 100 times a day, treat you like you're their best friend and the most important person on the globe. Don't mistake hot pursuit for attachment. With the media, it's short-attention-span theater. Once they've run their story, no matter how much they may love you, you're usually quickly forgotten and replaced by the next pretty face, the subject of the piece they're currently developing.

The Rules

You can't win the publicity game if you don't know the rules. Only fools play high-stakes poker without knowing whether a flush beats a straight. Yet that's precisely what you're doing when you don't know the rules that govern relationships with the media. You're an amateur sitting at the pros' table, you're playing in a game that's over your head—you're pouring hard-earned publicity dollars down a green-felt drain.

Since the media hold all the cards, they make the rules. If you want to play at their table, you have to adhere to their rules. If you do, the media will consider you a professional, someone they can rely on and with whom they'll do business. Ironically, there are only three rules and they're alarmingly simple:

1. You are a resource for the media.
2. It's never personal.
3. The media can always change the rules, but you can't.

 **GUERRILLA TACTICS**

Since the media consider you their resource, it's wiser to accommodate them than to try to convince them otherwise. Face it, their only interest in you is what you can do for them or their audience. Sorry if we hurt your feelings, but it's better to face reality and acknowledge the disparity in the relationship and make the most of it.

Become a volunteer. When you speak with your media contacts, ask what they're working on and see if you have information or contacts that might help. To become a media resource, alert them not only to items you want publicized, but also to items in which you have no stake. Convey the impression that you're looking out for their interests, become a member of their team.

Be available when your media contacts call. If you can't supply what they want, give them the name of someone else who might have the information they seek. If you don't help them out, someone else will. So make the most of the opportunity. It may pay off down the road. Give the media names to contact, leads to follow, and check with your network for others who might help.

Nothing Personal

Adjust your attitude. Understand that when your media contacts don't respond to or return your calls, it's not personal. You can't be thin-skinned, resentful, or easily hurt. Remember that you're on a mission—a mission to get your story told—which is all that really matters. As Groucho Marx said, "The secret of life is honesty and fair dealing. If you can fake that, you've got it made."

Be an actor. Remain pleasant and affable when you feel you're being blown off, treated rudely, or ignored. Put a smile in your voice and sound understanding, even sympathetic. Don't give up. Be persistent, because sooner or later you'll get through and your persistence and professional demeanor will be recognized and most likely rewarded. Often, the winner isn't the swiftest runner, it's the last one remaining at the end of the race.

Changing the Rules

When it suits their purposes, the media will change the rules. You can count on it. Actually, they can change more than the rules, they can change everything. Your story or appearance may be edited, rewritten, revised, chopped, bumped, postponed, or canceled.

When you have been disappointed with the changes in your story, take it in stride. Even though you're fuming inside, be professional, which in this case means act like you understand because, frankly in most cases, there's not a single thing you can do about it.

Salvage something from the situation that will benefit you. Instead of wasting time and energy arguing, complaining, and raising your blood pressure, mildly express your displeasure. Use the word "disappointed" rather than "angry" or "frustrated." Make your point once and then drop it. Resume being a team player.

Never show anger or threaten. Instead, immediately focus on finding bargaining chips to position yourself for the future. When you capitulate, gently slip in "Okay, you owe me one." and make sure your contact gets the message. During subsequent interactions with your contacts, plant subtle reminders by asking how the matter turned out.

Stay on Their Radar Screen

With the media, the saying, "Out of sight is out of mind," is a truism. So consider the following to remain in their minds:

- Follow writers' careers—note what they're writing and where they're working. Where are they focusing their energies? Are they concentrating on interviews, quotes, facts, analysis, or commentaries? Does their work appear in newspapers, magazines, or on the Internet. Track producers—see what types of programs they're running and the subjects they're covering. What do their features and guests have in common? Ask yourself what they may be lacking and determine whether any of your resources could bolster their coverage. If so, share your suggestions with them.

- Keep in touch. Periodically call, e-mail, and send information to remind your contacts that you're still alive, kicking, and available to them as a resource. They're more likely to call about stories, quotes, or guests in your field when they know you're around. Send them copies of your promotional materials, newsletters, and holiday cards. Mail handwritten thank-you notes whenever they cover you and when they get promotions, awards, and new jobs. If you know their birthday, drop them a card.

- Since everyone sends holiday cards, distinguish yourself by sending something they don't expect. For example, send funny post cards on odd, little known occasions or short notes just to say hello or that you were thinking of them.

 **GUERRILLA TACTICS**

When you make new media contacts, ask how they prefer to be contacted—e-mail, phone, fax, or carrier pigeon—and note their preference on your media list. Ask for their business cards and always verify that their contact information is up to date.

As we've mentioned, faxes can be unreliable because they get lost or misdelivered in frantic media offices. Your best bet is e-mail. E-mail is now the preferred form of communication because it's quick, direct, informal, cost-effective, and the least intrusive.

Remember

Although your media relationships should be mutually beneficial, the relationships aren't equal. The media holds the upper hand. If you want to play the game and be recognized as a professional, you must play by the media's rules. Become a media resource. Ask your contacts what they're working on, give them information or the names of people who can help, and always be available when they call. The most important thing you can do in these relationships is to stay on your media contacts' radar screen.

23
Design a Seminar

"By learning you will teach; by teaching you will learn."
—Anonymous

WHEN GIVEN THE CHOICE, most rational souls prefer to do business with the best, most highly regarded luminaries in their fields. And many people are willing to pay a premium to get the best. How many times have you heard someone say, "My surgery was performed by a world-renowned kidney surgeon"? You never hear them say, "This surgeon nobody ever heard of transplanted my kidney, but he gave me a really good a price."

Dealing with those who are best in their fields builds confidence, because people feel that it improves their chances for success. Doing business with the best is prestigious and gives you something to crow about. The slightest contact with celebrities makes some people think they're mini stars or that they're special because they were touched by stars. Experts can charge more, so being acknowledged as the best translates into big money. It puts you in the big leagues.

Seminars in your field can offer you a fast track to the top. Attending them can polish your skills, bring you up to speed on industry developments, introduce you to new areas, and help build your network. Everyone attending such seminars is in the same industry, has the same interests, and is a potential customer, client, partner, or media contact. At seminars, you can meet, learn from, and forge relationships with renowned experts and hang out with your peers.

 **GUERRILLA TACTICS**

To really capitalize on seminars, lead or teach them. Teaching peers increases your visibility, reputation, and stature in the industry. It establishes you as a respected authority—a leader in your field.

As a leader at the seminar, you will receive media attention and be exposed to more potential customers or clients. And as a result of your leadership, you become an acknowledged authority in your field, and you can charge more, a whole lot more!

As a seminar leader, you're on center stage demonstrating your expertise to business people who've paid a bundle to hear you and other experts. You can swap ideas and war stories with the finest minds and the most successful practitioners in your industry.

Start Your Own Seminar

Since appearing at seminars is so desirable, everyone wants to get in on the act. If you're not in demand, become a promoter. Organize or lead your own seminar. It's a proven formula that will get you to the top. Running your own seminar gives you experience and invaluable contacts. It also lets you see if you enjoy putting on seminars and whether you're good at it. The key is to start small, learn on the job, and work your way up to establish a track record. Starting small also limits your financial risk.

When you are first planning your own seminar, consider the following tips:

- Identify topics that can draw large audiences. If you're a financial planner, run a seminar on getting low-interest mortgages; if you're a psychologist, teach stress reduction techniques; if you're a chiropractor, explain how to eliminate back pain. Give practical, hands-on, how-to instructions so attendees return home with tangible benefits.
- Don't charge; put on free seminars. Consider them learning experiences and initial steps in your master plan. Either rent a room or convince a local charity, religious, civic, or social group to allow you to use their facility in exchange for a modest contribution and/or publicity.
- To promote your seminar, print up posters and fliers. Place posters in high traffic areas such as schools, universities, community centers, libraries, and businesses in or related to your field. Send announcements to local radio stations and related Web sites. Get names from your network, name lists (names of people sorted into specific businesses, interests, or characteristics), and local organizations. Send postcards or fliers announcing the event to your network, those on name lists, and your media contacts. Promote your seminar on the Web at sites such as *www.advertize.com.*

Work for Others

Running a seminar is hard, demanding work, so instead of trying to start or run your own, it might be advisable to offer your services as a lecturer to organizations that sponsor such events. Unless you've got a big reputation, don't even think of starting at the top. Instead, begin by volunteering your services to local organizations and then, as you gain skill and recognition, move on to bigger venues.

Service Clubs

Start with service clubs in order to get experience, understand the process, and make mistakes on a small scale. Think of it as the equivalent to a comedy club where comics, both experienced and novice, go to polish their material and try out new routines. It's where you can make mistakes and learn from them.

Volunteer to speak at events sponsored by the Elks Club, the Rotary Club, the Veterans of Foreign Wars, the chamber of commerce, Women in Business, or religious, business, or civic groups. Don't ask to be paid; chalk it up to your education. Consider these speaking engagements as opportunities to perfect your presentation, build your reputation, and meet potential customers or clients, contacts, and the media.

GUERRILLA INTELLIGENCE

Warning: Some local organizations appeal mainly to retirees. While events sponsored by these groups may provide opportunities to sharpen your presentation and your delivery skills, they're not good opportunities to network and get new business. So when you book engagements, factor in the audience profile. To generate business, appear before groups whose members are in the active working community.

Community Colleges

To get experience and build a reputation, teach a workshop or even a course for local educational institutions, such as community colleges or adult education programs. Teaching a course can be time-consuming and the networking and business opportunities are limited. However, the experience is wonderful, and today's students may be tomorrow's customers or clients.

Internet Conferences

Gain experience and exposure by participating in online conferences. Check search engines (AOL, Yahoo, Goggle, and so on) newsgroups, and PR services (PR Newswire, Business Wire) for upcoming conferences in your area of expertise. Find out whether you qualify to be a panelist or suggest topics that you could participate in or lead.

Promoters

When you're comfortable with your performances for local organizations, approach businesses that provide adult education and career-development courses. A wide spectrum of courses is sponsored by state employment agencies and private enterprises such as the Learning Annex, the American Management Association, and the Training Clinic.

Lecturers are paid. They're expected to be highly professional and are graded by audiences. These sessions can be a fertile source of new business opportunities. Lecturing at this level puts an impressive notch on your resume and can qualify you for larger, more lucrative bookings.

See *www.tasl.com* for comprehensive lists of classes and conferences sponsored by universities, industry associations, media, and training companies throughout the country.

Conferences and Conventions

Outside of the *Today* show, *The Oprah Winfrey Show,* or your own infomercial, conferences and conventions are the top. Trade and industry gatherings are held locally, regionally, nationally, and internationally. They offer extensive educational programs and are always in the market for dynamic, entertaining instructors and speakers.

Conferences and conventions provide unparalleled opportunities for visibility and advancement in your industry. Competition to lead seminars at national and international conferences is fierce. Only the most outstanding speakers are selected and invited to return. Speaking at major conferences puts you at the pinnacle of your industry. It says you've arrived. Besides interacting with and being treated as an equal by the top people in your field, you're the focus of attention by both the media and potential customers or clients.

Speakers and instructors usually receive an honorarium and their travel/lodging expenses are paid. Presentations are critiqued and leaders are expected to be accessible to attendees.

 **GUERRILLA TACTICS**

As a seminar leader or instructor, your first responsibility is to teach, but in doing so, you must be entertaining. The most popular leaders, instructors, and speakers are accomplished performers. They can rouse audiences, inspire and amuse them, and make them sign up for the next go round.

Ostensibly, seminars are about learning. In reality, they're equally about networking, socializing, and fellowship. Seminars are not school, they're more like a show or entertainment. They often entail travel and are expensive so audiences—who are used to lively, amusing, and instructive presentations—have lofty expectations.

Your use of the following tips will enhance your success as a seminar leader:

- Become a performer. Spice up your presentations with humor, anecdotes, and real-life stories.
- Be newsy. Everyone loves inside scoops about people, companies, and gossip in their business.
- Update the latest industry developments and make yourself available to those in attendance.
- Focus on a few hot topics that people in your industry should learn and cover them expertly.
- Encourage questions from the audience.
- Make yourself available after you've completed your presentation.
- Distribute copies of news developments, articles, examples, reading lists, and abstracts of presentations so that attendees feel that they're getting value.
- Provide a list of the names and contact information for those who signed up for your sessions.

Questions

Questions usually enhance presentations because they reflect the audience's concerns, reveal actual problems, and lead to stimulating exchanges. They also provide a rich source of examples that you can incorporate into future presentations.

Take questions during your presentation and after you've completed it. Also make yourself available for questioners during breaks and when you're not instructing.

Fielding questions is a skill that often requires delicacy. Every seminar has at least one individual who insists on asking an endless stream of questions that interest no one else. Although all attendees should feel free to question, no single person has the right to monopolize a seminar, but someone always tries. After a few questions, politely, but firmly, tell incessant questioners, "Let's give other people a chance."

Audience members often think that because they paid for the seminar, they're entitled to professional advice. They won't hesitate to pose personal questions that don't apply to or interest others. Usually, their questions are long and complex and are followed by a string of additional questions. Answer the initial question briefly and, if the questioner persists, offer to speak with the questioner during the break.

GUERRILLA INTELLIGENCE

Seminar promoters estimate that 20 to 25 percent of those who attend engagements buy speakers' goods. And, when the speaker is well known, even more attendees will purchase their materials. Product prices tend to be high because they're narrowly focused and purchasers may deduct the items purchased as business expenses. If you make five presentations to audiences of 500 people, you can expect to pull down substantial, additional money.

Sales

Although established speakers and authors, such as *Chicken Soup for the Soul* coauthor Mark Victor Hansen, command handsome fees to lead seminars and address conferences, they routinely make even more selling a wide assortment of materials during their appearances. For example, they sell books, audiotapes, videotapes, workbooks, calendars, and novelty items from the back of the room. They also get names for their mailing lists, which may have commercial value.

Veteran speakers frequently offer package deals at seminars. They might package three or four items that usually sell for $250 for half that price. To encourage sales, they'll autograph their wares, chat with attendees, pose for photographs, and dance with your spouse. Audiences inspired by rousing speakers gobble up goods that will remind them of or supplement the experience—especially when the speaker autographs them.

Remember

Seminars are a fast track to the top, and leading them can speed you to the top of your field. Gain experience and visibility by organizing small workshops on specific topics that you've mastered and then work your way up. As a seminar leader, your first responsibility is to teach, but in doing so you must also be entertaining. Take questions from the audience during and after presentations.

24
Get Published

"Take the top of the mountain."
—DAVID OGILVY, ADVERTISING GENIUS

PUBLISHING A BOOK CATAPULTS YOU to the upper strata. It gives you more than credibility, it gives you the elevated status of being an authority. Authoring a book awards you recognition as an expert, a leader in your business, and a star in your field. It puts you right on the top.

GUERRILLA INTELLIGENCE

Although many people think they've got a book's worth of things to say, few actually do. And, even fewer have the ability and the discipline to express their thoughts coherently, put them in writing, and get them published. Besides testifying that you're an expert, writing and publishing a book puts you among the elite because so few people actually complete all the steps to get their book published. Publishing a book demonstrates that you're special and can get things done.

Advantages of Authorship

A book is a powerful marketing tool. Authorship gets your name out to the public and implies that you're an expert. Authorship can make you a celebrity, and, in our celebrity-crazed world, people flock to be associated with celebrities.

The advantages of being a published book author are many:

- Authors are respected and sought after.
- Giving potential customers or clients a copy of your book tips the scales in your direction. It creates instant good will, and your writing a personalized message will thaw the most glacial personalities and convert total strangers into grateful, loyal, long-standing devotees.
- Once your book is published, your status as an expert becomes permanent; it can never be taken away. You're listed in the Library of Congress, in the Copyright Office, and with Amazon.com. The local media competes to interview you. You get cool invitations, and attract conference groupies. Being a published author is exciting and satisfying—it's fame lasts far more than fifteen minutes!
- The exhilaration of authorship is addictive. Once published, virtually all authors want to repeat the experience. Subsequent books reinforce their status and further their careers. Public admiration and respect is intoxicating.
- Books don't have to be lengthy. Frankly, most people never read them, so they don't know whether your book is long or short, good or bad, or in English or Mandarin. However, when they learn you've written a book, they're invariably impressed and usually try to get to know you.
- Most authors don't make money from selling their books, but their books help propel their careers. And, you never know, there's always a chance that your book will make the bestseller list, you'll appear on Leno or Letterman and hit the jackpot!

Getting It Down

Writing a book isn't easy. It takes knowledge, time, and discipline. First, you must have content—information to fill the pages. Clearly articulating your knowledge is time consuming, exacting, and requires dedicated concentration. It can be hard work.

Ideally, content should provide something new or express existing material better, but we all know that doesn't always happen. Great storytellers and gifted teachers know how to make boring old stuff come alive and take on new meaning.

Not everyone writes well and those who can't can hire ghostwriters. However, it's your book, so you have to tell ghostwriters what to write because they usually aren't experts in your field. Working with a ghost is a partnership. You provide the substance, and the ghostwriter puts it in publishable form. But when they've finished writing, it's all up to you. You must review every word, every sentence, and every idea because they all will be attributed to you. As the author, your name and reputation will be on the line.

 **GUERRILLA TACTICS**

To test the book-writing waters,

- Draft an outline. Jot down topics, list every possibility.
- Edit the list down to ten to fifteen important topics and organize them in a logical order.
- Set it up as if you're telling a story or explaining a skill.

The organized topic list will be your working outline—the table of contents—which is the structure for your book.

Writing a book is an evolving process. Everything is subject to change. Few authors write straight through. There's always editing, moving, adding, deleting, and rewriting text. Sometimes, it feels like a puzzle. Nevertheless, begin with a structure, even though it will change. Don't wing it. Create a structure and stick with it until you're convinced that it doesn't work. Then make whatever changes feel right.

Sit at your computer or with your tape recorder and express your thoughts. Forget about grammar, spelling, or logic. Just capture information. This isn't English class. *Get the stuff down!* Spill your guts. Put down everything that comes to mind, whether it makes sense or not. The idea is to get a flow, to build a rhythm, and express yourself. It can always be fixed later.

Don't write an introduction. Introductions are usually written after the entire text is completed. Begin with Chapter 1 and work through the outline in order, chapter by chapter. If you have thoughts about an introduction, note and save them. If you feel that introductory material is essential, that you can't begin without it, make that your first chapter. If you find yourself skipping around, rethink your outline. When you find certain material more appropriate for other chapters, get it down then and there, as soon as it comes to mind, or you'll either forget about it or lose it.

When you've completed a first draft of your manuscript, reread and edit each chapter in order. Try to read the entire manuscript before you rewrite; make notes as you read. Then revise the manuscript until you're satisfied. Recruit others to read and comment on what you've composed. Solicit lots of readers, both in and out of your field, and insist that they be honest and severely critical. Thank them in your book's acknowledgments.

Don't fall in love with your language unless you plan a career as an author. The purpose of the book is not to establish you as a literary figure, but to enhance your business status.

Publishers Versus Self-Publication

Entire books are devoted to whether to self-publish or go with an established publisher, so we'll cover it only briefly here.

Established publishers give a book greater prestige. However, that perception is rapidly fading especially with the advent of e-books and how easy self-publishing has become. If your audience is scholarly or academic, prestige is vital, but in pop culture books, prestige is less important.

Publishers have sales forces involved throughout the process. Their suggestions often contribute to larger sales. However, with noncelebrity authors, publishers usually print small first runs and seldom push sales. Publishers use in-house staff to promote their books, but their advertising and PR for first-time authors is usually weak. Authors often hire, at their own expense, their own PR people to work with and supplement publishers' in-house publicists. Publishers' books have a small, but better, chance of being reviewed. Self-published books are rarely reviewed.

> ### WARNING
> Publisher's sales forces are often committed to traditional marketing assumptions that may inhibit or not work for innovative and creative projects. Traditional marketing assumptions are (1) that consumers consider large books more desirable and a greater value than smaller volumes, (2) that readers buy on the basis of large first chapters, (3) publisher's sales forces tend to be overly conservative and risk adverse in regards to content and design, and (4) they want to stick with what has worked and are often adverse to change.

Publishers pay authors in advance against future royalties. Contracts generally stipulate three payments: (1) on contract signing, (2) at an intermediary stage such as completion and submission of half the chapters, and (3) on completion and submission of an acceptable manuscript. However, the payment schedule can vary.

Except for celebrities, first-time authors seldom receive royalties of more than 6 to 8 percent of the cover price. They may get small advances, but they usually don't receive additional moneys until the publisher has recouped all advances.

Publishers discount books, which cuts authors' royalty receipts. Publishers also withhold a percentage of royalties earned to cover books that may subsequently be returned.

Publishers take a piece of subsidiary rights, such as movie

versions, dramatizations, serialization, calendars, and cards. When you self-publish, you own 100 percent of these rights, but you may have to hire an agent or a representative to sell them. However, agents and representatives usually take a smaller percentage than publishers demand.

Publishers handle all accounting and bookkeeping and generally pay royalties twice a year, usually by the first of April and October. When you self-publish you have to keep the books, and money comes in irregularly.

Instead of receiving moneys up front, self-publishers invest in their books by fronting printing costs, which can be a book's greatest expense. Self-publishers must hire distributors to place their books, and agencies to market and promote them. Outside PR agencies are invariably more accommodating and outperform publishers' staffs. However, they don't come cheap. Finally, self-publishers get to keep the lion's share of the book's income, which can be an enormous amount if the book sells well.

Literary Agents

Literary agents are the gatekeepers for the publishing world. Some publishers don't accept unsolicited manuscripts, while others assign them to overburdened junior editors, who furiously speed read in order to keep abreast. To get a publisher's attention, hire an agent.

Agents will advise whether your book is publishable or if you're wasting your time. They'll recommend changes and resources such as ghostwriters, book doctors, researchers, independent editors, and indexers. Agents know which publishers might be interested in your particular book and how much to ask for it.

Since agents work on a percentage of your book earnings (usually 15 percent), they're skilled negotiators who try to get the best deal. They become your partner for the life of your book. Agents relieve you of time-consuming details, oversee the publisher's marketing, expedite promotional tours, monitor distribution, and protect your contractual rights. As book sales take off, agents will push for additional promotion from the publisher and begin talks for a second book.

Good agents earn their keep because they fight for your interests every step of the way. They don't just stop working for you once the book is on the shelves. Agents can be invaluable advisors, comrades in arms, and guides who can walk you through the Byzantine mazes of publishing and protect your interests.

A number of books list the names and contact information for agents. See *Writer's Guide to Book Editors, Publishers, and Literary Agents, 2001–2002: Who They Are! What They Want! And How to Win Them Over* by Jeff Herman.

Remember

Publishing a book establishes you as an authority and gives you a powerful marketing tool. Writing a book isn't easy. It takes knowledge, time, and discipline, but you can hire a ghostwriter. Authors have the option of self-publishing or going with established publishers. They also have the option of whether or not to hire an agent.

25
Prepare for the Unpleasant

"The expected rarely occurs and never in the expected manner."
—FORMER GENERAL VERNON A. WALTERS

ALWAYS EXPECT THE UNEXPECTED. Whenever you least expect it, the sky may fall in and disasters could occur. When preparing for interviews, prepare for questions that are hard, totally off the wall, just plain stupid, or hostile.

"The press's job [is] to dig . . . to pick at things that may not be pleasant or comfortable for the people involved, to try to get as much of the story as possible into the hands of the public so that the public can make decisions about how we want to run our lives."
—THOMAS BARR

Usually, interviewers are not out to get you. Most are content with a good, straightforward story, but interviewers know that confrontational clashes can make things more interesting. As a result, some interviewers prey on their subjects, try to rattle them, and make them look stupid. Such interviewers thrive on conflict, try to catch their subjects off guard, and agitate them. These mavericks have no scruples and will go to great lengths to make themselves look good at your expense.

GUERRILLA INTELLIGENCE
To protect yourself, always remember the following tips:

- *Nothing* is off the record—even when the media promises it is!
- Never say or write anything that you're not prepared to see blaring across the front page of a newspaper.
- When in doubt, hold your tongue.
- Silence is often preferable to saying something you might later regret.

Prepare, Prepare, Prepare

As we've stated, the major reason why people perform poorly in interviews is that they're unsure of their subject matter. Simply put, there's no substitute for knowing your stuff. Do not, under any circumstances, seek media coverage until you know your subject inside out!

Regardless of the interviewer's reputation, prepare to be attacked. The most gentle, genial host might be having a horrible day and subconsciously may need to punish someone. And, unfortunately, you happen to be close at hand. Confrontational interviewers probe for weaknesses, and when they find a soft spot, they move in like sharks for the kill. Your best defense is to know your material, to firm up those soft spots, and let your knowledge see you through.

The fact that celebrities shine in interviews isn't an accident. It's a product of training, coaching, and practice. Before Rick's clients are interviewed by the media, he coaches them and puts them through a series of mock interviews. Mock interviews test clients' knowledge, pinpoint their weaknesses, and identify where they need work. Clients are grilled during friendly interviews, hostile interviews, dumb interviews, and combinations of them to prepare them for all possibilities. After the training, they can waltz through the most hostile inquisitions with grace and poise.

When you're prepared, there are no hard questions. Every question is a setup, a golden opportunity to demonstrate your expertise, your charm, and the wonders of your product or service. They're openings to sell and make yourself look fabulous.

On the Attack

It's hard to stay composed when interviewers are out to upset, confuse, and discredit you. When we're attacked, our adrenaline flows, our hearts pump wildly, and we mobilize to protect ourselves. Instinctively, we want to lash out, to counterattack. Calmness under pressure isn't easy; it takes practice. It also takes focus and intense concentration to ignore assaults and remain calm.

> **GUERRILLA INTELLIGENCE**
> When under attack, always take the high road. Never stoop to your assailant's level by being combative, defensive, or nasty. Stay focused, remain dignified, and stand tall. If you leave with nothing else, leave with your dignity.

Remind yourself, before each interview, to stay cool and collected no matter what the provocation. Remaining under control lets you think more clearly and show interviewers that you're impervious to hostile attacks. Most interviewers retreat when their strikes are thwarted. The public admires, and responds to, people who remain poised under fire.

Wait for a three count before answering all questions. It gives you time to gather your thoughts and for a better response. Practice pausing until it becomes routine. Then, when you need to buy time to answer tough questions or to compose yourself, the pause will seem perfectly natural.

Admit when you don't know an answer. Never fake it or bluff! Instead, say "That's a good question and I honestly don't know the answer, but I'll find out." If you learn the answer before the interview ends, tell the audience. Audiences respect honesty. Conversely, they detest bluffers and usually can sense them.

Prepare for the worst—for example, if an interviewer states, "This is one of the worst products I've ever seen," "It's reported that you stole this process from your former employer," or "Is it true that you were arrested for child molestation?"

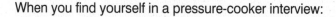

GUERRILLA TACTICS

When you find yourself in a pressure-cooker interview:

- Don't be defensive! Audiences are adept at reading body language; they focus on how you respond. Stay cool because your reactions speak louder than your words.
- Don't be argumentative, you don't want to get into a hostile encounter. If you disagree, disagree respectfully and courteously. Remain composed and dignified. Don't show annoyance, irritation, or anger. Remember, you're there to get publicity, not for a fight.
- Never repeat a negative question, even if you're trying to buy time, because the repetition reinforces negative implications. It's better to take a hit and quickly move on than to reinforce negative impressions.
- Look directly at the audience and the interviewer and immediately assert, "Everyone who tested our product absolutely loved it! Let me show you how great it works." "This process was originally developed by X Corp., but we overhauled it so it now works with all computer systems," or "No, that allegation is completely false!"
- Don't blame others or make excuses; it will turn people off. Prepare responses that deal directly with the allegations.
- Avoid the gory details. Make a firm, declarative statement and don't go into detailed explanations. If the interviewer persists, continue to be firm, polite, and brief.

Irrelevant Questions

Questions that that are totally off track may indicate that the interviewer doesn't understand your subject, is not prepared, has lost focus, or has his or her own agenda.

Unless you have reason to think otherwise, assume the interviewer is innocent of devious motives. As a media resource, your job is to protect the interviewer and make him or her look good. Give the interviewer the benefit of the doubt. Answer irrelevant questions with short, pleasant replies and try to steer them to your advantage. Subsequent questions will usually reveal whether the question was an anomaly or if the interviewer was unprepared, confused, or had his or her own agenda.

GUERRILLA INTELLIGENCE

If the interviewer doesn't seem to understand your subject, it could indicate a bigger problem. You may not be communicating clearly. If the interviewer doesn't understand, others could be in the same boat, which is the last thing you want, because your job is to clearly communicate the main points of your topic.

Respond by giving more precise answers and avoiding all assumptions and technical terms. Explain everything in clear, simple terms. Study the interviewer and audience for indications of whether they understand.

If the interviewer is unprepared, bail him or her out. Act as if the interviewer asked the world's most intelligent question and try to respond with an answer related to the question. Never hint that the interviewer is unprepared. Push your agenda when answering subsequent questions and if the interviewer catches on, great. If not, keep pretending that you're both on the same track.

With confused interviewers, try to spot where they went wrong. Don't articulate or discuss the error with them, correct them, or say that they're wrong or confused. Instead, steer the interview back on course by providing background information that will resolve the misunderstanding, but don't lecture! Then respond to the question within the proper context. Never embarrass the interviewer or the interview could dissolve into a disaster.

When interviewers insist on advancing their agendas, you're stuck! You have no choice but to go along. Follow their lead and give them what they want, as long as it doesn't hurt you. And, be gracious. Don't look as if you're swallowing medicine. Interviewers often switch gears and, with luck, satisfied interviewers will move on and help you deliver your message.

Murphy's Law

Every book seems to include a warning about Murphy's Law, so why should we be an exception. When you're working to publicize your product or service, whatever can go wrong will go wrong, and if you're not prepared to deal with it, it can take you down.

The media will make commitments in good faith. Usually, they intend to fulfill their promises, but you know what they say about good intentions! They'll tell you that your story will be featured in the Sunday magazine, on the evening news, or get a special Web page link. You'll get excited and alert your friends, family, and customers or clients. Then the bottom will drop out. Everything will change. The media won't deliver and you'll be left red-faced, trying to explain what went wrong.

When you deal with the media, you're getting involved in the news business and news always comes first. Your story could be the tastiest thing since vanilla-iced raisin bread, but it may be supplanted by some mundane, late breaking story merely because the story is news. It's how the business works. It's not personal. News takes priority over everything else. The newest and most recent events always take precedence.

Expect disappointments and be professional. Your stories will be cut, chopped, revised, and disfigured beyond recognition. They'll be postponed, bumped, rescheduled, rewritten, and canceled once again. Instead of praising your product, reporters may detest it and write editorials demanding that you be criminally prosecuted.

Don't blow your top, become depressed, or alienate media contacts because you were dumped from the morning show. Be a "good sport," even though you're aching inside. Take it in stride, be professional, and try to turn defeats into assets. Expect rejections, disappointments, and ambushes, and try to salvage the most from them.

Never take it personally. It's not you, your product, or service—it's simply the business. When you receive a rejection, try to learn the reason. Analyze your submission from the vantage point of the person of who rejected it. When you have answers, revise your submission to eliminate those problems. The best way to cope is to view every rejection as a lesson, an opportunity to strengthen your approach, and move a step closer to your goal. Remember, you're in a trial by fire in which the hardest steel must endure the hottest flame. Let the media's blows toughen your hide and your resolve. Then mix in a heavy dose of persistence and you'll be fine. You'll weather another storm and be the better for it!

Remember

Expect the unexpected and you won't be surprised. Nothing is off the record, even when the media promises it is! Be well prepared because the major reason why people perform poorly on interviews is that they're unsure of their subject matter. Remain composed if interviewers ask hard or unfair questions or questions that seem to push their own agendas.

26

Crisis Control— Confront Disasters and Turn Them Around

"You are the brand."
—Tom Peters, marketing guru

YOUR BRAND—your business or product name—is your most important asset and once you've established it, you must be protected at all costs! Accidents, disasters, and screw-ups are inevitable. Let's hope that yours are minor. But when they occur, act immediately. Fix them and face the public or else you'll lose the trust and confidence of both consumers and the financial community—and you might never get them back

 **GUERRILLA TALE**

When bottles of Tylenol were tampered with, the company immediately yanked every bottle off the shelves. As soon as the news broke, Tylenol called a press conference. It announced that although only a few actual tampering cases had been detected, it was pulling every bottle in distribution in order to protect the public's safety. Tylenol's prompt action is the textbook example

of how to respond to a PR disaster because it turned Tylenol into the most trusted name in America. Consumers knew that they could depend on Tylenol, because the company cared, was unwilling to compromise the public's safety, and would do, absorb, and spend what was required to resolve the problem. Ever since, Tylenol has enjoyed unprecedented public support and respect.

In contrast, revered stalwarts of American business, Firestone Tires and Ford Motors, steadfastly refused to accept responsibility for defects in tires that had been supplied as original equipment on some Ford vehicles. In reaction, consumers lost trust in both Firestone and Ford, and withdrew support of their products. Sales dipped and consumers went so far as to return Firestone products that were never suspected of being defective because they lost trust in the Firestone brand.

Similarly, Exxon's perceived reluctance to take responsibility for the infamous *Exxon Valdez* oil spill in Alaska resulted in a boycott from which the oil giant never recovered. Lifelong customers stopped buying Exxon's products because they were outraged by its apparent contempt for the environment and failure to behave like a responsible corporate citizen.

What to Do

In business, it's all about trust. Trust is a delicate jewel that takes years to create, but which can be destroyed in an instant. Although you're not running Ford, Firestone, or Exxon, the confidence of your clients is every bit as important. Your customers or clients want products that work, that won't fall apart, and that will do their job. They're entitled to it! It's what they're paying for. Furthermore, they want you to stand firmly behind your goods, without excuses or blame.

When disasters occur, your first concern should be to do everything in your power to restore your customers' confidence, because if you don't, you're gambling with your business future.

 **GUERRILLA TACTICS**

As soon as you learn of a disaster in your business confront it. Don't avoid it or hide. Call a press conference to inform the world that you're accessible and willing to face the world. Stand up and take your punishment.

At the press conference, show that you care by:

- *Admitting.* Own up that the problem occurred.
- *Apologizing.* State that it shouldn't have happened, express your sorrow, and explain what caused it, if you know.
- *Assuring.* Tell the public what steps you've taken to ensure that it won't occur again.
- *Announcing an investigation.* If you don't know why it occurred, tell the media that the cause has not yet been determined, but an in-depth investigation is underway. Immediately investigate the disaster to determine how similar disasters can be prevented.
- *Taking responsibility.* Clearly and specifically state how you're addressing the consequences of the disaster and the specific steps you're taking to ensure that it won't happen again.
- *Informing the media.* Keep the media informed on all changes and developments. When Odwalla juice was pulled from the market, the company held press conferences and issued press releases to inform the public of its test results and the specific steps it was taking to address problems.

People Understand

If you move swiftly and take responsibility, the public will be understanding. They know that people are imperfect, that they make mistakes, and that accidents happen. The public may forgive mistakes in judgment but not mistakes in motive.

When disasters occur, your customers or clients will stand by you. They'll even forgive you, if you admit that it happened, sincerely apologize, move quickly to fix the problem, and prevent future disasters. The public will not forgive you if you hide, avoid responsibility, and cover up. If you want the public's trust and confidence, be forthright, up front, apologetic, and take prompt remedial action.

Remember

Disasters will occur, and when they do you have to protect your brand and reputation. Immediately address the problem by calling a press conference. Admit that a problem occurred, apologize for it, assure the public that you've taken steps to prevent a recurrence, and begin a prompt investigation if you don't know the cause. If you take responsibility, the public will understand.

27
Grow Your Business with a Web Site

"When I took office, only high energy physicists
had ever heard of what is called the World Wide Web. . . .
Now even my cat has its own page."
—BILL CLINTON, FORMER U.S. PRESIDENT

FOR GUERRILLAS, THE INTERNET IS A BONANZA because it has expanded guerrillas' media opportunities exponentially. A Web site makes it possible for a guerrilla to reach wider target audiences more effectively and efficiently. The Internet gives the public direct access to Web sites, so anyone can get your information, not just the media. The content you provide isn't filtered through the media, who usually decide what's news and what gets printed, aired, and publicized. Before the Internet, publicists focused their time and energy courting the media. If they were lucky, the media told their story to the public, but the media usually added their own spin, which the publicists hoped was the spin they wanted.

The Internet offers guerrillas some key advantages over using traditional media to publicize their product or service:

- The Internet lets you tell your story directly and in the manner you want to your target audience.
- Your audience comes to you. Potential customers or clients visit your site because they're interested in viewing your information or forming a relationship with your company.
- Many visitors to your site are looking for more information than they get from newspapers. Before they do business with or invest in your company, they want to see all your press releases or financial statements. They don't want their information interpreted for them by others, they want to see original documents so they can draw their own conclusions.

Global Reach

In the past, when guerrillas began to publicize their businesses, they were forced to conduct local or regional campaigns. Usually, the cost of national campaigns was prohibitive, so guerrillas concentrated on promotions close to home. High costs limited their entry into other markets and slowed their growth. Well, that was in the past. Today, the Internet recognizes no such boundaries; the Internet erases boundaries.

A Web site blankets the globe. When you visit a site, you don't know whether it originated next door or in Timbuktu. Once your site is up, you can attract customers from all over the world. From the outset, the Internet gives you access to it all—local, regional, national, and international markets.

Global reach increases your possibilities exponentially. Before the Internet, guerrillas with narrowly focused specialties slaved for years to expand their customer base. Usually, they had only a small regional market. Today, simply by launching a Web site, those guerrillas can leapfrog regional borders and immediately offer their wares to a vastly larger, international clientele.

Unequaled Value

As a promotional tool, a Web site is an unequaled value. A Web site can reach an international audience for less than the cost of advertising in most local media. It's global reach and ability to target potential customers can lift a guerrilla from obscurity to riches faster and more economically than any other marketing method.

 **GUERRILLA TALE**

The Blair Witch Project *was essentially a home movie with a $40,000 budget that came out of nowhere to become a box office smash. Much of its success was attributable to the Internet.*

To promote the film, the producers conducted an Internet-based campaign centered on an eerie Web site and extensive online word of mouth. They spawned hundreds of fan and product sites, discussion groups, and rave reviews, which helped turn The Blair Witch Project *into a $2 billion property.*

Despite charges that the filmmakers' friends seeded the Web to create a favorable buzz, the success of The Blair Witch Project *stands as positive proof of the Web's power as a promotional tool. Net publicity inexpensively created a ground swell and the motion picture industry took notice. Salon.com (July 16, 1999) quoted Gordon Paddison, director of New Line Cinema's interactive marketing, as saying: "Internet marketing is the most inexpensive and efficient mode of marketing around. And it's available to those with limited resources. Online is all about word of mouth."*

The point is that through the Web, obscure, small-capitalized ventures can reach colossal target audiences that have gigantic purchasing power and the power to shape public opinion. Since The Blair Witch Project, *you seldom see promotions for movies that don't have Web sites or include well-planned Internet-based publicity campaigns.*

Specialization

Web sites also speed guerrillas' ability to shape the direction of their careers. It lets them focus their marketing efforts on more sharply defined areas. In the past, it took years to establish your niche, but now guerrillas can, from the outset, use the Web to proclaim that they're specialists.

GUERRILLA TALE

In law school, Mark showed an aptitude for copyright law, a field dominated by powerful law firms and corporations. Upon graduation, he took a job as a licensing attorney with a major publishing company. He worked hard, got great experience, and after a year opened his own, one-man office. Although he only had a handful of clients, Mark had a friend who was a Web site designer. Mark put up a Web site that promoted him as a copyright specialist for authors and from the get-go clients poured in. Mark's site quickly established him as a specialist.

Twenty-First-Century Player

A Web site also places you in the twenty-first century. It testifies that you understand the new economy, that you're using the latest tools, and providing the most easily accessible information.

Your Web site is the first resource that prudent potential customers, clients, or peers examine to find out more about you and your product or service. It speaks directly to the businesses you want to attract—innovative businesses that are blazing trails into the new millennium. It shows that you're a kindred spirit, a player in the twenty-first-century economy. It also tells them who you are, what you're doing, and where you're headed. Remember, most people prefer doing business with people who are on the same wave length. Don't you?

Make Friends with the Internet

For those of you who aren't familiar with the Internet, stop here and get to know it. In fact, get to know it well. Visit a wide variety of sites. Experiment, play, and try it out. Examine content, design, speed, and ease of use. Don't be afraid to make mistakes, they're part of the process. Then decide what would work best for you.

WARNING

A bad Web site can be worse than no Web site at all. Visitors won't waste time with sites that are weak in content, poorly designed, or slow, difficult, or unreliable to navigate. A bad Web site will be a blot on your reputation and will cost you business. So, don't jump rashly into the Web site waters. If you plan to promote your business with a Web site, do it right!

GUERRILLA TACTICS

Before designing a Web site, ask the following questions:

1. Who is my target audience?
2. How do I best reach them?
3. What information do they need to know?
4. What is the intended result?
5. What is the best way to achieve that result?

After you've answered the above questions, start planning your Web site being sure to consider your goals and needs in terms of the following three perspectives: marketing, technology, and art/creative.

Then answer the following questions from all three perspectives:

- Who is the site being created for?
- What are their technical needs?
- What is their access speed?
- Should the site have video or animation?
- What size screen will it work with?
- What are the visitors' needs and expectations?
- What information do visitors want?

- How do you want to communicate with them?
- How do you lay out the site so it's easy and intuitive to navigate?
- How do you organize the site?
- How will visitors get to my Web site?
- Why will visitors return to my Web site?

Dan Janal's Start-up Suggestions

If you're starting a Web publicity campaign, Internet marketing guru, Dan Janal, author of *Dan Janal's Guide to Marketing on the Internet*, recommends the following:

- Register your Web site with search engines. A listing of search engines and search engine promotion services can be found at *www.guerrillapublicity.com/searchengines.*
- Register under the proper category and related categories.
- Register each of your products and/or services.
- Create compelling keywords.
- Add meta tags (code used by search engines to categorize Web sites) for keywords and descriptions.
- Link to complementary sites (and have complementary sites link back to your site).

Getting Publicity Using Internet Resources

To get publicity from the print media, notify the press about your new site, when you add new content, and when you receive awards and distinctions.

KEY SITES

Key sites for notifying the press about your Web site include:

- PR Newswire—*www.prnewswire.com*
- Business Wire—*www.businesswire.com*
- Canadian Corporate Newsnet—*www.cdn-news.net*

For online publicity:

- Encourage other sites to reprint your articles or to link to your articles. Have a main article page with a list of available articles and a reprint permission form. For example see: *www.planetlink.com/articles.html.*
- Create an e-mail signature file (See Chapter 31, "In Praise of E-Mail.")
- Post notices and answer questions in discussion groups. (See Chapter 29, "Join Internet Communities.")

Increase Your Site's Traffic

It's important to increase the traffic on your site because the more hits your site gets, the more people will view your publicity, which in turn will increase your business. To get more traffic, you may want to create a media center, use distribution services or registration systems, or ask visitors to assist.

Media Center

Make your Web site function as a press center or a press room. Provide content for the media and make it easy for them to use. Prominently display the words "Media Center," "News Room," or "Press Room" on all your site's pages and prominently on the front page; link them to a series of pages or subsections with:

- A listing of all your press releases and articles by their headlines. Place the headlines in reverse chronological order, with the most recent release at the top of the list. Link each headline to the full text of the press release, which visitors can view and print. You can also provide files to be downloaded.
- Format your Web pages so that visitors can print them in easily-readable, printer-friendly versions.
- Provide supporting documents to give visitors more information about your company and product or service. Such items may include spreadsheets, fact sheets, multimedia

photographs of products and employees, company and management biographies, logo, client list, testimonials, awards and recognition, events and programs, links to other sites, and other information that visitors can download. List date-sensitive material in reverse chronological order and group documents according to categories. Consider creating a separate page for each category.

• Give contact information and include your logo on every page. It's amazing how many Web sites don't provide the phone number, fax number, or e-mail address for the site. Don't force visitors to search madly when they want to contact you.

GUERRILLA INTELLIGENCE

Warning: Don't post financial or any other type of sensitive information on your Web site if you're concerned about your competitors getting access to it. However, if you wish to provide limited access, your site can be constructed to let you designate who has access to sensitive information.

Make it easy for the press to use information from your site. Include information about your product or service on your Web site's "About Us" section or in separate product or services sections. Include a request form on your site that visitors can complete and submit in order to ask questions or get information.

KEY SITES

For examples of outstanding online press rooms, visit:

- *www.ge.com/news*
- *www.janal.com/new.html*
- *www.ibm.com*

Distribution Services

Internet distribution services circulate press releases to thousands of reporters and media outlets. Send your releases to one of the following services:

- PR Newswire (*www.prnewswire.com*)
- Business Wire (*www.businesswire.com*)
- Internet Wire (*www1.internetwire.com*)
- Internet News Bureau (*www.newsbureau.com*)
- eReleases (*www.ereleases.com*)

GUERRILLA INTELLIGENCE

Warning: Send your press releases to only one distribution service, because they all reach virtually the same audiences and charge similar fees. The media doesn't want or need to receive the same releases from multiple services.

Registration System

Create a registration system on your press center through which the press can tell you who they are and what material they wish to receive. Get registrants' names, e-mail addresses, and topic areas, such as general news, financial reports, or new product news. Categorize the data according to the media they represent (radio, TV, press, and Web) and the interests indicated. Build in the capability for visitors to subscribe to your e-mail list(s). Systems can be added to your Web site that will automatically send messages, including promotional messages, to list members.

GUERRILLA INTELLIGENCE

Warning: Registration systems that require detailed information can be barriers, because many visitors will log off your site rather than complete them. Ask as few questions as possible, and clearly post your privacy policy.

Ask Visitors to Help

You can increase your Web site traffic by asking visitors to bookmark your site, make your site their starting page, and sign up to be on your mailing list.

Making a Site Effective

Visitors to Web sites are demanding, and they have plenty of options. If your site has problems, they won't waste their time with it and usually won't return. They might even turn to your competitors' sites. So don't put up your site until it's well tested and easy to navigate, and you're convinced that it's effective.

To ensure visitor pleasure, make sure that your site is always easy to use, quick to download, informative, and attractive—and that it reflects your mission.

Easy to Use

Make your Web site easy and intuitive to use. If not, visitors won't stay or return. Visitors have loads of other options, and if they have to jump through hoops to use your site, they won't waste their time. Waiting for your site to appear will frustrate and anger visitors. It will undermine your hopes of turning them into satisfied customers or clients. So, make your site simple to use!

Before launching your site, test it on friends or family members who have little computer/Web experience, and note the problems they encounter. Assume that others will incur the same problems and that the problems are with your site, not with your visitors. Don't accept excuses or explanations from Web designers. Care only that your site is easily navigable by everyone from novices to experts. The bottom line is that the site must be easy to use. Make sure that your site works smoothly with all operating systems and browsers. And finally, fix all problems.

When your site is online, continually monitor it to make sure that all links work. Nothing is more frustrating than being detoured to a totally irrelevant site instead of the promised destination. If links don't work, visitors won't return to your site.

Informative

Your Web site should be the repository of vital information about your business—it must be informative. A good design may attract visitors, and ease of operation will keep them happy, but content, features, and functions will bring them back. Ultimately, visitors want value. They want to see who you are, what information you provide, and how it can benefit them.

Use your Web site to describe your business, its history, specific projects you are working on or have successfully completed, financial information, and product and service information. Web sites can also be used to display your portfolio, staff biographies, staff photographs, customer/client lists, testimonials, news, newsletters, games, contests, privacy and security policies, audio, video, and links to other sites.

If your business involves selling a product, your Web site can include product descriptions, product specifications, price lists, photographs, illustrations, shopping cart and online order processing, ordering information, shipping instructions, and direct e-mail links for questions and comments. See *www.lefile.com* for reviews of Web sites. On this site you can learn what to include and what to avoid as determined by people who are knowledgeable and well regarded.

Quick to Download

As previously stated, visitors to Web sites hate to waste their time. "The site took too long to download," is a consistent complaint that Web designer Steve Lillo of Planetlink (*www.planetlink.com*) hears. According to Steve, slowness is a major turn off.

To be successful, Web sites must download fast! If visitors have to wait long—most won't stick around, especially if they have other options—they'll be off and running to other sites, including those of your competitors. The most terrific, prize-winning site won't attract many visitors if it takes forever to view. Slow downloading can be expensive, it can cost you customers or clients.

In the past, a site could either be downloaded quickly or be graphically exciting, not both. You had to make a choice.

Fortunately, that's no longer true. Today, Web designers can give you the best of both worlds—sites that download fast and look great.

Web designers know how to best use color, optimize and compress images, and judiciously incorporate graphics to make your site "lean and mean" and visually appealing. They can write code that tells your browser how the Web page looks while taking minimal space and using downloadable files such as Java applets sparingly.

Attractive

A Web site is an electronic calling card or billboard in cyberspace that everyone can see. It's intended to grab visitors' attention, get them to respond positively to your product or service, and return to your site.

GUERRILLA INTELLIGENCE

Design—a site's look and feel—is the first thing visitors notice. Site design reflects how you would like to be perceived, whether classical, traditional, modern, progressive, or avant-garde. Bold design featuring unusual colors or color combinations and typefaces can signify a dynamic, aggressive, and vigorous approach. However, it can also come off as distracting, visual noise. Web site design is akin to dressing appropriately for a job interview. It may not get you the job, but without it you decrease your chances of making it to the second round. What constitutes appropriateness depends on the audience you hope to reach. Also, Web design isn't just about looks. It also controls many other features including the site's structure, organization, and ease of navigation, which are essential if a site is to succeed.

Reflects Your Mission

Remember, the purpose of your Web site, the reason for its existence, is to support your mission. It's easy to be seduced by the glitter of new, exciting technology, brilliant writing, startling color combinations, and ground-breaking design. But what value do they provide if they divert visitors from your site's main purpose—to support your mission?

Identify your site's mission. Be specific. Your site should reflect and support the mission of your business. For example, if the mission of your business is to sell tools, create a Web site that supports your business of selling tools. On your site, give visitors information about your tools and make it easy for them to buy your tools online. Also make it clear to them why it's to their benefit to buy your tools.

If the mission of your site is to convey information, give visitors easy access to your information. Make your content easy to read, understand, print, and send to others.

GUERRILLA INTELLIGENCE

Remember, if your Web site doesn't help to build your business, you may be better off without the site.

GUERRILLA TACTICS

Web designer Steve Lillo (*www.planetlink.com*) shared his secrets on how to assure that visitors come back to your site. They are:

- Always tell the truth. State the facts clearly and avoid hype, buzz words, and jargon. If you're stating your opinion, make it crystal clear that you're merely giving your opinion, not quoting facts.
- Employ appropriate technology to insure that every element of your site is easy to use. Keep in mind that use of the latest technology doesn't always produce the most effective Web site. Ease of use is especially important with large, complex sites. Make sure all links connect properly.
- Make your site lively and entertaining. Create great content that visitors will look forward to reading. Give advice, the latest news, and explain how visitors can perform basic

tasks involved in your field. (Filling out forms, performing mechanical tasks, baking pies, and developing photographs.) Include anecdotes, jokes, industry news, tips, contests, surveys, and discussion groups. Award prizes and give discounts on merchandise.

- Keep content updated so that the information you provide is always correct. Remember, your Web site is also a research tool. Visitors will depend on you for reliable information and won't use your site if your information isn't current. Provide information that's updated regularly such as daily tips or monthly articles.

- Notify people via e-mail about significant news developments, updates to your site, and other information that may be of benefit or interest to them. Create a link from your e-mail message to your site, so that your site is only a "mouse click away" from your customers or clients.

- Deliver what you promise—if you can't deliver it, don't promise. As previously stressed, results are ultimately what count, and once you get past the glitter, results are what visitors to your site want. If you don't provide as advertised, you'll lose credibility and most likely your business.

- Update the look of your Web site so it's consistent with your other marketing materials. If your business look or branding changes, update your site to reflect the change. Periodically freshen it by changing colors, type, graphics, and layouts.

- Never litter the Web with spam (electronic junk mail or junk news group postings). Don't host or use services that specialize in circulating spam. The wide distribution they offer is more than offset by the resentment they arouse. Sending spam can also cause you to lose your Internet account, which can result in lost business.

- Provide added value. What information or services can you provide that will cause visitors to return to your site? Fill your site with newsletters, industry analysis, calendars of events, industry directories, and other interactive services. Create a Web site that visitors will want to return to and recommend.

Remember

The Internet is a bonanza for guerrillas because it has expanded their media opportunities exponentially. Before designing a Web site, identify your target audiences and their needs. Register your site with search engines, create a media center or press room, and make it easy for the press to use information from your site. Test it thoroughly to make sure that it's easy to use, informative, quick to download, and attractive, and that it reflects your mission.

28
Research the Information Superhighway

*"If it keeps up, man will atrophy all his limbs
but the push-button finger."*
—FRANK LLOYD WRIGHT

WHERE, OTHER THAN ON THE INTERNET, CAN PEOPLE—
from the comfort of their homes, cafes, or vacation resorts—find
everything they need to know about an industry, a business, or a
competitor? The Internet has become an unsurpassed information
source. More and more professionals, especially those in the
media, are going online to find sources and information. It saves
time and it's convenient and easy to use. All a user has to do is go
to a search engine, type in a keyword, and pull up the material.

In conducting your research, you may want to consider
looking at the following sites for the information you need:

- **Trade Associations**
  DMOZ—*http://dmoz.org/about.html*
  Google—*http://directory.google.com/Top/Business/
  Resources/Associations/TradeAssociations*

The Internet Public Library, Associations on the Internet—
www.ipl.org/ref/AON
Yahoo—*www.yahoo.com/Business_and_Economy/*
Organizations/Trade_Associations

GUERRILLA INTELLIGENCE

Although the Internet removes boundaries and enables you to publicize your product or service throughout the world, it also lets you identify and pitch highly specialized audiences. Through the Net, you can identify highly specific markets, such as collectors of Venetian carnival masks, street luge aficionados, or people devoted to Paul Auster novels. You can get feedback from select groups on how they feel about your products, services, promotions, and pricing.

So, before you begin to promote your business, you need to conduct research. Get to know the turf and learn exactly what you're getting into. The Internet can direct you to information about your industry, market, and competitors. It can give you data that will be essential in shaping a successful publicity campaign.

- **U.S. Government Agencies**
  Copyright Office—*www.loc.gov/copyright*
  Federal Web Locator—*www.fedstats.gov*
  General Accounting Office—*www.gao.gov*
  Library of Congress—*www.lcWeb.loc.gov*
  Patent and Trademark Office—*www.uspto.gov*
  U.S. Census Bureau—*www.census.gov*
  U.S. Securities and Exchange Commission—*www.sec.gov*
- **Financial Information Sites**
  Annual Report Gallery—*www.reportgallery.com*
  Corporate Financials Online—*www.cronews.com*
  Hoover's—*www.hoovers.com*

- **Business School Sites**

  Haas School of Business, University of California—
  www.haas.berkeley.edu

  Kellogg Graduate School of Management, Northwestern
  University—*www.kellogg.nwu.edu*

  Stanford Graduate School of Business—*www.gbs.stanford.edu*

  Wharton School of the University of Pennsylvania
  www.wharton.upenn.edu

- **Discussion Groups**

  http://messages.yahoo.com

  www.ewatch.com

  www.delahaye.com

  www.groups.google.com

  www.liszt.com

  www.paml.net

- **Newspapers and Magazines**

  Business 2.0—*www.business2.com*

  Forbes—*www.forbes.com/magazines*

  New York Times—*www.nytimes.com*

  News Directory.com—*www.ecola.com*

  Wall Street Journal—*www.wsj.com*

  Wired—*www.wiredmagazine.com*

- **Directories of Directories**

  Reference Desk—*www.referencedesk.org*

  ReferencePage.com—*www.referencepage.com/*
  referencepage.html

  The Channel Guide—*www.thechannelguide.com/*
  reference.htm

  The Info Service—*http://info-s.com*

  Virtual Sites—*www.virtualfreesites.com/search.html*

- **Media Directories**

  Bacon's MediaList Online—*www.medialistsonline.com*

  Burrelle's Media Directory—*www.burrelles.com/*
  indexmd.html

  Media Finder—*www.mediafinder.com*

MediaMap Online—*www.mediamaponline.com*
Online Public Relations—*www.online-pr.com*
* **Distribution Services**
  Business Wire—*www.businesswire.com*
  eReleases—*www.ereleases.com*
  Internet News Bureau—*www.newsbureau.com*
  Internet Wire—*www1.internetwire.com*
  PR Newswire—*www.prnewswire.com*
* **Miscellaneous Sites**
  Finding print media—*http://mediafinder.com*
  Foreign translations—*www.babelfish.altavista.com*
  Hits on your site—*www.hitometer.com*
  Internet statistics—*www.eMarketer.com*
  Internet surveys—*www.nua.ie/surveys*
  Resources for Economists—*http://rfe.wustl.edu/OrgsAssoc/
    index.html*
  The Virtual Reference Desk—*www.lib.purdue.edu/reference*
* **Guerrilla Sites**
  Guerrilla Marketing—*www.jayconradlevinson.com*
  Guerrilla Publicity—*www.guerrillapublicity.com*
  The Guerrilla Group—*www.guerrillagroup.com*

Online Clipping Services

For most guerrillas, the task of monitoring the Internet for mentions of their product or service is overwhelming. Few can do it by themselves. When you use a search engine—the primary monitoring tool—to find Web sites, you may get thousands of hits, each of which must be reviewed and that can take a lifetime. Too often, these hits are out of date, inaccurate, or insignificant.

Fortunately, a number of clipping services have sprung up that can save the day. They include:

Bacon's Information, Inc.—*www.baconsinfo.com*
Clip Explorer—*clipexplorer.com*
CyberAlert—*www.cyberalert.com*

DeepCanyon—*www.deepcanyon.com*
eclip.com—*www.eclip.com*
eWatch—*www.ewatch.com*
Luce Press Clippings—*www.lucepress.com*
PressAccess—*www.pressaccess.com*
Webclipping.com—*www.webclipping.com*

Media Calendars

Online services provide searchable databases of items on media editorial calendars from thousands of publications. Contact information—e-mail addresses and phone and fax numbers—for the appropriate editors and reporters are also supplied. The calendar information is continually updated. Databases can be searched by topic, keyword, publication name, circulation, and location.

If you're pitching a story or looking to tie into upcoming features, search media calendar databases to find good fits. Calendar services also provide the editorial profile for magazines, including their editorial thrust and target audience. Key sites for media calendars are:

Bacon's International, Inc.—*www.bacons.com/mcalendars/
mcalendars.asp*
Media Map—*www.edcals.com*

Reporters' Questions

The Information Superhighway is a two-way thoroughfare. Not only can you conduct research on the Internet but also reporters can come to you. Reporters can post questions on:

ProfNet—*www.profnet.com*
Direct-PR—*www.direct-PR.com*

about articles they're developing and have them e-mailed to subscribers who might have the answers.

Subscribers to these services receive and can answer questions by e-mail. Reporters are usually looking for information and/or quotes on esoteric topics. If you can furnish them, they'll credit you, which can be great publicity. They may even contact you directly when they're working on features on your area of expertise.

For an updated list of categorized links for information and services visit *www.guerrillapublicity.com.*

Remember

The Internet is an enormous information source that you can easily use from the comfort of your office or home. The Net enables you to identify and target specific audiences for niche products and services. You can also obtain additional information and ask specific questions via e-mail.

29
Join Internet Communities

*"Communities of like-minded people form on the Internet
just as naturally as cliques form in high school."*
—DANIEL S. JANAL,
ONLINE MARKETING AUTHOR

INTERNET COMMUNITIES are interactive forums where members with similar interests exchange ideas and information. According to estimates, well over 100,000 Internet communities now exist and that number is rapidly rising. They include discussion groups, newsgroups, mailing lists, bulletin boards, message boards, and chat rooms. Although the term "discussion group" usually denotes a two-way conversation and the other terms refer to one-way dialogs, in this book, we'll simply use the term "discussion groups" to refer to all Internet communities and groups.

Businesses create discussion groups to keep in contact with customers, suppliers, and the media. They can learn from discussion groups how people feel about their products or services, test new ideas, target messages, and build strong relationships.

In discussion groups, people from all over the world come

together and conduct electronic conversations to explore solutions to problems of mutual interest, demonstrate their expertise, build relationships, build reputations, learn, and help one another. Group members can actively participate by posting and responding to comments or simply sit back and silently observe.

When you join a discussion group, you generally don't know the other members: who they are, what they do, and why they're in the group. But as you get in deeper, group members become friends, confidants, mentors, advisors, and disciples who can sing your praises and advance your cause.

Market Research

Monitor discussion groups to learn what customers are saying about your product or service and similar products and services. Monitoring discussion groups will also give you a feel for:

- Marketplace trends and conditions
- Needs and concerns of prospects and customers
- Problems with products and services
- How problems can be corrected
- Ideas for new products and applications
- Misinformation or rumors you can dispel.

Submit your own questions to discussion groups to get valuable feedback.

You can find groups covering topics that interest you using the search engines or sites listed below:

- **Search Engines**
  NorthernLight—*www.northernlight.com*
  AltaVista—*www.altavista.com*
- **Sites**
  www.groups.google.com (newsgroups)
  www.liszt.com
  www.paml.net

Posting

Publicize your product or service by posting items with discussion groups. However, before submitting items, follow the group for a minimum of several days. During this time, learn their rules and conventions. Determine whether that group includes your target audience. Remember, each group is different and groups continue to change as they take on new members and as developments take place in technology, the marketplace, and in society.

GUERRILLA INTELLIGENCE

Know your group! When you post an item to a discussion group, you're essentially jumping into a conversation; you're entering a community where the residents have established their own structures and rules. You will want to:

- Get a feel for how the group members communicate and the type of postings that are apropos. If your postings violate its rules, you could lose your right to post with the group; or worse, irate members could bombard you with retaliatory messages called flames.
- Find out the group's advertising and promotion policies. Often, the policy is set by the group or business, not a service provider. Many groups won't accept advertising or blatant self promotion. In a number of groups, screening is loose or nonexistent, so ads can end up running even though they're prohibited.
- If prohibited ads slip through, you could be set upon by hordes of angry, even vicious, e-mailers. Angered members could boycott your product, service, or Web site or launch hate campaigns against you. So, be careful and publicize only where you're sure you're welcome.

 **GUERRILLA TACTICS**

When posting information, commenting, or replying to news or discussion groups, observe the following guidelines:

- Write short messages that do not exceed one computer screen (24 lines or about 240 words).
- Study and follow the format used by members, including appropriate abbreviations.
- Address the topic on the subject line. It's considered rude when responses aren't on the topic being discussed.
- If you want to discuss a different topic, go to the appropriate group, send a private message, or send a new message with a different subject, which starts a new "thread," and be sure the subject line reflects your message.

Some discussion groups are happy to receive press releases, while others are not. Even if they don't accept your press release, you can still get your news out simply by contributing to the group, asking questions, or answering member's questions.

Essentially, discussion groups are intended to inform, not to sell or promote. To protect yourself from boycotts or hate campaigns:

- Edit and rewrite pieces to comply with the group's rules.
- Minimize the commercial aspects and maximize the informational aspects.
- Comment, answer questions, and make recommendations, so that you build both relationships and your credibility.
- Demonstrate your knowledge and expertise.

Don't alienate the group and jeopardize your credibility and relationships to blatantly plug your goods or services.

 **GUERRILLA TACTICS**

Add a signature file at the end of all postings to discussion groups as well as to all outgoing e-mails. A signature file contains your name, the name of your business, and your contact information. It also can include your business message, as shown in Jill's signature file below.

Jill Lublin
Promising Promotion
P.O. Box 5428
Novato, CA 94948
Voice: (415) 883-5455   FAX: (415) 883-3299
Web address: *http://www.promisingpromotion.com*

"Creating powerful public relations that catapult your business into the public eye."

Link your e-mail signature file to your Web site. It can build traffic for your site.

Web Rings

Web rings are groups that connect Web sites that have particular interests. For example, the Sensational Snowglobe ring includes over 130 sites about snow globes from making them and marketing them to information about them. When you form or join a Web ring, your site is linked to the other ring members' sites. Through these links, visitors to any site in the ring can easily access the other sites in the ring. Web rings are usually free.

Starting or joining a Web ring is great way to publicize your product or service. It groups you with other business people who have similar interests and with whom you can form alliances and business arrangements. Besides increasing traffic on your site, Web rings attract quality visitors—those specifically looking for the type of information provided on your site. Directories of Web rings can be found at Ring Surf—*www.ringsurf.com* and Yahoo Web Ring—*www.webring.yahoo.com*

Remember

Over 100,000 Internet communities are estimated to exist. Monitor discussion groups to discover what customers are saying about your product or service and similar products or services. Publicize your business by posting items with discussion groups, but first be sure to know how the group operates. Write short postings. And always add a signature file at the end of all postings and all outgoing e-mails.

30
Online Publicity Strategies

*"A fundamental new rule for business is that
the Internet changes everything."*
—BILL GATES, MICROSOFT COFOUNDER

IT'S EASY TO GET STAMPEDED by the elephantine mass of
information on the Internet, and it's frustrating to sift through
the outpouring of content when you are searching for what you
need. You have to know where to look. Therefore, we're
including lists of sites that may be helpful and suggested strategies for their utilization.

Posting Press Releases
Announce and post your press releases to your Web site.
Summarize each press release with a brief story on the main page
of your site's press release section. Then link the summary to the
full text of the release.

Simultaneously send your press release to:

- Your media list (See Chapter 10, "Media Lists: Play the Numbers Game.")
- Online distribution services
- Everyone in your organization
- Discussion groups (See Chapter 29, "Join Internet Communities.")

Add links to your press release to connect it with information on your Web site and information on other sites that might interest your visitors. For example, link to financial statements, government statistics, and prior press releases.

Distribution Services

Distribution services circulate press releases to thousands of media outlets. Many of them also offer other services including providing contact information for journalists, editors, and industry analysts, while continually supplying updated news reports and financial information, and furnishing links to other information.

 **GUERRILLA TACTICS**

Don't send the same press release to more than one distribution service because most of them send items to the same media outlets. Bullet key points in electronically distributed press releases so that they'll pop right off the page.

Distribution services may be found at:

Business Wire—*www.businesswire.com* (online and offline distributions)
NewsHub—*www.newshub.com*
Imediafax—*www.imediafax.com* (fax distributions)
Internet News—*www.internetnews.com*

InternetNewsBureau—*www.newsbureau.com* (online distributions)

InternetWire—*www1.internetwire.com* (online distributions)

Media Map—*www.mediamap.com*

NewsHub—*www.newshub.com*

Newslinx—*www.newslinx.com*

PRNewswire—*www.prnewswire.com* (online and offline distributions)

PRWeb—*www.prweb.com* (e-mail distributions)

Online Publications

Submit promotional materials to publications or create your own publication. The big advantage of creating your own online publications is that you make the rules. Becoming a publisher is a powerful way to show the world who you are, what you know, and how you can help people.

It will help you build name recognition and credibility. You can demonstrate that you're a respected, dedicated, principled, articulate, clever, visionary, and expert, who is well connected and well liked. With your own publications, you can build a following and increase your business.

GUERRILLA INTELLIGENCE

Successful publications reflect their creators. So, develop a newsletter, e-zine, or mailing list service that is an extension of you. Use it as a platform to express your insight, ideas, knowledge, sense of humor, passion, conviction, and world view. Remember, as we stated way back in Chapter 1, "You are the product!"

But be careful not to be too self-serving. Remember, that it's not only about you. Fill your publication with information that will benefit your target audience so that they'll depend on your publication and look forward to reading it.

As the publisher, editor, or whatever you want to call yourself, you select the content and decide how to present it. Unlike discussion groups, you can include whatever content you want. You can dedicate your entire publication to promoting your own goods unabashedly or even to knocking your competitors. You can write it and edit it yourself, or contract the whole thing out—it's up to you. The major disadvantage of creating your own publication is that it's a tremendous amount of work, which can divert you from more important tasks.

Online Newsletters

Newsletters usually are industry-, product-, or interest-specific. They're information intensive, but may carry advertising. Most newsletters are all business with little fluff. They assume that subscribers want and need their information in a quick easy-to-read format, so they get straight to the point.

Newsletters come in all sizes, shapes, and approaches and thrive on alerting subscribers to developments in their fields. Subscribers read them to stay up to speed. Some newsletters go into exhausting detail while others are brief. They merely report developments that subscribers can explore elsewhere in greater depth.

Generally, online newsletters occupy a separate section of a Web site and, in some cases, are password protected. Most of the time, access is free, but they can also be fee-based.

Subscribers like newsletters because they're so specifically focused, can be quickly read, and easily printed, circulated, transported, and stored. Most newsletters are published in-house and intentionally avoid the formalities of traditional magazines and newspapers. They are more loosely written and edited, which may make them easier and more enjoyable to read.

Publish new editions of your newsletter on a regular basis—at least quarterly. Marketing experts suggest following the rule of 75/25: Provide information of worth and value in 75 percent of the newsletter and sell stuff with the remaining 25 percent. Find a ratio that fits your needs and those of your readers.

Don't charge for access to your newsletters, unless you're prepared for a big drop-off in subscribers. However, if your information is essential and not otherwise available, your readership may hold, or even grow, when you charge.

Before starting a newsletter, become familiar with other newsletters. Surf the Web for newsletters in your field and other fields. Examine them closely. Note features you like, dislike, or wish had been included, and develop a template of your own. If your newsletter appeals to a large number of readers, you may attract advertisers.

PR newsletters can be found at the following sites:

Internet.com—*www.channelseven.com*
InternetPRGuide—*www.internetprguide.com*
Media Map—*www.mediamap.com/webpr*
Ragan Communications—*www.ragan.com*

E-zines

E-zines (or zines, if you really want to sound cool) are electronic newsletters delivered via e-mail. They're similar to online newsletters, except they are sent via e-mail. Usually, they're free of charge and published by companies to support their business. However, some are like printed magazines, in that advertising supports them. Most e-zines are sent to subscribers on a regular schedule, but many others are published sporadically.

The content of e-zines runs the gamut of human imagination from the highly specialized to the diverse and eclectic. E-zines often contain articles submitted by authors in exchange for publicity, which is an option for you. Or you can get publicity through e-zines by creating your own e-zine.

If you decide to create your own e-zine, you will need to build an audience for your publication. Use all the available sources:

- Solicit subscribers from your Web site, by e-mail or postal mail, and through seminars, conferences, and speaking engagements.

- Ask your customers, suppliers, colleagues, friends, and family to subscribe. Seek to build a loyal following for your e-zine instead of inflating your circulation figures. Remember, the goal is to reach those people who are interested in your product or service.
- Don't twist arms, or force subscriptions down anyone's throat. Send it only to those people who actually want to receive it. If you charge for access to e-zines, expect to lose subscribers. However, as with online newsletters, your readership might hold or even grow if your information is essential and not otherwise available.

A word of caution: think twice about selling the names on your subscriber list. Your subscribers probably are not interested in receiving spam. Likewise, don't inundate subscribers with additional mailings.

To get a feel for how other e-zines look, check out the following sites:

Guerrilla Publicity—*www.guerrillapublicity.com*
Guerrilla Marketing Online—*www.jayconradlevinson.com*
Web Digest for Marketers—*www.wdfm.com*
The Tenagra Apogee—*www.apogee.tenagra.com*

Directories listing e-zines can be found at:

e-zines.com—*www.e-zines.com*
eZineSearch—*www.ezinesearch.com*
Ezine Universe.com—*www.bestezines.com*

Mailing List Services

Mailing lists are hybrids between publications and Internet communities. They're easy to use and ideal for beginners. Basically, mailing lists are interactive discussion groups in which members send e-mails on subjects of mutual interest that are automatically circulated to the other list members. Some lists moderate or screen messages, while others distribute messages unscreened.

As with other publications, you can get publicity by contributing to mailing lists or starting your own. If you start your own mailing list, it can be purely commercial. You can freely send press releases and distribute information or promotional materials. Mailing lists solidify your contacts with business associates such as employees, customers or clients, suppliers, retailers, and the media. Plus, they enable list members to communicate directly with one another.

When you start a mailing list, you also set the rules and chart its direction. However, the interactive nature of mailing lists makes them operationally more like discussion groups. Things can change quickly. And, like discussion groups, mailing lists' tone, direction, and nature can shift with the addition and deletion of members, internal and external developments, and time.

Some key sites for mailing lists can be found at:

Liszt—*www.liszt.com*
Publicly Accessible Mailing Lists—*www.paml.net*
Tile.Net/Lists—*www.tile.net/listserv*

After you set up your mailing list, contact the sites directly above to list your mailing list if you want it to be publicly available.

FAQs and Fact Sheets

Write a list of frequently asked questions about an element of your product or service and their answers (FAQs). Similarly, you can also write instructions explaining how to perform specific tasks or fact sheets on your area of expertise, products. or services. Be informative. Attract attention by displaying your knowledge and let your knowledge sell you.

Be sure to put your FAQs, instructions, and fact sheets on your Web site, but remember to update them when you make changes in your product or service. Also consider submitting them to discussion groups that permit them or turning them into articles for the media.

Many discussion groups allow FAQs and information that's useful. FAQs and factual info are archived, (See Internet FAQ Archives—*www.faqs.org.*) referenced, and further circulated. They can build name recognition and establish you as an authority. Again, distribute FAQs only to discussion groups that accept them, because you don't want the group to turn on you.

Add a form to your FAQ page so readers can e-mail questions to you that the FAQ may not have addressed. When you receive questions submitted on your form, you will know that they came from your FAQ page, which makes it easier to manage the information. And, you can also get the questioners' names, contact information, and see if they want to subscribe to your publications.

When questions are submitted that your FAQs has not addressed, answer those questions directly, and obtain the individual's contact information. Add the question and answer to the FAQ list. Hard questions alert you to problems with your products or instructional materials, so formulate a policy for addressing problems because they will arise.

Remember

Announce and post your press releases to your Web site. Place a summary of each press release on the main page of your site's press release section. Link each summary to the full text of the press release and send all releases to a distribution service. Submit promotional materials to publications or create your own publication, such as online newsletters, e-zines, mailing lists, FAQs, instructions, and fact sheets.

31
In Praise of E-mail

"If you took a course in how computers can aid your marketing, your first insight would be how e-mail can boost your profitability."

— JAY CONRAD LEVINSON

GUERRILLA INTELLIGENCE

At the end of the year 2000, there were 514.25 million e-mail addresses, according to Messaging Online's "Year-End 2000 Mailbox Report," an increase of 88 percent from 1999. "U.S. e-mail service subscribers grew by 73 percent in 2000, but the rest of the world experienced 109 percent growth."—eMarketer.com

IF THIS CHAPTER HAD A SUBTITLE, it would be "Fifteen Reasons Why Guerrillas Love E-Mail."

1. E-mail Is Efficient

It's quick, easy to use, and conserves time, which always seems to be in short supply, and it gets the message across. It links you directly with recipients, there are no middlemen—unless you want them. Messages are transmitted immediately and can be easily shared, forwarded, answered, printed, or saved. E-mail's reply feature encourages recipients to respond promptly, and they usually do. Address book files eliminate the need to remember complex e-mail addresses. Saved e-mails provide lasting records.

TIP In e-mail, state the most important information first where it will be most likely to be read. Many readers skim or don't read the entire message. So, keep your messages short and to the point. Make sure that the subject reflects the content.

2. E-mail Gets Through

You can reach busy, powerful people, who won't ordinarily take or return your phone calls, via e-mail. People in power regularly read their e-mail because they want to be in touch with the world and because they understand e-mail's value. Producers and editors read their e-mail. Today, everything has changed, e-mail is now one of the most powerful business tools; it's the best way to reach people.

TIP E-mail the head honchos, the top people. It improves your odds of getting through to the decision makers.

3. E-mail Has Become the Publicists' Most Powerful Tool

Sending short, gentle reminders helps publicists balance the need to continually follow up and the danger that in doing so they might alienate important media contacts.

TIP Write short paragraphs, which are easier to read; bullet important information and keep the entire e-mail brief.

 **GUERRILLA TACTICS**

Before you send important e-mails, send them to yourself. Despite miraculous programs that make us all good spellers, embarrassing typos and mistakes have a way of slipping through. However, many are easily caught when you take a fresh look.

Also, e-mail messages sometimes read more harshly than intended; reading them again gives you an opportunity to soften them up.

4. E-mail Gets Right to the Point

E-mail etiquette discourages time-consuming preliminaries, extraneous niceties, and small talk, which are expected in other modes of communication. Instead, e-mail etiquette encourages brevity and precision. If you wish, add pleasantries or personal comments, but in many business situations it's not considered cool.

TIP Capitalize words sparingly. Caps are considered discourteous; they're read as shouting. Capping first letters is okay, but not entire words unless you mean to shout or convey anger.

5. E-mail Allows for Quick, Clear Messages

E-mail allows you to quickly and clearly convey precise information that often gets butchered in telephone messages, such as numbers, formulas, technical terms (medication and scientific names), and the correct spelling of names.

TIP Confirm or document critical information discussed in meetings or telephone conversations with e-mails. When replying to e-mails, don't delete the original e-mail message. Recipients who get lots of e-mail, or don't immediately reply to them, need context, so always include the original text for them to reference.

6. E-mail Can Contain Links to Your Web Site or Other Sites

E-mail links let you reference and give recipients easy access to information that you did not send in the body of your e-mail message or in an e-mail attachment. E-mail can link to pages in your Web site.

TIP Use e-mail to get people's attention. Send the media brief query e-mails and provide a link back to your home page or your press-room page so they can obtain additional information.

7. E-mail Lets You Transmit Bulky Files Instantly

Photographs, charts, lists, and spreadsheets are often too big and time consuming to fax. With e-mail, you don't have to stand around feeding pages into a copier or a fax machine nor do you need to stuff them in envelopes or pay for postage or overnight delivery. All you have to do is add or attach them to your e-mail, and zip, off they go.

TIP Send your press release via e-mail to group lists. That's the most efficient method.

> ### GUERRILLA INTELLIGENCE
> Warning: People are wary about attachments because they may contain viruses, so use them judiciously. Large files can slow down or tie up e-mail transmissions, so make them downloadable from your Web site and send an e-mail that contains a download link.

8. E-mail Delivers Even When Unread

When recipients don't read their e-mail, they usually check to see what came in and who sent it. The subject line on e-mail menu inboxes provides a forty-two-character space in which you can convey the gist your message. This keeps you on the recipients' radar screens, even if they don't open your e-mail. Through the subject line, you can provide gentle reminders without being perceived as a pest.

TIP Write precise, succinct subject lines. Besides describing content, recipients use subject lines to categorize their e-mails, to decide whether to open e-mail, and when scrolling to find old e-mails.

 **GUERRILLA TACTICS**

Think of e-mail subject lines as if they were book titles. You wouldn't buy a book that didn't have a title, because you couldn't tell what the book was about. Similarly, many recipients won't open e-mail unless they know what the e-mail's about.

Make your subject line interesting and intriguing—like a book title—to fire the recipient's curiosity. Practice writing subject lines as if they were headlines.

9. E-mail Eludes Electronic Fences

Getting past answering machines, voice mail, secretaries, and screeners can be murder, but e-mail slips through. Although we've been conditioned to prefer personal phone contact, it's often impossible. When your phone messages aren't answered, don't feel rejected—use e-mail. The objective is to get your message through, and e-mail accomplishes the task. The rest is up to the recipient.

TIP Use e-mail when other channels are blocked.

10. E-mail Is a Versatile Marketing Tool

It's ideal for sending fliers, newsletters, and other promotional materials without incurring the costs of printing and mailing, which can be substantial. And, recipients who want hard copies can easily print them out.

TIP E-mail bulk distributions. It's fast, easy, and saves trees.

11. E-mail Domain Names Can Promote Your Business

Include the name of your business in your domain name. For example, johns@planetlink.com. Many Internet service providers supply such customized domain names for a nominal charge. When you sign up with a provider, make sure that if you switch to another provider you can keep your domain name.

TIP Invest in a domain name that includes the name of your business.

12. E-mail Signature Files Are the Equivalent of Letterheads on Stationery

Besides giving recipients your name, the name of your business, and your contact information, other material such as your message (sound bite) can be included in a signature file to promote your business.

TIP Include your contact information, Web site address, and sound bite as a signature file.

13. E-mail Demonstrates That You're Firmly in the Twenty-first Century

It shows that you're versed in the standard tools used in the business world today.

TIP Include your e-mail address and your Web site address on your stationery, business cards, and promotional materials to show that you're up to date.

14. E-mail Shifts the Cost and Burden from Senders to Recipients

With regular mail, senders put letters in envelopes, buy and attach stamps, and deposit them in mailboxes. With e-mail, recipients have the burden of opening them, and run the risk of receiving spam or viruses.

TIP Don't send spam or attachments that are large without getting the recipient's permission. Sending spam is a short-sighted publicity approach.

15. E-mail Has Revived the Lost Art of Letter Writing

Although most e-missives may not be literary masterpieces, they're often creative, expressive communiqués. E-mail's directness and brevity has created a new way of writing and given form to a new preciseness of thought.

TIP Try your hand at fiction.

32
Growing Pains—How to Hire the Right PR People

"Winning isn't everything, but wanting to win is."
—ARNOLD PALMER, GOLF IMMORTAL

SO YOU'RE CRUISING ALONG. You've put the principles of this book in practice and they're working beautifully. Your publicity campaign is generating tons of business. In fact, it's producing more work than you can handle. To keep abreast, you're virtually living at the office. Your spouse is threatening to leave you, your kids seem like strangers, and the dog acts as if you're an intruder.

Something's got to give. Obviously, you can't process all the new work, run your PR campaign, and please the folks at home. You also can't afford to turn down new business. It's senseless to stop a campaign that's paying big dividends. But taking more time away from the family isn't an option. What to do, what to do?

Clearly, you need help. You can hire additional staff, but finding and training good workers takes time. In the meantime, the hole you're digging is becoming a crater.

 **GUERRILLA TACTICS**

Instead of hiring additional workers for your business, it may be smarter to seek help from publicity professionals. Hiring professionals can allow you to concentrate on your business, which after all is your expertise, while the pros see that your PR campaign is running smoothly. Since you've now learned so much about publicity, you can monitor their work without surrendering overall control.

For help with publicity, you have basically three options: PR agencies, consultants, or in-house publicists.

1. **PR Agencies.** We know large PR firms can cost a fortune, because most large agencies are geared to corporations, not guerrillas. However, size isn't everything and it's easy to get lost among the redwoods. Many smaller agencies are reasonably priced and can provide more personal service targeted to your needs. PR firms are usually well staffed. They can handle every aspect of your campaign in-house and don't have to contract out. Firms usually work on monthly retainers, but many will take you on a project basis and charge an agreed-upon, set fee.

GUERRILLA INTELLIGENCE

Warning: Be wary of agencies that claim to do more than just PR, i.e., PR and advertising or PR and branding. They seldom do each well. PR is a unique discipline that takes special talents. So if you want PR, go to a firm that specializes in PR only.

2. **Consultants.** Freelance PR professionals usually are a one-person operation without staff. Generally, consultants worked for large PR agencies or corporations and then went out on their own. Since they seldom have staff, you'll probable incur additional expenses for services

they aren't equipped to perform. Consultants are usually less expensive than agencies because they have lower overhead. Often, they will work out of your office or place of business. More information on consultants is included at the end of this chapter.

3. **In-house Publicists.** You can hire experienced PR specialists to become employees on your staff. Generally, guerrillas can't afford in-house publicists and their resources are better spent concentrating on their core business. However, you could hire a part-time in-house publicist for a percentage of job fees, or you could trade services.

Guerrilla Resources

Do your homework. Check *O'Dwyer's Directory of Public Relations Firms* that lists 2,400 of the largest firms worldwide, in the United States, and in twenty-four cities or regions. O'Dwyer's, which is available in hard copy or online (*www.odwyerpr.com*), lists firms geographically, by size, and by eleven specialty areas.

Identify firms and/or consultants that specialize in your products or services and in the type of promotions you envision. PR is highly specialized. Firms and consultants concentrate in areas including health care, technology, pharmaceuticals, nonprofit businesses, and crisis control. Although firms may claim to do everything, few do everything well. The key is to match the type of services firms provide and the clients they represent with your objectives. Check out their Web sites.

Select four or five firms and/or consultants to interview. Before you contact any firms or consultants, define your needs and objectives. Determine how much you're willing to spend for PR annually. Then meet and interview each firm and consultant. During the interview pay attention to your gut feeling for the firm or consultant. Observe how they work and listen carefully to the results they promise to deliver. Ask for client names and contact them to get feedback on how they judge their working relationship with the firm or consultant.

Experience

After you've signed on with a PR agency, you may discover that the impressive gentleman, who always had the right answers, isn't working on your account. Instead, your publicity is being handled by a novice six months out of school, who still doesn't know where to find the pencil sharpener.

 **GUERRILLA TACTICS**

Before you hire an agency, learn who will actually work on your campaign and his or her experience. If it's a newer employee, ask who'll be supervising your account and to what extent he or she will be monitoring it.

Experience is important, but it isn't everything. It can also pose problems. Publicists, like anyone else, get into ruts. They tend to stick with what traditionally worked in the past and can be reluctant to change. They may be committed to assumptions that no longer apply or lack the boldness to distinguish you and make your campaign fly.

Using outsiders is often effective. New faces can bring fresh ideas, new approaches, excitement, and flair. Often outsiders can see what others may have been too close to notice. For example, a publicist who worked only with automotive clients might be just the right person to create a breakthrough campaign for a nonprofit hospital.

Obtain the names of recent and current clients. Specifically request the names of those who worked with the people who'll be handling your account. Call them. Learn how they liked working with the agency and the individuals, and if they were pleased with the results. Ask them to list the agency's strengths, weaknesses, and what they would change. Find out how promptly agency personnel return calls.

Ask the agency what it will bring to your account. Is it creativity, large agency backing, entrepreneurial background, media placement, or booking speaking engagements? Find out what you can expect.

Get a written statement explaining how much you will be charged for each service you might receive.

Interview Checklist

The questions that you should ask prospective publicity professionals will vary project to project. However, in most cases you should ask the following basic questions:

1. Who will lead my account?
   What is his or her experience?
   How much time will he or she spend on my account?
2. Who will work on my account?
   What is his or her experience?
   How much time will he or she devote to my account?
3. Who will supervise the work on my account?
   What is his or her experience?
   How much time will he or she put in on my account?
4. What is the plan for my campaign?
5. How long will my campaign run?
6. How much access will I have to strategists who design my campaign?
7. How much input will I have in my campaign?
8. Will I receive weekly communications about my account?
9. How often will I get updates on my account?
10. How many calls to whoever needs to be called will be made on my account?
    Each week?
    Each month?
11. What specific results will I receive?
    After one month?
    After three months?
    Upon completion of the project?
12. How do I measure results?
13. What can I do if I don't receive the results promised?
    Can I fire you?

Will you refund fee payments?

If so, how much?

What will I be charged?

Will I receive extra work at no charge?

14. What specific results have you created for past, similar clients?

15. What are your strong points and your advantages over other agencies?

Be Proactive

You are always the expert. No one knows or cares as much about your business as you. You must be involved in your campaign and make or approve all major decisions. Stipulate that you must be notified in advance and approve of all decisions that will cost more than a stated monetary amount. To stay involved, insist on receiving weekly updates. Updates will inform you whether your campaign is proceeding on schedule and what problems occurred. Updates will also help you make quick adjustments to address problems.

However, in your involvement take care to avoid interfering, preventing, or making it more difficult for the publicity professionals to do their jobs. Such involvement will be counterproductive, breed resentment, and your campaign will suffer. Leave the details to the professionals. Assume the role of a consultant, an advisor, or a resource who has inside knowledge that can enhance the PR experts' performance.

 **GUERRILLA TACTICS**

If you decide to hire consultants, make sure you hire the top consultants. To identify the experts in your industry, go to bookstores, libraries, and the Web to find out who wrote the best books in your field. Find out who ran a PR campaign that impressed you. Check out the most effective instructors on the seminar circuit and at schools and universities. Ask your friends and peers.

Obtain and study publications written by experts before you approach them. Contact information is usually given at their speaking engagements or can be found on their publications or Web sites.

When you contact these experts, be willing to pay for their knowledge. Don't try to pick their brains. Tell them, "I want to buy some of your time. I've read your books and I want to hire you as a consultant to walk me through this project. I want you to tell me exactly what to do." This approach will show them that you're professional and that you understand that their time is valuable. They'll also treat you as a professional.

If consultants refuse to charge you, send them a gift equal to or of greater value than the fee they normally charge. This small gesture will buy good will and insure that you have access to those experts in the future.

Although hiring the top authorities as consultants may be expensive, it's usually a great investment. Most experts are familiar with most problems, because they know the industry, the short cuts, the players, whom to approach, how to get the best results, and can prepare you for changes that you might otherwise not discover.

Remember

When you hire publicity professionals, you can concentrate on your business while the pros run your campaign. You can hire, work with, and supervise PR agencies, consultants, or in-house publicists. Identify those that specialize in your products or services and in the type of promotions you envision; then interview them. In hiring and working with a PR professional, keep in mind that you're the expert—no one knows or cares as much about your business as you.

33
Summing Up

*"An idea can turn to dust or magic, depending
on the talent that rubs against it."*
—WILLIAM BERNBACH,
ADVERTISING LEGEND

NOW THAT YOU'VE READ THIS BOOK, and it's fresh in your mind, it's time to act—to move from the theoretical to the practical. It's time for you to take the information that we've provided on how to create a successful publicity campaign and rub it vigorously against your ideas, objectives, and talent. It's time to make some magic!

Before you begin, we would like to stress some final points that bear repeating. Although we've covered these points in the book, keep them in mind because they pervade virtually every aspect of publicity. Understanding them should give you a better perspective from which to apply the information you've learned and deal with the situations that you're going to face.

1. *Think publicity.* Publicity must become a mindset, a constant and instinctive focus in your life. Always look for

opportunities to publicize your products or services. Not just when you're in your office, but when you're home, out with the family, or at social events. Continually ask, "How can I publicize my restaurant, my book, or my dog-walking service?" "How about this newspaper, magazine, station, Web site, or event?" "How should I approach them?" "Who do I know who can help me?" and "What is the best strategy?" When you come across other promotions, always ask, "How could it work for me?"

2. *Credibility is everything.* You are the product, so never claim to be what you're not or promise what you can't deliver. Ultimately, consumers want results. A clever pitch may initially amuse them, but they want products that work and services that provide the tangible results promised. When people don't believe or even doubt you, they won't support your efforts. Your failure to deliver will alienate customers or clients and quickly destroy a lifetime of credibility and good will. To compound the problem, it's infinitely harder to regain lost credibility and good will than it is to first establish them.

3. *Build for the long run.* Choose your battles judiciously. Don't wage a life-or-death struggle on every issue or you may not get the chance to do battle tomorrow. That doesn't mean that you should always give in easily or not make repeated efforts. It means that you shouldn't press an issue with a media contact to the point where you could destroy the relationship. Take the long-term view. Remember that you may need that contact down the road. Think in terms of campaigns, rather than ads; in terms of careers, instead of jobs; and in terms of decades, rather than days, months, or years.

4. *Media relationships are not equal.* In your relationships with the media, the media holds the upper hand because they can deliver publicity. Don't take it personally when your media contacts don't respond. The fact is, they're usually busy. The media has a short attention span and

once they have your story and you're not on their schedule, you're no longer in their minds. Don't fall apart when your new best friend pulls away. Instead, maintain the friendship by becoming a media resource. Since the media is a voracious machine that must be fed, feed the media. Serve your contacts heaping portions of your stories, information, and contacts, even after they keep chewing them up and spitting them out.

5. *Send killer press releases.* The media demands press releases, even though they may not always read them. Sending great press releases is the mark of a true professional, and people in the media prefer to deal with professionals. Learning to write great press releases sharpens your focus and shapes the direction of your publicity campaigns. Writing press releases is a critical publicity skill. Practice until you master writing compelling one-page press releases with attention-getting headlines and bullets. In press kits, press releases are the beef; the rest is simply gravy.

6. *Follow up on everything.* Persistence is the key to publicity. Without persistence your story probably won't be told. Follow-up can be the difference between languishing in the crowd and emerging into the spotlight where you can shine. Remember the rule of seven: it takes seven calls to get a yes. When following up, don't be a pest and never be rude! Tread lightly, but give the media repeated, gentle reminders to keep your project on their minds. Make following up a regular part of your business, not just an occasional, haphazard practice. Set aside a time each day to follow up and maintain a follow-up log to record your efforts on all campaigns.

7. *Never give interviews unless you're totally prepared.* The major reason people mess up interviews is that they lack command of their subject. First, learn your subject expertly. Prepare five main points to cover in every interview and another fifteen to twenty subpoints, or three to four under each main point. Strengthen and spice up those

points by using anecdotes, stories, jokes, and statistics. Practice, practice, practice—in front of the mirror and in front of your friends and family. Have people grill and pepper you with questions. Consider a hiring media coach or taking media training.

8. *Become an authority.* Learn you discipline expertly, and then increase your visibility by teaching, speaking, and/or writing about it. Design, organize, lead, teach, and partici- pate in seminars or workshops. Publish materials on narrow subjects that you've mastered and clearly explain your knowledge to others. As a recognized authority, you'll meet and spend time with other experts and your peers. You'll expand your knowledge, your contacts, your network, and your business.

9. *Master the Internet.* Explore both the Internet's research and marketing capabilities. Begin by playing. Visit a wide array of Web sites to get a full understanding of the range of sites that exist and the approaches they use. Then draw from sites that excite you to create a Web site that will support your business objectives. Make your Web site easy to navigate, informative, and attractive. Check out the competition's sites and participate in Internet commu- nities. Use e-mail for both correspondence and to dis- tribute information, including publicity materials.

10. *Maintain contact with the publicity community.* Attend trade shows, conventions, and conferences. Contact the authors of this book. Send us your comments on this book and information that we might include in future versions. Tell us about your own experiences, insights, and stories.

Contact us at: *www.guerrillapublicity.com*
Jay Conrad Levinson: *www.jayconradlevinson.com*
Rick Frishman: *www.plannedtvarts.com*
Jill Lublin: *www.promisingpromotion.com*

Appendix A
Sample Materials

THE BALLANTINE PUBLISHING GROUP

A Division of Random House, Inc., 1540 Broadway, New York, N.Y. 10036

Contact: <u>Planned Television Arts</u>
Brian Feinblum 212-583-2718
Christina Semmel 212-715-1678
Patricia Blythe 212-583-2776

<u>Celebrating 40 years of success with Harvey Mackay, who is forever...</u>

PUSHING THE ENVELOPE

"His previous career-advice books....combine catchy titles, solid advice delivered in sound-bite style and entertaining personal tales. I like his approach to networking."
—WALL STREET JOURNAL, columnist Hal Lancaster

"Mr Mackay preaches the gospel of self-improvement, hard work, ingenuity and fair-but-fierce competition. The message is delivered in short, homiletic chapters covering the art of managing, selling and being a leader."
—NEW YORK TIMES, Deborah Stead, columnist

Harvey Mackay, labeled by *Fortune* magazine as "Mr. Makes Things Happen," is celebrating 40 years of career success with the new paperback release of his fourth *New York Times* best-seller, **PUSHING THE ENVELOPE: All The Way To The Top (Ballantine Books, May 2000)**. Mackay is a true business titan who is respected as one of today's leading motivators, inspirers, and CEO's with a proven track record that meets anyone's bottom line.

Practical and entertaining, Mackay triumphs in offering scores of avenues to pursue success. Pushing boundaries—and yourself—**PUSHING THE ENVELOPE** teaches us to consistently deliver in an always-changing world. The clear message from one of America's leading business and civic leaders includes commentary on the following:

The art of negotiating—sometimes you get what you want by calling it another name
25 creativity killers—how corporations extinguish innovation
Deal-making—if you can't say *yes*, it's *no*
10 areas to improve—new year's resolutions to make today
How to get a raise—negotiating is selling, so prepare a sales pitch
10 attributes of a great salesperson—they can see things from a customer's eyes
Retail is detail—beware the naked man who offers you his shirt
10 tips on managing—how to win at liar's poker
Leadership—leaders are truthful even when it hurts
Fail-safe steps to move up the corporate ladder

"When you're pushing the envelope, you're looking to maximize your advantage," writes Mackay. "You're looking for the edge...the angle...the window. It's there." Indeed, the man *Success* magazine calls the "World's Greatest Networker," is about reaching out, making the extra effort and paying great homage to detail, respect and etiquette. He finds the edge in common sense. **PUSHING THE ENVELOPE** offers Mackay's latest life lessons and business advice that can only come from someone who leads a successful professional and personal life. It delivers the product of his diverse experiences and shares the inimitable wit and savvy that led Toastmasters International to name him as one of the world's top 5 speakers.

His career highlights include:

✓ **He bought a failing envelope-manufacturing company at age 26, and it now has annual sales of $85 million. It employs 550 people and manufactures over 6 billion envelopes annually. The seven most senior workers have been with him for a combined 250 years. Every employee, regardless of rank, is consulted for input by the company president for up to 30 minutes each.**

✓ **His books have sold 8,500,000 copies in 80 nations, translated into 35 languages, including four *New York Times* best-sellers and another that was a national best-seller *(Sharkproof)*.**

✓ ***The New York Times* ranked the best-selling motivational books of all time and named two of Mackay's #1 NYT best-sellers in the Top 15—*Swim With The Sharks Without Being Eaten Alive* (#10) and *Beware The Naked Man Who Offers You His Shirt* (#13). He was joined by Covey, Peale, Carnegie, Chopra and others, and was just the fourth author with multiple books.**

✓ ***Dig Your Well Before Your Thirsty* jumped to the *NYT* best-seller list within 12 days of its release and remained there for five months.**

✓ **Millions read his daily United Feature Syndicate column, which is circulated to over 50 papers nationwide, including the *Denver Post, Detroit Free Press,* and the *Minneapolis Star Tribune.***

✓ ***Sales & Marketing Management* named him as one of the 80 most influential people in sales and marketing: "Mackay just might be the business world's ultimate motivator."**

Mackay's book tells us when conventional wisdom needs to be secondary to gut instinct, such as his policy on hiring workers back even if they were fired or left to go into business for themselves and wound up in Chapter 11. Recognizing talent and emotional stability doesn't always go hand in hand, so Mackay says he hires people he doesn't like personally as long as they can get the job done professionally. He also says the customer isn't always right.

His company's mission statement is simple: "To be in business forever," but he details the values that should be promoted in any organization. He tells us about hiring right—and the need to let people go so that the company can grow ("I finally realized it was the people we didn't fire that made our lives miserable"). He also tells us the nation's 14 million salespeople don't have to fear losing their jobs to the Internet ("You can take your talent wherever you go. You will always be in demand"). He warns us: "Don't neglect the little things" and reminds us: "You really can't go it alone." He encourages risk-taking, exhorts us to contribute to the community and asks us not to neglect our family in pursuit of the almighty dollar.

Mackay tells us about famous people who began as failures and smart people who do dumb things. He talks frankly about trust, determination, winning, and forgiveness, while deriding the lack of attention paid to details in business and assailing customer-service surveys. He humorously tells us how to ruin a great sales force, offers the right questions to ask a potential customer, and reveals how to close not just today's sale but tomorrow's. There is commentary on quick-thinking and long-range planning as well as on the pricing of products and how to limit phone tag, leave strong messages and answer the phone professionally.

Sprinkled liberally with his aphorisms and "Mackay's Morals," **PUSHING THE ENVELOPE** enlightens, leads and shows us the way Harvey Mackay has done things for over four decades. "Two of the lessons I teach," says Mackay, "are know the competition, and you can always learn something from someone." Indeed, we learn a lifetime of something from someone who is continually **PUSHING THE ENVELOPE.**

Publication Data: Ballantine Books May 2, 2000; ISBN: 0449-00669-7; $16.00; 348 pages; paperback
A *main selection* of the **MONEY BOOK CLUB**
Visit our Web site at www.randomhouse.com/bb/ or www.mackay.com

Contact: Scott Piro @ 212-593-6439
piros@ruderfinn.com

Victoria Principal

The "Living Principal": Looking and Feeling Your Best at Any Age

Victoria Principal shares her secrets for living youthfully through motivation, beauty, and overall mind-body health in *Living Principal: Looking and Feeling Your Best at Every Age* **(Villard Books)**. In nine simple, straight forward chapters (focusing on diet, exercise, hair and skin care among other components of well-being), Victoria has created a program to guide those women who truly desire to better themselves one step at a time.

When Victoria turned forty-two, she was caught off guard. She began seeing signs of aging, and began to experience unexpected insecurities. Instead of playing the blame-game and creating excuses for her problems, Victoria took responsibility and reinvented her life.

Living Principal can be used as a complete anti-aging plan, or each individual chapter can be used to meet specific goals or needs. Beginning with taking charge of your attitude and committing yourself to complete mind-body health, Victoria outlines the need for routine and balance in one's life.

Victoria Principal Can Discuss:
- •How to groom skin and hair as you age
- •Two beauty essentials often overlooked: EYE & TEETH CARE
- •Her easy-to-follow "30 DAY DIET TO LOSE"
- •In depth analysis of HORMONES & PLASTIC SURGERY
- •How to look and feel sexy at any age
- •How women can "tend to their souls" and other SPIRITUAL ADVICE

Ultimately, Victoria has outlined a 30-day plan to begin the journey to whole-health that can last a lifetime!

About the Author:
Victoria Principal, known to the world from the hit television series *Dallas,* has gone on to establish herself as a phenomenally successful entrepreneur with her Principal Secret skin and beauty care line and her film and television production company. She is also the author of the best-selling books *The Body Principal, The Diet Principal,* and *The Beauty Principal.* She is fifty-one years old and lives in Los Angeles with her husband, Dr. Harry Glassman.

VICTORIA PRINCIPAL IS AVAILABLE FOR INTERVIEWS
WEDNESDAY, APRIL 11, 2001
FROM 7:00—11:30 AM EST
CONTACT SCOTT PIRO @ 212-593-6439

Laugh to:
Relieve Stress
Enhance Communication
Enrich Relationships
Diffuse Conflict
And More....

LAUGHTER

Enda Junkins is a rate commodity—a laughing psychotherapist. Known as the Laughter Guru, she has been speaking on laughter internationally for over ten years, sharing her unique, practical, and memorable tools for creating laughter to enthusiastic audience response. A leading national expert on laughter, her wit, wisdom and flexible approach to using laughter with a wide range of serious topics has made her presentations effective for businesses, organizations, and the personal arena as well. When she speaks, Enda's warm, powerful, fun-loving personality draws her audiences to her and keeps them anxious to participate. Participants leave her presentations feeling energized and positive. They also take with them the potential for lower stress levels, tools for clearer communication, and a stronger connection to one another. Enda's laughter expertise developed over more than 25 years as a practicing psychotherapist using laughter in the healing of serious issues. Her work with laughter has been enthusiastically received by her professional peers who consistently rave about her presentations on "The Power of Laughter in Therapy" and her "Belly Laughter for Couples." She is the author of one book and three videos on laughter.

EDUCATION
BA Baylor University
MA Baylor University
MSW University of Illinois

LICENSES AND CERTIFICATIONS
Licensed Master Social Worker-Advanced Clinical Practitioner
Licensed Marriage and Family Therapist
Academy of Certified Social Workers
Board Certified Diplomate
NASW Diplomate in Clinical Social Work
Certified Hypnotherapist

ABBREVIATED CLIENT LIST
The Associates
Sprint
U.S. Army
The Cooper Institute
Southwest Airlines
AT&T
Human Resources Southwest Conference
MCI
Southwestern Bell

TYPES OF PRESENTATIONS
Keynotes
Seminars/Workshops

PRESENTATIONS
"Laughter: The Light Solution for Stress" is a highly entertaining, unique approach to the wearisome problem of stress. Enda Junkins crates laughter to reduce stress in the moment and provides specific tools to keep her audiences laughing long into the future.

"Laughter Is the Bridge to Understanding" elaborates on the role of laughter in providing clarity in communication. Enda provides a compelling framework for communication without anxiety. The presentation is funny and educational with specific suggestions on how to "lightly" enhance communication about serious topics.

It's impossible to be angry and laugh at the same time. **"If You Roll with Laughter, You'll Roll with the Punches"** focuses on specific laughter techniques that diffuse conflict and allow people to ease through those awkward, tense moments when they disagree. In this laughter-filled presentation, participants experience the relaxation of laughter for themselves.

"Belly Laughter for Couples: Something Else Positive Below the Belt" is a presentation for couples which is truly unique. Take all the important factors in relationships, examine them with zany, practical, effective techniques and sit back for a relationship ride that will last

PARTICIPANTS:
Are less stressed and more energized.
Become more open to change and learning.
Feel more positive and communicative.
Have new skills to promote laughter daily.

Enda Junkins teaches us to use laughter as a very powerful tool. Her style is fun, witty, and direct. Her message works both personally and professionally. She delivers a terrific life lesson." *Laura Canbakis, Director-Executive Meetings and Events, GTE Corporation.*

Phone: (972) 255-Laff (5233) email: <u>ejunkins@lauaghtertherapy.com</u>   <u>www.laughtertherapy.com</u>

THE BALLANTINE PUBLISHING GROUP
A Division of Random House, Inc., 1540 Broadway, New York, N.Y. 10036

HARVEY MACKAY
BIOGRAPHY

Harvey Mackay has written five books in the past dozen years—all best-sellers. He has appeared on *Larry King Live* and *Oprah,* been featured in the *Wall Street Journal* and *New York Times,* and interviewed by hundreds of leading news media outlets.

He has owned an envelope manufacturing company for nearly 40 years that now has annual sales of $85 million, employs 550 people and creates 20 million envelopes per day.

As one of the most sought-after speakers by Fortune 500 corporations, he has worked with or spoken to hundreds of leading corporations, associations and major universities, including: Amway, Arthur Andersen, AT&T, CitiCorp, Century 21, Dupont-Merck, Ford, IBM, Merrill Lynch, Pepsi-Cola, Prudential, Visa, Waldenbooks, Wal Mart, National Automobile Dealers Association, and the American Bankers Association.

He has received endorsements and the adulation of many high-profile individuals, including: Charles Schwab, Stephen Covey, Al Neuharth, Larry King, Ted Koppel, former President Gerald Ford, Harvey Golub and Tom Peters.

He is a graduate of the University of Minnesota and the Stanford University Graduate School of Business Executive Program. He is an avid runner and marathoner, and a former #1 ranked tennis player in Minnesota.

Mackay is the past president of the Minneapolis Chamber of Commerce. He is an active member in the Envelope Manufacturers Association of America, the University of Minnesota National Alumni Association and the Chief Executives organization.

He currently is a director of Robert Redford's Sundance Institute, the Minnesota Orchestral Association and the University of Minnesota Carlson School of Management. He has been a guest lecturer at various universities and business schools, including Harvard, Stanford, Michigan, Cornell, Wharton and Penn State.

Mackay's civic duties include having played a key role in bringing the 1992 Super Bowl to Minneapolis, along with obtaining an NBA franchise (Minnesota Timberwolves), getting the Hubert H. Humphrey Metrodome built, and bringing in Lou Holtz to coach the University of Minnesota football team.

Mackay, 67, lives with his wife of 39 years in Minneapolis. They have three children .and six grandchildren.

For more information, consult his official Web site at www.mackay.com

The GIRLS' GUIDE *to* POWER *and* SUCCESS

AMACOM, 1601 Broadway, New York, NY 10019 • *For publicity information*, call: (212) 903-8315 *or* e-mail: ktimbrell@amanet.org

Contacts: Carolyn Lipkins, 212-593-6403, lipkinsc@ruderfinn.com
Carrie Kreiswirth, 212-593-5869, kreiswirthc@ ruderfinn.com
Beth Mellow, 212-583-2777, mellowb@ ruderfinn.com

The Facts Behind the Myths About Working Women

A persistent and prevailing attitude exists that women will quit work in a heartbeat to get married and raise a family. Here are the facts:

• Today, a mere 13 percent of America's families fit the 1950s model of husband as bread-winner and wife as homemaker. According to the U.S. Bureau of Labor Statistics, more than 60 percent of all marriages are dual-career marriages, making up 45 percent of the working population and representing the largest single group of families in the workforce.

• Working wives contribute substantially to family incomes. In 1997, the median income for married couples with the wife in the paid labor force was $60,669, compared with $36,027 for those with only the husband as wage earner.

• According to the U.S. Bureau of Labor Statistics, 40 percent of all women in the workforce have children under the age of eighteen. As for women in senior executive positions, a recent nation-wide Catalyst research survey found that 72 percent are married and 64 percent have children.

• A national Catalyst research survey found that more than 80 percent of new mothers return to the labor force within six months after childbirth.

• Today, women are earning the majority of college and master's degrees. Women also comprise approximately 40 percent of the students in professional schools, and that number is growing rapidly.

• Statistics from the National Foundation for Women Business Owners show that women now own an estimated 40 percent of all businesses in the United States. The nation's 9 million women-owned businesses employ nearly 25 million people and contribute more than $3.6 trillion to the U.S. economy.

• Studies consistently show that men and women equally want more flexibility in arranging their own day-to-day schedules and innovative support from their employers to successfully balance their work and their personal lives. When Baxter Medical surveyed its employees, for example, the company learned that 49 percent of men versus 39 percent of women were looking for a new job because of work/life conflicts.

• According to a national Catalyst research survey, 67 percent of married working women say they would continue to work even if there were no financial need to do so.

***

Adapted from **THE GIRLS' GUIDE TO POWER AND SUCCESS** by Susan Wilson Solovic (AMACOM; May 29, 2001; $22.95 Hardcover).

MYSTIKAL

SEAGRAM'S GIN LIVE

JUNE 2001
Kansas City, MO.....6/12
Memphis, TN.......6/14
New Orleans, LA.....6/15
Houston, TX........6/16
Dallas, TX.........6/17
Dallas, TX.........6/18
Austin, TX.........6/19
Lafayette, LA......6/20
Columbus, OH.....6/22
Cleveland, OH.....6/23
Flint, MI..........6/24
Milwaukee, WI.....6/25
Minneapolis, MN....6/26
St. Louis, MO......6/28
Detroit, MI........6/29
Grand Rapids, MI....6/30
JULY 2001
Chicago, IL..........7/1
Augusta, GA.........7/3
Huntsville, AL......7/4
Jackson, MS........7/5
Atlanta, GA........7/6
Birmingham, AL.....7/7
Fayetteville, NC.....7/8
Chattanooga, TN....7/10
Savannah, GA......7/11
Raleigh, NC........7/13
Jacksonville, FL.....7/14
Miami, FL..........7/15
Orlando, FL........7/16
Hampton, VA......7/18
Columbia, SC......7/19
Richmond, VA......7/20
Washington, DC.....7/21
Indianapolis, IN....7/22
New Haven, CT......7/25
Boston, MA.........7/26
Philadelphia, PA...7/27
New York, NY......7/28
Baltimore, MD.......7/29
AUGUST 2001
Los Angeles, CA......8/2
Oakland, CA.........8/3
Las Vegas, NV.......8/4
Sacramento, CA......8/5

SEAGRAM'S GIN LIVE

FACT SHEET

WHAT: **Seagram's Gin Live,** the hottest concert tour of the summer featuring **Mystikal,** the "Crown Prince of the South," premier vocal quartet **Jagged Edge** and new soul sensation **Jaheim.** The 40-city tour will showcase the innovative artistic styles of today's leading hip-hop and R&B artists. The tour will travel to theaters and other mid-size venues across the country, allowing fans to experience the extraordinary talents of these artists live in an intimate setting.

Seagram's Gin will donate a portion of the ticket sales to **One Hundred Black Men, Inc.,** a national, non-profit social service organization dedicated to fostering economic, educational and technological development initiatives in communities across the country.

WHO: Jive recording artist **Mystikal,** So So Def's **Jagged Edge,** and Divine Mill/Warner Bros. Records **Jaheim**— three leading artists whose music captures the enduring tradition of R&B and the excitement of hip-hop. Also featured on the tour are Public Announcement, City High and vocalist Nivea. More exciting acts will be added.

WHEN: The two-month tour kicks off on June 12 in Kansas City and concludes August 5 with a series of performances on the West Coast. A complete tour schedule is enclosed.

CONTACT: Helen Shelton / Philip Ramirez
Ruder Finn, Inc.
212-593-6443 / 212-583-2795

301 EAST 57TH STREET, NEW YORK, NY 10022

Jagged Edge

THE BALLANTINE PUBLISHING GROUP

A Division of Random House, Inc., 1540 Broadway, New York, N.Y. 10036

26 Suggested Discussion Points and Questions
for Harvey Mackay

1. Harvey, you've been inspiring and motivating so many people for four decades. What is missing from the work ethic today that you value greatly?

2. You have worked with and trained numerous leaders and great managers. What would you identify as the greatest characteristics of successful people?

3. You identify 25 "creativity killers"—those things that stop others from taking the initiative—such as "We never did it that way before" to "It's not in the budget" to "Our competition doesn't do that so why should we?" Why does this type of negative thinking pervade most of the corporate culture? What can someone do to overcome those who block innovation?

4. How does a company go about differentiating itself from all others in the face of global assimilation and Internet-induced homogenization or product and price?

5. You emphasize the practice of "fuzzy logic," espousing the avoidance of rules and to never play simply by a set of numbers and determined boundaries. Why do you say the best decisions are those made at the last possible instant?

6. The skills of selling and networking, you suggest, are enhanced by becoming a fundraiser for a charity. What other ways can one benefit by becoming active in the community?

7. What are some of the attributes of a truly great salesperson?

8. How does one become the person you identify as being a "fixer"? You claim every company has such a person, the one who can call in favors, pull some political muscle or just come up with those hard-to-get tickets to a sold-out concert.

9. Can you give us examples of famous people who at first failed miserably before breaking through to experience wild success? Who are your heroes who identify with your definition of the secret of success: "You need to be a hungry fighter and a hungry fighter never quits"?

10. You identify time-wasters such as telephone tag, stating you never leave your name for a return call without a designated time you can be reached. You also point at how too much time is wasted when co-workers swap stories with each other, noting "When was the last time you got an order from another salesperson?" What other time-eaters should be avoided?

11. Your envelope company produces over six billion envelopes annually and with annual sales of $85 million. But there was a time when it almost filed for Chapter 11 because you said you made a decision based solely on emotion and ego and not on sound business reasoning. What advice would you give others to avoid the same mistake?

12. Sometimes smart people do stupid things like giving an answer to a question they have no clue about, just so they can give an answer. What can be done to prevent such things?

13. Why do you say the telephone receptionist is the most important salesperson in your company? What tips can you share regarding telephone skills?

14. What do you mean when you tell people to take their work—but not themselves—seriously?

15. What mistakes do workers make when seeking a raise?

16. Share some of your best negotiating tips with us and explain why we should never cut a deal with someone who has to go back and get the boss' approval?

17. What's the best deal you never made?

18. Do companies need mavericks or more rank-and-file who "follow-the-leaders"?

19. What do you mean when you say: "Dumb companies remain enmeshed in structure, processes and politics. They have meetings to see if they should have meetings"?

20. In your new book you write: "It is not the guy you never met before who offers you the business opportunity of a lifetime that you have to worry about. It's the buy who has the locker next to yours at the country club who makes the same kind of offer." Does this mean we can't trust our friends, acquaintances or business associates?

21. As one of the premiere speakers on the circuit, share with us some of the ways to make a speech go off smoothly?

22. Is it true one should not go into business with a friend?

23. How can one use laughter as a productivity tool?

24. How do you balance work and family without one suffering as a result of the other?

25. You offer tips on business travel and the art of doing lunch. Can you share some now?

26. In PUSHING THE ENVELOPE, you wrote: "Companies that concentrate just on satisfying their customers and whipping competition to a pulp miss the easiest audience of all: their own employees. Focus on them, and the rewards are huge." How does a manager or executive go about doing this?

PLANNED TELEVISION ARTS

15 Suggested Interview Questions
Dr. Kevin Leman
THE BIRTH ORDER CONNECTION

(1) Dr. Leman, you've been reporting on the role birth order plays in our lives for the past two decades. Your best-selling landmark book, BIRTH ORDER, has forever changed us. Tell us what is innately true about birth order and what makes it such a reliable indicator of one's personality and behavior?

(2) Tell us what some of the traits are for each of the birth orders: first-born, middle child, baby and the only.

(3) In your new book, THE BIRTH ORDER CONNECTION, you now relate your research specifically on how birth affects the connections we make with others, particularly potential spouses. Does this mean we should uncover one's birth order before even thinking about dating him or her?

(4) But don't numerous factors play a role in whether the chemistry between two people will last— such as values, finances, looks, religion, age?

(5) Now, you're the youngest in your family. Are we in trouble taking advice from a member of the group you see as the party animals of society?

(6) So, if two people wanted a long-lasting relationship, which birth order pairings make for the best match?

(7) Which birth order member is the most likely to have a critical eye, as in finding fault in others easily?

(8) What significance does having a critical parent have?

(9) Does sibling gender or parental birth orders further influence one's personality and relationships?

(10) One of your chapters highlights questions people should ask each other on a date. You ask people to describe their childhood memories, parents and siblings. What should one be looking for?

(11) THE BIRTH ORDER CONNECTION also offers great advice on things to look for in a potential mate. You ask people to make note of their partner's views on children, money and spirituality, and to observe their levels of passion and intelligence. Are we blinded by an overwhelming physical attraction?

(12) You also warn us of various red flags to watch out for—their relationship to their parents, a violent temper, immaturity, a need to control, selfishness, wandering eyes, etc. Why are some of these obvious problem areas too difficult to manage and so easy to ignore?

(13) You note that people marry for the wrong reasons—to please their parents, fearful no one else will ask, to obtain financial security, because this person is exactly like—or are opposite Mom or Dad. Why do so many of us fall into these traps and how do we avoid them?

(14) What are some tips for each of us to handle our middle-born spouses?

(15) You met your wife while working as a janitor in the men's restroom. You took her to dinner, which consisted of splitting a McDonald's cheeseburger. Is this proof romance can blossom anywhere?

1110 Second Avenue New York, New York 10022
212.593.5820 Fax: 212.715.1664

Publicity Department
Two Penn Plaza
New York, NY 10121-2298
Tel 212 904 5951
Fax 212 904 4091

McGraw-Hill

A Division of The McGraw-Hill Companies

10 QUESTIONS FOR DAVID D'ALESSANDRO
CEO OF JOHN HANCOCK FINANCIAL SERVICES

1. What inspired you to reveal branding strategies in **BRAND WARFARE**? Is there a risk in sharing branding secrets with the competition, especially when you suggest it is a battle out there for market share and name recognition?

2. Your background is in marketing and public relations. How does one make the rare leap to CEO, especially in becoming the youngest one in the 139-year-history of John Hancock?

3. Under your tutelage as CEO of John Hancock Financial Services, the company certainly has lifted its profile. How did you implement branding at Hancock?

4. Some companies build their brand around slogans, images or logos. Others brand themselves around an individual sports icon or an event such as the Super Bowl. Based on your experiences with major athletic events and sports leagues, what method offers the best bang for your buck?

5. Would you rather spend millions in advertising on news media or would it better be spent on sponsoring a big event, such as when John Hancock sponsored the Olympics? How does a company choose what works for it?

6. **BRAND WARFARE** revolves around 10 principles for building a killer brand. Can you elaborate on a few and share one of your unique stories with us?

7. Hancock sponsors the Boston Marathon and we are told you actually got them to change the course so that it ends close to the Hancock Tower—and not at the base of your competitor. Is this what branding is all about – not just paying for advertising, but dictating changes?

8. Your firm began sponsoring the Olympics in 1994. Amidst scandal concerning the IOC over the granting of host city rights, Hancock was the only major corporate sponsor to be critical of the IOC. What lessons did you learn in the process of being linked to such a huge, expensive and potentially disastrous event? What is the 'Hancock clause'?

9. Hancock, as you mention in the book, could have been ruined by a scandal that plagued the insurance industry in the early 1990s. What should a company do to protect its brand?

10. **BRAND WARFARE** hits the advertising industry pretty hard. What should a company look for when working with an agency? You have orchestrated some successful advertising campaigns for Hancock. What makes for successful advertising as it relates to building a brand?

LET ME TELL YOU ABOUT

EVERYTHING®

OVER 150 *EVERYTHING®* TITLES, INCLUDING:

The Everything® After College Book
The Everything® Astrology Book
The Everything® Baby Names Book
The Everything® Bartender's Book
The Everything® Bedtime Story Book
The Everything® Bicycle Book
The Everything® Casino Gambling Book
The Everything® Cat Book
The Everything® Christmas Book
The Everything® College Survival Book
The Everything® Crossword and Puzzle Book
The Everything® Dating Book
The Everything® Dessert Cookbook
The Everything® Dog Book
The Everything® Dreams Book
The Everything® Etiquette Book
The Everything® Family Tree Book
The Everything® Fly-Fishing Book
The Everything® Games Book
The Everything® Get-a-Job Book
The Everything® Get Ready for Baby Book
The Everything® Golf Book
The Everything® Guide to Walt Disney World®, Universal Studios® and Greater Orlando
The Everything® Home Buying Book
The Everything® Home Improvement Book
The Everything® Internet Book
The Everything® Investing Book
The Everything® Jewish Wedding Book
The Everything® Low-Fat, High-Flavor Cookbook
The Everything® Money Book
The Everything® One-Pot Cookbook
The Everything® Pasta Book
The Everything® Pregnancy Book
The Everything® Sailing Book
The Everything® Study Book
The Everything® Tarot Book
The Everything® Toasts Book
The Everything® Trivia Book
The Everything® Wedding Book
The Everything® Wedding Checklist
The Everything® Wedding Etiquette Book
The Everything® Wedding Organizer
The Everything® Wedding Shower Book
The Everything® Wedding Vows Book
The Everything® Wine Book

THE EVERYTHING® PREGNANCY ORGANIZER
Monthly Checklists, Calendars, Schedules, and More
by Marguerite Smolen
Publication Date: July 24, 2000
Price: $15.00 trade paperback; spiral bound with tabs & pockets
Pages: 322
ISBN: 1-58062-336-0

Contact: Carrie Lewis
Publicity Director
(781) 607-5210

THE EVERYTHING® PREGNANCY ORGANIZER
Monthly Checklists, Calendars, Schedules and More
by
Marguerite Smolen

Let's face it—when a woman is pregnant not only are hormones raging, but she is exhausted, uncomfortable and often nauseous. Not the best time to organize one of the most important events in her life—the pregnancy itself! The **EVERYTHING**® series once again comes to women's rescue by providing them with a handy planner, covering all the topics a new mother-to-be needs to know.

THE EVERYTHING® PREGNANCY ORGANIZER (July 24, 2000; $15.00 trade paperback; 322 pages) by **Marguerite Smolen** offers dozens of worksheets, checklists, pockets, and loads of helpful hints to help new mothers organize every aspect of their pregnancy. From keeping track of doctor's appointments and medical results to creating shopping lists and planning a nursery, this organizer is a new mama's best friend.

Arranged chronologically, **THE EVERYTHING® PREGNANCY ORGANIZER** includes complete medical information on every aspect of pregnancy for each month. It covers such important topics as:
Tracking physical and emotional changes
Diet and exercise programs
Birthing options
Choosing the perfect name

- more -

ADAMS MEDIA CORPORATION
57 LITTLEFIELD STREET, AVON, MA 02322 / PHONE: 800-872-5627 / FAX: 800-872-5628

Pregnancy is a time when women should relax, rest up, and take care of themselves and the new life inside them. **THE EVERYTHING® PREGNANCY ORGANIZER** helps them do just that, with no worries and plenty of reassuring advice.

ABOUT THE AUTHOR:

Marguerite Smolen is a former writer for many national magazines. She lives in Bethlehem, PA.

# # #

Related Titles in the EVERYTHING® Series:
($12.95 trade paperback; 8" x 9¼"; two-color with illustrations)

THE EVERYTHING® PREGNANCY BOOK
THE EVERYTHING® BABY NAMES BOOK
THE EVERYTHING® GET READY FOR BABY BOOK
THE EVERYTHING® BABY SHOWER BOOK
THE EVERYTHING® BEDTIME STORY BOOK

Related Titles in the *all new* EVERYTHING® Mini Books Series:
(October 2000; $4.95 trade paperback; 4" x 5"; two-color with illustrations)

THE EVERYTHING® PREGNANCY MINI BOOK
THE EVERYTHING® GET READY FOR BABY MINI BOOK
THE EVERYTHING® BABY NAMES MINI BOOK
THE EVERYTHING® BEDTIME STORY MINI BOOK

Visit Adams Media Corporation on-line at:
www.adamsmedia.com

April, 2001

Dear Interviewer/Reviewer:

Business leaders face the difficult task of reconciling their personal beliefs with the bottom-line demands of their business obligations. Often, it seems like the conflict between short-term business strategies and their desire to "do the right thing" pull them in opposite directions. In order to get through these trying situations, many business execs are turning to spirituality. *Business Week* recently wrote a cover story discussing religion in corporate America claiming that it's presence was "exploding." The article found that "spirituality minded programs in the workplace not only soothe workers' psyches but also deliver improved productivity."

With this trend increasing, Adams Media is proud to publish **GOD IS MY CEO:** *Following God's Principles in a Bottom-Line World* (April 10, 2001; $19.95 Hardcover; 280 pages; ISBN: 1-58062-477-4) **by Larry Julian**. This business book understands business leaders and provides spiritual guidance in a non-threatening way. It provides no one-size-fits-all prescriptions, but instead helps managers and executives to meet their own challenges through questioning, prayer, self-examination, and the application of Biblical principles. This book is not about preaching religion, nor is it a debate about what is right or wrong. Rather, this book is about helping leaders make the right choices in challenging circumstances.

Each chapter includes four elements:
1) Help readers gain insight and perspective on their present situations by helping them understand the underlying roots of their issues.
2) Share God's principles as an alternative way to help them make wise decisions in the midst of challenging circumstances.
3) Help leaders gain ideas and encouragement from real-life stories of leaders who have faced the same challenges.
4) Provide a simple and practical daily plan to move forward with a sense of purpose.

GOD IS MY CEO offers readers a variety of practical tools and applications, which are based on both Biblical principles and sound management practices. Through Julian's work conducting executive retreats and CEO discussion groups, he has built in true stories of contemporary leaders who faced difficult dilemmas and turned to God for guidance including:

◆ Horst Schulze, CEO, The Ritz Carlton Hotel Company
◆ Ken Melrose, Chairman and CEO, The Toro Company
◆ Robert O. Naegele Jr., Former Chairman and Co-owner, Rollerblade
◆ Al Quie, Former Governor, State of Minnesota
◆ C. William Pollard, Chairman and CEO, The ServiceMaster Company

These examples, coupled with questions and exercises, provide a process for integrating these tools into the reader's personal life.

Larry Julian is a successful consultant and speaker who specializes in leadership development. He has trained thousands of business leaders, and his clients have included 3M, AT&T, General Mills, Honeywell, Mayo Clinic, US West, and hundreds of other large and small organizations. He lives in Plymouth, Minnesota.

Enclosed is a copy of the book and more material for your review. If you need further information or would like to speak with Larry Julian, please contact me directly at (781) 607-5210 or Carrielewis1@aol.com.

Best regards,

Carrie Lewis McGraw
Director of Publicity

ADAMS
MEDIA CORPORATION

GOD IS MY CEO
Following God's Principles in a
Bottom-Line World
by Larry Julian
Publication Date: April 10, 2001
Price: $19.95 Hardcover; 280 pages
ISBN: 1-58062-477-4

Contact: Carrie Lewis McGraw
Director of Publicity
(781) 607-5210
Carrielewis1@aol.com

Advance Praise for

GOD IS MY CEO
by Larry Julian

"**GOD IS MY CEO** – a fact that becomes reality as you comprehend the fabulous insights of this timely book! **Larry Julian's** passion is played out through the ingenious sharing of life's journeys of some of our nations top CEO's."

■ Naomi Rhode, Past President, National Speakers Association

"**Larry Julian** has written a gameplan to help all of us score a touchdown in life. The stories in this book serve to motivate, encourage, prepare, and teach us how to make the right choices in our lives. Whether you are a football coach, self-employed, or Chairman of the Board, the principles in **GOD IS MY CEO** can help you define the champion within."

■ Dan Reeves, Executive Vice President of Football Operations and Head Coach, Atlanta Falcons

"**GOD IS MY CEO** is a gem of a book. It sure challenged me in my role as a leader and it will do the same for you. A powerful read."

■ Pat Williams, Senior Vice President, Orlando Magic

"**Larry Julian** provides 20 examples of leaders who excelled in the real world by placing trust in the Lord and allowing Him to lead their lives."

■ Jim Lindemann, CEO, Emerson Electric Company—Emerson Motors Corporation

"**GOD IS MY CEO** should be read by all CEOs or anyone in a leadership position. If your company is driven by mission rather than the bottom-line, this book will strengthen your position. It will encourage all of us to be ethical in all our business dealings and to see the value of biblical based principles."

■ Anne (Auntie Anne) Beiler, Founder and CEO, Auntie Anne's Hand-Rolled Soft Pretzels

"This book should be read by all who are seeking the truth of God's wisdom and how it applies in the workplace. Newcomers to the business world will find nuggets of gold in these pages and the more seasoned traveler will find an oasis where they can be rejuvenated."

■ Stan Geyer, President & CEO, Flouroware

-more-

MEDIA CORPORATION

"Having reviewed **GOD IS MY CEO**, I am impressed with its simple and clear directions. It is a book of purpose. Read it and learn from it. I did."
- ■ Richard M. DeVos, Co-founder, Amway Corporation

"The practical approach of having CEOs give their answers to real life situations is an extremely practical way to give advice. What's most important, however, is the biblical foundation which has been authenticated in the lives of the men and women highlighted in your book."
- ■ Wes Cantrell, Chairman of the Board and CEO, Lanier Worldwide, Inc.

"To have balance in our lives we must deal with the physical, mental and spiritual in our personal, family, career and financial lives. For those in leadership positions who must lead by word and deed, **Larry Julian** tells them how—put God in the center of each phase of your life. **GOD IS MY CEO** is direct, on target, beautiful and convincing. Excellent!"
- ■ Zig Ziglar, Author/Motivational Teacher

"Unlike the countless leadership books on the market, this one will never be out of date because the biblical principles offered in this book are timeless."
- ■ Marc Belton, Senior Vice President, President, Big 6 Cereals, General Mills

57 LITTLEFIELD STREET, AVON, MA 02322 • (508) 427-7100 • FAX: (508) 427-6790 • INTERNET: WWW.ADAMSMEDIA.COM

MEDIA CORPORATION

GOD IS MY CEO
Following God's Principles in a
Bottom-Line World
by Larry Julian
Publication Date: April 10, 2001
Price: $19.95 Hardcover; 280 pages
ISBN: 1-58062-477-4

Contact: Carrie Lewis McGraw
Director of Publicity
(781) 607-5210
Carrielewis1@aol.com

GOD IS MY CEO
Following God's Principles in a Bottom-Line World
by Larry Julian

A time comes when every leader's intellectual and business logic is tested beyond their perceived limit—a time when the latest leadership practices cannot provide the answers to a challenge and dilemma that is deep inside of them. There are times when critical business decisions have no correct answer and can only be made by a leap of faith by the leader alone. **Larry Julian** is here to change that by providing the much-needed aid with his book, **GOD IS MY CEO:** *Following God's Principles in a Bottom-Line World* (April 10, 2001; $19.95 Hardcover; 280 pages; ISBN: 1-58062-477-4).

Unfortunately, most of us live in two separate worlds: a deeply personal, private, and spiritual world and a public, demanding competitive business world. These two worlds clash in their values, beliefs, and principles and we are caught in the middle. The elements of this dilemma look like this:

Unwritten Business Rules	God's Principles
◆ Achieve results	◆ Serve a purpose
◆ What can I get?	◆ How can I give?
◆ Success = dollars	◆ Significance = people
◆ Work to please people	◆ Work to please God
◆ Fear of the unknown	◆ Living with hope
◆ Leadership is being first	◆ Leadership is being last
◆ Take charge; surrender means defeat	◆ Let go; surrender means victory
◆ The end justifies the means. Get to the outcome regardless of how you accomplish it.	◆ The means justify the end. Do the right thing regardless of the outcome.
◆ Short-term gain	◆ Long-term legacy
◆ Slave to the urgent	◆ Freedom of choice
◆ You can never produce enough	◆ Unconditional love

We seem to be presented with a disturbing choice: either embrace bottom-line success and turn from God, or accept and live by God's Principles and suffer whatever negative business consequences come our way. We are challenged by questions like "Can I do what's right and be successful in a competitive, bottom-line world?" and "Can I be both ethical and profitable?"

-over-

God's principles and bottom-line success are not opposites. Yes, you can live God's principles and be successful. Yes, you can be both ethical and profitable. And yes, you can honor God, serve others, and fulfill your professional obligations.

GOD IS MY CEO offers readers a variety of practical tools and applications; all based on Biblical principles and sound management practices. Through Larry Julian's work conducting executive retreats and CEO discussion groups, he has built in true stories of contemporary leaders who faced difficult dilemmas and turned to God for guidance. Some of the featured leaders include:

- ◆ Bill George, CEO, Medtronic
- ◆ C. William Pollard, Chairman and CEO, The ServiceMaster Company
- ◆ Jerry Colangelo, Owner, The Phoenix Suns and The Arizona Diamondbacks
- ◆ Al Quie, Former Governor, State of Minnesota
- ◆ Linda Rios Brook, Former President & General Manager, KLGT-TV
- ◆ Horst Schulze, CEO, The Ritz Carlton Hotel Company
- ◆ Bob Buford, Founder, The Leadership Network
- ◆ S. Truett Cathy, Founder and Chairman, Chick-fil-A
- ◆ And many more

Their personal accounts, coupled with practical tools, applications, and a discussion guide will provide a process for the reader to succeed personally and professionally.

GOD IS MY CEO demonstrates that managers need not choose between managerial success and God's principles. Indeed, the book shows that alignment with God's Word can enhance one's ability as a manger, and be good for one's soul and one's organization.

<u>About the Author:</u>

LARRY JULIAN is a successful consultant and speaker who specializes in leadership development. He has trained thousands of business leaders, and his clients have included 3M, AT&T, General Mills, Honeywell, Mayo Clinic, US West, and hundreds of other large and small organizations. He lives in Plymouth, Minnesota.

GOD IS MY CEO
Following God's Principles in a Bottom-Line World
by Larry Julian
Publication Date: April 10, 2001
Price: $19.95 Hardcover; 280 pages
ISBN: 1-58062-477-4

Visit Adams Media Corporation On-line at:
<u>www.adamsmedia.com</u>
and
<u>www.businesstown.com</u>

57 LITTLEFIELD STREET, AVON, MA 02322 • (508) 427-7100 • FAX: (508) 427-6790 • INTERNET: WWW.ADAMSMEDIA.COM

MEDIA CORPORATION

GOD IS MY CEO
Following God's Principles in a
Bottom-Line World
by Larry Julian
Publication Date: April 10, 2001
Price: $19.95 Hardcover; 280 pages
ISBN: 1-58062-477-4

Contact: **Carrie Lewis McGraw**
Director of Publicity
(781) 607-5210
Carrielewis1@aol.com

A Conversation with Larry Julian

Q: Why did you write GOD IS MY CEO?
As a consultant and speaker, I have observed hundreds of leaders struggle with professional issues such as downsizing and personal issues such as finding a correct work/life balance. Today's business leaders feel vulnerable and alone as they struggle to do the right thing. They are encouraged to seek God on Sunday, but when they need to trust God Monday through Friday, they often succumb to the bottom-line demands of their business.

Most of today's leaders feel caught in the middle with nowhere to turn. Their churches don't understand business and most leadership books don't address the tough moral, ethical, and spiritual dilemmas leaders face. I wanted to write a book that would get leaders talking and connecting on the deeper, more meaningful issues they face rather than the surface day-to-day issues.

Q: What is the book about?
Leaders live in two worlds, a deeply personal, private, and spiritual world and a public, demanding, and competitive world. They don't know how to reconcile the two worlds and, as a result, they struggle and often succumb to their dilemmas. **GOD IS MY CEO** shows leaders that following God's principles can help them solve their most difficult dilemmas and overcome their toughest issues.

Q: How does your book help the reader solve their business problems?
After conducting hundreds of leadership programs and executive retreats, I have identified what I believe are the top 10 issues facing business leaders today. Every chapter will identify a specific issue and provide a biblical solution and, in the process, do three things for the reader:
1. Learn from 20 leaders how they utilized God's principles to overcome their challenges
2. Develop a better understanding of how to apply biblical principles to solve his or her business dilemmas
3. Challenge his or her thinking through a discussion guide to help put his or her thoughts into action

**Q: Your book openly shares biblical principles as the source for leadership success. How do you
        address the diversity of other faiths or even atheists?**
My book is not about preaching religion or telling people what to do. Rather, the book is intended to be a resource to help people struggling with a business dilemma, regardless of their faith. I built the book on the premise that every individual can freely think and, thus, has the freedom to choose. I believe biblical principles are the foundation for wise choices in life and in business. Therefore, through case studies and examples, I offer alternatives and options to help the reader think through their dilemmas to make sound business decisions.

Q: What is the greatest misconception you see regarding dilemmas?
We commonly view our moral and ethical dilemmas as an internal struggle between right and wrong—either we embrace bottom-line success and turn from God or accept and live by God's principles and suffer whatever negative business consequences come our way. We are challenged by questions like "Can I do what is right and be successful in a competitive, bottom-line world?" and "Can I be both ethical and profitable?"

-over-

If you trust in God, live by His principles, and have the patience to wait on His timing, then I believe the answer to these questions is "Yes!" Yes, you can live by God's principles and be successful. Yes, you can be both ethical and profitable. And yes, you can honor God, serve others, and fulfill your professional obligations.

Q: Tell us about you and your passion for this topic.
I've heard that people usually speak on topics they struggle with. That's certainly true for me. I spent 17 years in the hotel business before I became a speaker and consultant. Beginning as a corporate trainee, I worked my way up the ladder from sales manager to Director of Sales and Marketing with Hyatt, Doubletree, and Omni Hotels. I was driven by the bottom-line and was driven to succeed. The bottom-line was my god. Everything else was secondary—my family, my health, and my personal life. My defining moment came in June 1989, when I was fired. Caught in a political crossfire between management and ownership, as the top marketing person I was offered up as a sacrifice. I was devastated. I had spent my career working 80 hour weeks trying to feed the insatiable bottom-line god and wound up with a divorce and flat on my back with severe back pain.

I was born Jewish, but not particularly religious. I had been seeking God at the time but didn't know anything about Him. Nonetheless, I cried out to God to save me from this mess. Through the process, I formed a deep personal relationship with Jesus Christ. My life completely changed as I came to realize that I was not alone.

Since then, I have been blessed in so many ways and feel called to help others who are in the same position. Now as a speaker and consultant, I work in the trenches of the business world in the areas of leadership, strategic planning, and teambuilding. My true role is that of peacemaker. Through leadership coaching, I help people find peace as they discover who they really are and as their ambassador, I help people form better partnerships with their employees, customers, and owners.

Q: How do you share your faith in a business setting?
I'm not hired to share my faith; I'm hired to solve a problem. It's important that I remain impartial, a facilitator focused on the greater good versus one side or another. I do, however, bring my whole self to a consulting project, fully utilizing my God-given talents and skills to be the best consultant, facilitator, and speaker I can be. Oftentimes, I work in highly political and intense circumstances. By bringing my whole self, love, compassion, understanding, wisdom, patience, and courage accompany me.

For example, I was recently hired to coach a leader who was struggling to build credibility within a 600-employee organization. Her job and career were on the line. She was facing resistance from all professional sides—the executive team, her employees, and the other division leaders. She looked towards an uphill climb fraught with pressure but was willing to do whatever it took to improve. Two weeks into the process, the CEO of the organization phoned me. My client's husband had died suddenly of a heart attack while her family was on vacation in Alaska. Professionally, her sensitive situation had just become almost impossible. She knew that she and her organization had to move forward, but in light of the circumstances, how? In coaching her through the situation, I never preached to her, but I prayed for her, was available to her, and helped her with the love and compassion my faith provides.

Q: How is your book different from other leadership books?

Very few leadership books address the deeper moral, ethical, and spiritual dilemmas leaders face. How many books help leaders deal with the emotional pressure of downsizing? How many books share stories of how CEOs have struggled and overcome their personal and professional issues? Most leadership books focus on success and how to achieve it. **GOD IS MY CEO** challenges our thinking and helps people choose the path that is best for them. I don't prescribe quick fix solutions. Instead, I help leaders build a long-term path filled with meaning and purpose.

ADAMS
MEDIA CORPORATION

GOD IS MY CEO
Following God's Principles in a
Bottom-Line World
by Larry Julian
Publication Date: April 10, 2001
Price: $19.95 Hardcover; 280 pages
ISBN: 1-58062-477-4

Contact: Carrie Lewis McGraw
Director of Publicity
(781) 607-5210
Carrielewis1@aol.com

About the Author

LARRY JULIAN, President of the Julian Group, uses his experience consulting with the corporate, government, and community sectors in successful speaking, facilitating, and coaching engagements. Over the past several years, Larry has facilitated hundreds of strategic planning retreats, teambuilding retreats and leadership development programs. In addition, Larry has conducted several leadership surveys and has written numerous articles to help leaders find deeper insight and meaning to their leadership roles.

His clients have included 3M, American Express Financial Advisors, Amoco, AT&T, General Mills, Honeywell, Mayo Clinic, PepsiCo, US West, and hundreds of other large and small companies.

He is a member of National Speakers Association and Minnesota Speakers Association and is a graduate of Michigan State University School of Business. He lives with his wife in suburban Minneapolis, Minnesota.

About Larry's passion to write GOD IS MY CEO:

After years of work within the trenches of corporate America, Larry observed that people in all positions, from CEO to line employee, were searching for meaning and purpose in their work. In particular, leaders were desperately looking for guidance for the tough moral and ethical decisions yet there were no books that addressed these deeper issues.

"I have observed that people want to do the right thing, but are challenged by and succumb to the bottom-line demands of daily business. While we are encouraged to seek God on Sunday, we are not equipped or supported to trust God in order to make the right decisions in the trenches Monday through Friday. I have discovered a huge number of business leaders who are searching for spiritual guidance to help them through the tough dilemmas. My passion is to help the leader seek God for guidance and, as a result, find personal and business success."

57 LITTLEFIELD STREET, AVON, MA 02322 • (508) 427-7100 • FAX: (508) 427-6790 • INTERNET: WWW.ADAMSMEDIA.COM

MEDIA CORPORATION

September, 2001

Dear Interviewer/Reviewer:

America is in a beef crisis—we cannot afford to go through what Europe has been devastated by. With the daily reports of Mad Cow's disease, lysteria, e.coli, and cancer-causing hormone injections in the news every day, millions of Americans have grown concerned about the meat they are eating, and rightly so.

- ◆ Just this past month 530,000 pounds of beef were recalled because of possible contamination.
- ◆ A number of the country's largest meatpacking plants still fail to meet federal inspection guidelines to produce meat free of disease-carrying substance.
- ◆ Thousands of families are being stricken by meat contamination each year.
- ◆ Safety in meat-packing plants and restaurants is lacking but is the public being made aware?
- ◆ The daily scares involving beef are an issue we cannot ignore—our lives depend on it.

How many more people have to die before this issue is controlled? It's time for the consumers to educate and protect themselves. Just in time for our New Year's Resolutions, Adams Media will be proud to arm the public with **BEEF BUSTERS** (January, 2002; $23.95 hardcover; 288 pages; ISBN: 1-58062-638-6) **by Marissa Cloutier, MS, RD with Deborah Romaine, and Eve Adamson**. This important health book will help everyone understand the dangers of beef and what we can all do to ensure our safety. It will be the first all-in-one guide and planner to finally give the public control over this raging epidemic.

Comprehensive throughout, **BEEF BUSTERS** gives readers all they need to steer clear of steer, with the latest medical findings on the various epidemics spreading because of bad beef, plus everything one needs to know to reduce beef intake and lose weight, clobber cholesterol, and satisfy protein cravings. Yet, if people just "can't" give up beef, the authors guide them on how to be "responsible" beef eaters by incorporating it carefully into their diets.

Along with featuring substitutes for popular beef recipes and caloric, fat, and cholesterol tables on beef products, this substantive guide will cover:

* What the latest info is on Mad Cow, etc.	* Other meats, dairy, and fish too…
* What the risks are	* Weight loss and a balanced diet
* What beef to avoid	* Eating vegetables without being a
* Digestion and metabolism	vegetarian
* High beef consumption and your health	* How to bust your family free
* Protein and iron	* Four steps to busting beef cravings
* Fat and cholesterol	* Beef buster menu planner

Let's help America get through the scare of beef due to the encompassing epidemics. **BEEF BUSTERS**—it's time to take control.

Enclosed is an advance galley for your review. Marissa Cloutier has had extensive media experience and is available for interviews. She is ready to advise your audience on how to protect themselves and their families. If you are interested in serial rights, please contact Michael Kelly at 508-427-6716 or mjkellyamc@aol.com.

Best regards,
Carrie Lewis McGraw, Director of Publicity
508-427-6725 or Carrielewis1@aol.com

57 LITTLEFIELD STREET, AVON, MA 02322 • (508) 427-7100 • FAX: (508) 427-6790 • INTERNET: WWW.ADAMSMEDIA.COM

MEDIA CORPORATION

BEEF BUSTERS
by Marissa Cloutier, MS, RD, with Deborah Romaine
and Eve Adamson
Publication Date: January, 2002
Price: $23.95 hardcover; 288 pages
ISBN: 1-58062-638-6

Contact: Carrie Lewis McGraw
Director of Publicity
508-427-6725
Carrielewis1@aol.com

BEEF BUSTERS FACTS

- In the first six months of 2001, the USDA issued more than three dozen recalls for meat products that tested positive for bacterial contamination. Recalled products included **1.1 million pounds** of ground beef contaminated with E. coli and **14.5 million pounds** of lunchmeat, sausage, and hotdogs that tested positive for listeria. Access recall information on the USDA Web site at www.fsis.usda.gov/OA/news/xrecalls.htm.

- The U.S. Centers for Disease Prevention and Control (CDC) reports that foodborne illnesses strike **76 million Americans each year**, hospitalizing 325,000 and killing 5,200 of them.

- Each year **73,000 Americans** become ill with *E. coli* O157:H7 infections; 600 of them die. Yet the USDA has a "zero tolerance" policy in place for fecal contamination of meat products, the primary source of the bacteria that causes these infections.

- Nutritionists consider a serving of beef to be about 3 ounces (cooked). Most restaurants serve burgers that are anywhere from 4 ounces to 16 ounces or more, and steaks that are 8 ounces to 32 ounces. Steak houses even feature "special" cuts that weigh in at as much as 48 ounces – that's four *pounds* of beef!

- A meat-based diet is known to be a contributing factor in developing colorectal cancer, prostate cancer, and possibly endometrial cancer and breast cancer.

- Two Americans die every minute from heart disease, the leading cause of death in the United States, and one in five – **60 million** – has some form of heart disease. Health experts believe up to 80 percent of all heart disease could be prevented through lifestyle changes to improve diet, increase exercise, and stop smoking.

- The first case of "mad cow" disease was identified in Britain in the mid-1980s. By the time veterinarians realized ten years later that not only was this deadly disease contagious but also that a form of it could infect humans, more than 200,000 cows had already died from it. By 2001, over 100 people had been diagnosed with vCJD, the human form.

- Even though BSE has not been detected in American cattle, a 2001 Gallup poll found that the potential of eating "mad cow" contaminated beef has caused **20 percent** of Americans to cut back on beef in, or eliminate beef from, their diets.

- Meat and bone meal feed containing the ground remains of slaughtered cattle was banned in the United States because of the risk of BSE-contamination, for use in feeding to cattle, in 1994. Yet in 2001, 22 tons of such feed, which still is permitted for feeding to pigs and poultry, were mistakenly shipped as cattle feed. The feed was recalled but not before 1,200 cattle ate it, forcing the government to quarantine them.

-more-

MEDIA CORPORATION

- In 2001, a physician reading the label of a nutritional supplement being sold at a retail store discovered the product contained animal brains, testicles, and other organs banned from import into the United States because of the risk they could carry BSE. Even though such ingredients are illegal, there are no procedures in place to prevent products containing them from making it to store shelves.

- In a further effort to prevent the spread of "mad cow" disease's human form, vCJD, into the United States, in 2001 the FDA banned blood donations from people who lived in Europe for six months or longer between 1980 and 1996.

- In ten years of random testing of cow brains for BSE, U.S. officials have examined the brains of 12,000 cows and found no evidence of BSE. By contrast, Western Europe health officials test 200,000 brains *a year* and identified about 1,000 new cases in 2001 – five years after declaring the epidemic under control.

- The United States lacks any uniform or consistent policies and procedures for testing for BSE in cattle. Although Europe has completely banned feeds containing the animal remains, which many health experts believe were pivotal in allowing BSE to overcome the British cattle industry, the United States still allows their manufacture and use for feeding to "nonruminants" such as hogs and poultry.

- The official report investigating the "mad cow" epidemic in Britain, released in October 2000, severely criticized British officials for downplaying the risk the disease posed to humans and for failing to implement a coordinated effort to stop the disease's spread among cattle. The report castigated the government for insisting that the nation's beef supply was safe for human consumption, when in fact 90 people had already contracted BSE's human form, vCJD, by the time officials acknowledged a risk for human infection in 1996.

- Despite federal legislation mandating "humane slaughter" procedures, secretly recorded videotapes have shown cattle being stripped of skin and meat while still conscious and alive. A series of articles in *The Washington Post* (April 9-11, 2001) quoted one worker as saying, "They die piece by piece."

- British feed manufacturers exported over 200,000 tons of potentially contaminated meat and bone meal feed to over 100 countries around the world before health experts fully understood the spread and risks of BSE.

- U.S. officials acknowledged in early 2001 that fewer than a third of the 9,500 American feed manufacturing plants inspected during 2000 were in compliance with federal regulations designed to prevent the spread of BSE in the United States.

57 LITTLEFIELD STREET, AVON, MA 02322 • (508) 427-7100 • FAX: (508) 427-6790 • INTERNET: WWW.ADAMSMEDIA.COM

MEDIA CORPORATION

BEEF BUSTERS
by Marissa Cloutier, MS, RD, with Deborah Romaine
and Eve Adamson
Publication Date: January, 2002
Price: $23.95 hardcover; 288 pages
ISBN: 1-58062-638-6

Contact: Carrie Lewis McGraw
Director of Publicity
508-427-6725
Carrielewis1@aol.com

About the Authors

Marissa Cloutier, M.S., R.D., is a registered dietician with a Master of Science in human nutrition and metabolism from Boston University. She is a food and nutrition instructor at Briarwood College in Southington, CT. She is the author, with Eve Adamson, of *The Mediterranean Diet,* and has written articles for the *Tufts University Health & Nutrition Newsletter* and for a Boston University "healthy aging" Web site. She trained at The Beth Israel Hospital in Boston, a primary teaching hospital of the Harvard University School of Medicine, and was a clinical dietitian at the Faulkner Hospital in Boston, a teaching hospital of the Tufts University School of Medicine. She is a member of the American Dietetic Association, the Connecticut Dietetic Association, and the American Medical Writers Association. Marissa and her family enjoy the many wonderful flavors and health benefits of a beef-free, primarily vegetarian, Beef Buster diet. Marissa currently lives in Connecticut.

Deborah S. Romaine has authored, co-authored, or contributed to fourteen books, including *Syndrome X: Managing Insulin Resistance,* with Jennifer B. Marks, M.D., and *The Complete Idiot's Guide to Healing Back Pain,* with Dawn E. DeWitt, M.D. She has published more than 350 articles. She specializes in writing about health and lifestyle topics, and collaborated with Marissa on the health and nutrition chapters of *Beef Busters.* Deborah has a Master of Arts degree in English and creative writing from the University of Washington. Although Deborah already eats a diet low in fat and cholesterol, after researching this book she doubts she'll ever be tempted to bring beef back as a mainstay on the family table. She lives in Washington State's Puget Sound area.

Eve Adamson has authored or co-authored 14 books, including *The Mediterranean Diet,* with Marissa Cloutier, M.S., R.D., and *The Complete Idiot's Guide to Zen Living,* with Gary McClain, Ph.D. She has a Master of Fine Arts degree in creative writing from the University of Florida. Eve collaborated with Marissa on the recipes and menu planner for *Beef Busters.* Although never crazy about beef to begin with, working on this book has helped Eve and her family to swear off beef completely. "Even if I can be almost positive a given piece of meat is safe to eat, there are so many other implications for me: What if this is the first bad batch and they discover it because my family gets sick? Is the momentary pleasure of a burger worth the health risk, from food-borne contamination, from saturated fat, or from the unknown danger of mad cow disease? Do I want to contribute to the consumption of animals, when I'm not comfortable with the way most of those animals are kept and killed? Do I want to feel healthier, have more energy, and feel more in harmony with the world around me? These days, I'm much more likely to make my decision based on questions like these. I find the diversity in flavor, texture, color, and nutritional value of plant foods much more interesting and conducive to creativity in the kitchen." Eve lives in Iowa City with her two sons.

-more-

57 LITTLEFIELD STREET, AVON, MA 02322 • (508) 427-7100 • FAX: (508) 427-6790 • INTERNET: WWW.ADAMSMEDIA.COM

About the Contributors

Foreword writer **Nancy A. Tarantino** received a Bachelor of Science degree in biology from West Virginia Wesleyan College and a Master of Science degree in health administration from New Jersey City University. She is licensed by the New Jersey Department of Health and Senior Services as a Registered Environmental Health Specialist and Health Officer, and has worked a health inspector for the Hoboken, New Jersey Health Department since 1989.

Technical editor **Glenn Rothfeld, M.D., M.Ac.,** served as a clinical fellow at Harvard University School of Medicine after his training in family medicine. He is trained in nutritional and herbal medicine and has a Master's degree in acupuncture. Medical director for WholeHealth New England, Dr. Rothfeld is also clinical assistant professor of community health and family health at Tufts University School of Medicine. Dr. Rothfeld is the author several books, most recently *The Acupuncture Response.*

In addition to her online business at *www.onlinedietician.net,* **Linda Horning, R.D.,** enjoys a career in community nutrition, both as a WIC nutritionist for the USDA Supplemental Nutrition Program for Women, Infants, and Children, and as a Head Start nutrition coordinator. More recently, her work providing nutritional analyses of menus, including those presenting in *Beef Busters,* has enabled Linda to see how easy it is to plan healthy meals when the focus is on fruits and vegetables. Plant-based diets contain all of the cancer and heart disease fighting properties, while leaving out those that lead to weight gain and poor nutrition. In an age when over nutrition is more of a concern than under nutrition, Linda will always support efforts that help us to curb our appetite for beef.

57 LITTLEFIELD STREET, AVON, MA 02322 • (508) 427-7100 • FAX: (508) 427-6790 • INTERNET: WWW.ADAMSMEDIA.COM

October, 2001

No, It's Not Just Another *Chicken Soup* Book

Dear Editor/Writer:

So Adams Media is publishing a new series of "feel good," inspirational stories. I know what you're thinking—do we really need another addition to the *Chicken Soup for the Soul* genre? **A CUP OF COMFORT: *Stories that warm your heart, lift your spirit, and enrich your life*** (October 2, 2001; ISBN: 1-58062-524-X) is *not* just another addition to the genre—it is the book that will transform the genre and set new standards for inspirational writing. The stories in the **CUP OF COMFORT** series are "longer, more enriching, and truly uplift the spirit in a way that no other competitive title does," says Scott Watrous, Chief Operating Officer for Adams Media.

Searching for the best inspirational writing available, editor Colleen Sell posted submission calls in a variety of print and online media. Each writer would receive $100 if his or her story was selected, with the writer of the best story receiving $1000 and leading placement in the book. The result was an onslaught—thousands of submissions. After an extensive (and exhausting!) process, 50 stories made Colleen's final cut. The contributors are an eclectic mix of first-time writers, journalists, published novelists and poets, oral storytellers, even a circus trapeze artist.

When we say these stories far surpass the competition, it's not an exaggeration. Consider this synopsis of "The Lady in the Blue Dress" by Edie Scher, winner of the submission contest:

> Edie tells the true story of a close family friend, Bridget, who discovered a lump in her breast. After a mammogram confirms the worst, her doctor schedules a biopsy. The night before her surgery, Bridget experiences a vision of her deceased mother who appears in the hospital to comfort her. (Bridget's mother died of breast cancer years before.) The next morning Bridget's doctor prepares to operate, only to discover that her lump has completely vanished.

Now this is a moving story, and if you were reading *Chicken Soup*, it would probably stop here. But the **CUP OF COMFORT** stories are more remarkable than that. Edie's story contains an unbelievable, final twist that will delight and amaze its readers. I won't ruin the surprise here.

Booksellers are already anticipating an enthusiastic reception from their customers when this book hits the shelves in October. The initial sales orders, from both independent bookstores and chains alike, are flooding in. "I have never seen such an immediate, positive response to a new series before," says Amy Collins, Adams Media Director of Trade Sales. **A CUP OF COMFORT** is poised to redefine the marketplace.

For more information or to schedule an interview with one of the available contributors (see attached list), please contact me directly at **508/427-6757**.

Best Regards,

Sophie Cathro
Associate Publicist

ADAMS
MEDIA CORPORATION

A CUP OF COMFORT: *Stories that warm your heart,*
lift your spirit, and enrich your life
Edited by Colleen Sell
Publication Date: October 2, 2001
Price: $9.95 trade paperback; 324 pages
ISBN: 1-58062-524-X

Contact: Sophie Cathro
Associate Publicist
508/427-6757

From the publisher of the nationally bestselling *Small Miracles* and *Heartwarmers* series . . .

A Cup of Comfort
Stories that warm your heart,
lift your spirit, and enrich your life

Edited by
Colleen Sell

Adams Media Corporation introduces a unique and exciting new collection of "feel good" stories that will transform the lives of its readers. **A CUP OF COMFORT:** *Stories that warm your heart, lift your spirit, and enrich your life* (October 2, 2001; $9.95 trade paperback; 324 pages; ISBN: 1-58062-524-X) edited by **Colleen Sell** is the flagship book in an original series that sets a new standard in inspirational writing.

After an extensive search, **Colleen Sell** scrupulously selected each of the 50 stories in **A CUP OF COMFORT** from thousands of submissions. She sought out stories that were richer, deeper, longer, and more uplifting than others in the genre. The result is a charming collection sure to tug readers' hearts and leave them with a warm, cozy feeling—just like a warm cup of comfort on a chilly winter day! Make some hot chocolate, grab a blanket, curl up with **A CUP OF COMFORT**, and cherish dozens of amazing true stories, including:

❦ A young couple is outbid on their dream house—by a lot. But the owners realize the appreciation and love the couple has for the house, and they accept the lower offer.

❦ A teenager learns the value of hard work when he spends the summer working for his grandfather.

❦ Family members rejoice when their sick infant is able to come home from the hospital on Christmas Day.

❦ An aunt helps her four-year-old nephew overcome his fear of lightning, creating a life-long bond between the two of them.

❦ An ER nurse aids an elderly couple and discovers that the woman is her long-lost mother.

(more)

The stories in **A CUP OF COMFORT** are remarkable for their warmth, compassion, and inspirational resolutions. The writers touch on such themes as:

- ❧ Family
- ❧ The bond of friendship
- ❧ The witnessing of miracles
- ❧ Profound life-changing moments

- ❧ Overcoming incredible odds
- ❧ The forces of nature
- ❧ Extraordinary acts of humanity

Take comfort in the goodness of life with **A CUP OF COMFORT**.

Excerpt from "Listen to Your Heart" by Susan Marie Lamagna in **A CUP OF COMFORT**:

My students filed in, put away their backpacks and coats, and dropped their homework into the homework box. The day went well. After story time, we did the calendar, and I told them, "Today we are celebrating the birthdays of Juan and Cynthia."

I brought out the pieces of cake I'd bought earlier that day and lit the candles, and then we sang "Happy Birthday" to the birthday kids. Cynthia and Juan beamed with happiness; their faces glowed brighter than the candles. The birthday boy and girl enthusiastically blew out the candles, and the children sat patiently while I quickly sliced each of the four pieces into five little slivers. While usually parents provide cupcakes for their children's birthdays, some unseen force within me that morning had directed me to a bakery that normally sold only pre-ordered cakes, where I spent my last few dollars on four slices of cake to split among 20 five-year-olds.

After the children finished eating their snack, I stood by the trash bin to make sure all the plates, spoons, and napkins went into the container. Juan was still smiling when he tossed his plate and said, "Teacher, I never had a birthday party before!"

About the Editor:
Colleen Sell has long believed in the power of story to heal, guide, enrapture, and transcend the human spirit. She is a professional author, book editor, magazine editor, copywriter, publicist, essayist, and screenwriter. She lives in Eugene, Oregon.

# # #

A CUP OF COMFORT:
Stories that warm your heart,
lift your spirit, and enrich your life
Edited by Colleen Sell
Publication Date: October 2, 2001
Price: $9.95 trade paperback; 324 pages
ISBN: 1-58062-524-X

Visit Cup of Comfort online at
www.cupofcomfort.com

Visit Adams Media online at
www.adamsmedia.com

MEDIA CORPORATION

Are you interested in **A Cup of Comfort**, but not sure how to use it in a segment? Consider one of the following life-affirming **themes**. Colleen Sell and contributors are available across the contry to discuss their stories and the importance of this new book series.

Readers can use A Cup of Comfort when they need to restore their faith in . . .

The Innocence of Children

Read stories:

Make a Wish, Mommy (p. 11) *The Crying Chair* (p. 16) *A Daughter's Trust* (p. 85) *The Walk of Courage* (p. 145) *Monsters of the Sky* (p. 151) *The Greatest Christmas Gift* (p. 196)

The Value of Life's Lessons

Read stories:

Of Needs and Wants (p. 56) *Maddie's Rose* (p. 102) *The Colors of Prejudice* (p. 174) *The Sweet Pea* (p. 207) *Ah, the Dandy Lions* (p. 306)

The Occurrence of Miracles and the Intervention of Angels

Read stories:

The Lady in the Blue Dress (p. 1) *In the Arms of Grace* (p. 96) *A Softer Heart* (p. 124) *A Voice in the Storm* (p. 163) *An Angel's Voice* (p. 191) *Miracle Fish* (p. 226) *Guiding Lights* (p. 246)

The Kindness of Strangers

Read stories:

Finding Our Home (p. 29) *A Heaping Helping of Thanksgiving* (p. 89) *Gratitude Harvest* (p. 118) *A Special Day* (p. 260) *The Kindness of Strangers* (p. 280)

The Transition to a Comforting Afterlife

Read stories:

An Angel's Kiss (p. 23) *Quiet Courage* (p. 35) *A Gift from Christmas Angels* (p. 132) *The White Dress* (p. 182) *I Heard the Bells of Heaven* (p. 291)

The Existence of Everyday Heroes

Read stories:

Listen to Your Heart (p. 79) *Not Alone* (p. 114) *My Dad, the Pink Lady* (p. 236) *Bowling Alley Hero* (p. 241) *The Saint of Subsidized Housing* (p. 273)

Contact: **Sophie Cathro**
Associate Publicist
508/427-6757

Tour Dates for
THE BOOK OF RUDY
by Rudy Boesch

October 4 & 5	New York, NY
October 15	San Diego, CA
October 16 & 17	Los Angeles, CA
October 23	Boston, MA
October 24	Philadelphia, PA
October 25	Baltimore, MD
October 26	Washington, DC
October 30	Richmond, VA
November 1	Norfolk, VA
November 2	Virginia Beach, VA
November 5	Atlanta, GA
November 7	Tampla, FL

To schedule an interview with Rudy, please contact:
Carrie Lewis McGraw
Director of Publicity
Tel: 508-427-6725
CarrieLewis@aol.com

MEDIA CORPORATION

THE BOOK OF RUDY:
The Wit and Wisdom of Rudy Boesch
By Rudy Boesch with Jeff Herman
Publication Date: October 4, 2001
Price: $5.95 trade paperback; 160 pages
ISBN: 1-58062-613-0

Contact: Carrie Lewis McGraw
Director of Publicity
(508) 427-6725
Carrielewis1@aol.com

THE BOOK OF RUDY
The Wit and Wisdom of Rudy Boesch

by Rudy Boesch
with Jeff Herman

> "Rudy Boesch is a true patriot . . . "
> -- Governor Jesse Ventura, Minnesota

RUDY. You've seen him on TV. You've heard his catch phrases repeated at home, in the office, and even from total strangers sitting next to you on public transportation. Known for such comments as "I gave my word, and my word is good," Rudy was also rated by *People* magazine in 2000 as one of the "sexiest men in America." But what are his real thoughts on the issues we face today? And, most important, what does a snake really taste like?

Unrehearsed, uncensored, and unabashed, Rudy speaks out on sudden fame, politics, the military, family life, and so much more in his book, **THE BOOK OF RUDY: *The Wit and Wisdom of Rudy Boesch*** (October 4, 2001; $5.95 Trade Paperback; 160 pages; ISBN: 1-58062-613-0) **by Rudy Boesch**. You may find you'll agree with him on topics you'd be surprised about, possibly disagree with him on others, and obtain a few good chuckles along the way.

Whether you agree with him or not, Rudy couldn't care less. "These are all my opinions. You can take them or leave them." As a Navy SEAL Master Chief, television personality, and all-around curmudgeon, Rudy is his own hero. "I'm proud of everything I did and everything I'm still going to do. I'm not done yet."

Kids love him. 20-, 30-, 40- somethings love him. Grandparents admire and respect him. Rudy Boesch is our favorite warm, slightly cantankerous uncle—tough, experienced, loyal, blunt, and funny. Rudy is Clint Eastwood, Jimmy Stewart, and W.C. Fields all rolled into one. And now, for the first time, Rudy's words and reflections are captured in one thought-provoking, often hilarious compendium.

-more-

MEDIA CORPORATION

Through a question-and-answer format, Rudy speaks his mind on…

- Survival
- Abortion
- Religion
- Relationships
- Television

- The media
- Family
- WW II, Vietnam, Persian Gulf
- Rudymania and being a celebrity
- And much, much more

THE BOOK OF RUDY is Mr. Boesch at his philosophical best: wise, honest, and always controversial. This revealing book uncovers the heart, mind, and soul of a true American hero who represents everything this great country stands for.

ABOUT THE AUTHORS:

RUDY BOESCH is a popular television personality and 73-year-old retired Navy SEAL Master Chief. He performed 45 combat missions in Vietnam during his years of service and was awarded the Bronze Star with Combat V. His highest award is the Defense Superior Service Medal. Rudy is a resident of Virginia Beach, Virginia, where he lives with Marge, his wife of 46 years.

JEFF HERMAN is the owner of The Jeff Herman Literary Agency, LLC, based in New York City and Columbus, Ohio.

THE BOOK OF RUDY
The Wit and Wisdom of Rudy Boesch
By Rudy Boesch with Jeff Herman
Publication Date: October 4, 2001
Price: $5.95 trade paperback; 160 pages
ISBN: 1-68062-613-0

Visit Adams Media Corporation online at:

www.adamsmedia.com

www.everything.com

www.businesstown.com

www.careercity.com

ADAMS
MEDIA CORPORATION

Publishers Weely
BookExpo America Show Daily
Firday, June 1, 2001

The Tribe
Has Spoken

Think you have what it takes to be a survivor? Ever wanted to be part of the new reality TV? Want to learn more about the necessary qualifications?

If so, stop by the Adams Media booth (1135) tomorrow between 4:30 and 6 .p.m. and join the party to honor Rudy.

Yep, you guessed it—that's Rudy as in Rudy "I gave my word, and my word is good" Boesch, the 73-year-old retired Navy SEAL Master Chief, ex-*Survivor* contestant and one of *People* magazine's "sexiest men in America" for 2000.

On hand to promote his upcoming title, *The Book of Rudy: The Wit and Wisdom of Rudy Boesch*, Boesch—whom *People* dubbed an "affable curmudgeon" and who is already

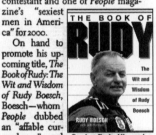

Survivor Rudy: His word is good.

booked on the *Today* show for the early October pub date—will sign postcards and pose for photos with his fans on Saturday from 2–3 p.m. at Table 22.

Gary Krebs, director of series- and single-title publishing for Adams Media, considers the acquisition quite a coup. "My hands were shaking with excitement as I read over his proposal," he admits. Calling Rudy "a national treasure," Krebs continues, "I admire Rudy and I know how many millions of people across the country admire him."

Short and to the point at 120 pages, the book showcases Rudy's trademark blunt philosophy on everything from food, sex and the military to "life, death, and a host of other issues," he says.

—HEATHER FREDERICK

57 LITTLEFIELD STREET, AVON, MA 02322 • (508) 427-7100 • FAX: (508) 427-6790 • INTERNET: WWW.ADAMSMEDIA.COM

MEDIA CORPORATION

www.usatoday.com

USA TODAY

Life

SECTION D

Tuesday, April 10, 2001

Lifeline

Rudyisms fill ex-Survivor's new book

Survivor's outspoken grumpy old man, Rudy Boesch, 73, is putting his deep thoughts down on paper. *The Book of Rudy: The Wit and Wisdom of Rudy Boesch* will be published this fall by Adams Media Corp. The outspoken ex-Navy SEAL will write about sex, religion, the military and the media. AMC says the book "will uncover the heart, mind and soul of a true American hero."

[INSIDE]

Survivor II may be quickly wiping the memory of the original *Survivor's* quasi-celebrities from pop-culture consciousness, but **Rudy Boesch** isn't going down just yet. **Adams Media** editor **Gary Krebs** will publish *The Book of Rudy*, in which Boesch will speak his mind on subjects such as sex, religion, television, politics and the media. (Perhaps there will even be a catalog of Rudyisms.) Incidentally, the former Navy Seal Boesch has his own GI Joe-like action figure, with bids for a signed limited edition doll reaching almost $60 on eBay).

Chicago Tribune
June 6, 2001
THE BOOK OF RUDY
by Rudy Boesch

Tying up loose leaves of BookExpo

Some final observations after a week in which Chicago was the temporary residence of some 20,000 publishers, writers, agents, publicists, book sellers and assorted other publishing professionals at BookExpo at McCormick Place:

Survivor of the week: Rudy Boesch wears fame well. And, for an hour Saturday, tanned and clearly enjoying himself, he pressed the flesh with his fans. One after the other, they came up to his table to stand, often with an arm over his shoulder, to have their photograph taken with perhaps the most recognizable star of the first "Survivor" show — and get from Boesch an autographed postcard promoting his upcoming book from Adams Media.

In October, Adams will publish "The Book of Rudy: The Wit and Wisdom of Rudy Boesch," co-written with Jeff Herman. Actually, it's a series of questions from Herman and answers from Boesch on subjects such as family, religion and sex.

So, he was asked, what's it like being an author? "Is that what I am? I voiced my opinion on certain things they asked me," he said.

And why was the first "Survivor" show so popular? "The mix of people," he said. "They had 15 messed-up people and one normal person, and that was me."

Survivor II may be quickly wiping the memory of the original Survivor's quasi-celebrities from pop-culture consciousness, but Rudy Boesch isn't going down just yet.

57 LITTLEFIELD STREET, AVON, MA 02322 • (508) 427-7100 • FAX: (508) 427-6790 • INTERNET: WWW.ADAMSMEDIA.COM

MEDIA CORPORATION

October 26, 2001

To: Events Office
        Book Passage
Tel: 415-927-0960
Fax: 415-924-3838

From: Carrie Lewis McGraw
Tel: 508-427-6725
Fax: 508-427-6790

Pages: 3

Dear ,

Patricia Evans last was on the book tour circuit with her bestselling title *The Verbally Abusive Relationship*. In January, she'll be coming out with her next book, **CONTROLLING PEOPLE**.

We've already received the first endorsement:

"**CONTROLLING PEOPLE** offers a fresh perspective on the dynamics of verbal abuse, and give explanations for some of the most perplexing aspects of this destructive behavior. This book may prove particularly valuable to those who have escaped the abusive relationship, but who still hear the echoes of their abuser's words, and wonder 'why me?'"

■ Irene Weiser, Founder, www.stopfamilyviolence.org

To follow is press material on this groundbreaking new book.

Patricia will be available for speaking engagements in January, February and on. I'm wondering if you'd be interested in scheduling an event with her.

Please let me know if you have any questions or need further information.

Best regards,

Carrie Lewis McGraw
Director of Publicity
Carrielewis1@aol.com

MEDIA CORPORATION

Date

Dear ,

For some people, the holiday season doesn't mean *Joy to the World* or even a *Silent Night*. It is just another season to watch others revel in true happiness, while they put on a happy face in an irrational, tense-filed place they ironically call home.

Many people become depressed at the holidays. For those who are under the influence of a controlling relationship the pressure of the holidays can become even more immense—they are not allowed to be depressed. The method of control in an "abusive" relationship can be so severe that the controller also dictates the person's happiness by telling they the must be happy even if they're not during this joyous season. Controllers can come in many forms through couples' relationships, co-workers, parents, friends, and even acquaintances. They can have such a tight grip on people that they often become unaware of their behaviors.

Bestselling author Patricia Evans can help ease the pain and confusion in her latest book, **CON-TROLLING PEOPLE:** *How to Recognize, Understand, and Deal with People Who Try to Control You* (January, 2002; $12.95 trade paperback; 320 pages; ISBN: 1-58062-569-X). This book will help the victim unravel the senseless behavior that plagues both the controller and the victim.

As the author of two thought-provoking books about verbal abuse, *The Verbally Abusive Relationship* (hailed by *Newsweek* as "groundbeaking") and *Verbal Abuse Survivors Speak Out*, Evans has brought the importance of properly responding to verbal abuse into the mainstream. Now she's bringing the magnitude of controlling people to the forefront.

She'll answer the most frequently asked questions about controlling people, how to recognize them, and how to protect yourself from their senseless behaviors. Patricia Evans has single-handedly brought the importance of properly responding to controlling people into the mainstream. She has helped men, women, and children rebuild lost self-esteem, change life patterns and escape situations of escalating danger. By making us more aware, she has saved lives.

In addition to her interviews with *Newsweek* and numerous other publicaitons, Patricia has appeared on hundreds of television and radio programs including *Oprah*, *Sally Jessy Raphael*, *Larry King Live*, and on national CNN radio with Jim Bohannon. Her books have been translated into Spanish and German.

Enclosed is a copy of the book and further information for your review. Please call me directly if you need further information or would like to interview Patricia.

Together let's try to bring the missing joy back into others' lives.

Best regards,

Carrie Lewis McGraw
Director of Publicity
508-427-6725 or Carrielewis1@aol.com

MEDIA CORPORATION

September 28, 2001

Dear James,

Here's a **Hot Deal** for you:

Adams Media Corporation is proud to announce that we will publish the first book on Laura Bush in March, 2002 titled **LAURA:** *An Intimate Look at America's First Lady* **by Antonia Felix** ($19.95; Hardcover; 256 pages and 8-page photo insert; ISBN: 1-58062-659-9).

The book will have an **exclusive interview with Jenna Welch, Laura's mother**. It will cover her life from infancy to the present, and will include recent events that promise to reshape her role as First Wife and First Lady.

Executive Editor Claire Gerus acquired the book with world rights through agent Tony Seidl of T.D. Media.

Author Antonia Felix has written three previous biographies: *Christine Todd Whitman; Andrea Boccelli*; and *Silent Soul: The Miracles and Mysteries of Audrey Santo*. Whitman commended Felix for her research into her life calling it "the most thorough I've ever seen."

Adams Media will roll out an extensive campaign of promotional fanfare in March, 2002.

If you need further information or would like to speak with Claire Gerus, please give me a call at (508) 427-6725.

Best regards,

Carrie L. McGraw
Director of Publicity
Carrielewis1@aol.com

MEDIA CORPORATION

To: Sandy Sandburg
         KEYL
Fax: 320-732-2284
Date: January 12, 2001

Dear Sandy:

There's no question that sleep is imperative to our physical and mental health. It's also important for our education. "People who interrupt sleep, even with a single all-nighter, may find that the memory hasn't been stored in the cortex, one part of the brain involved in learning new material," says a recent *USA Today* article (Nov. 27th). But wouldn't it be nice to go to bed with an issue and wake up the next day with a solution? Well now you can—in fact you've always been able to—it's just a matter of learning how.

Dr. Eric Maisel, who has been on your station before, has devised a revolutionary pro-gram that makes use of your brain's power to think while you sleep—to help you solve your problems, make decisions, and improve your relationships. His book **SLEEP THINKING** (January 2, 2001; $10.95 trade paperback; 240 pages) is sure to help anyone and everyone who has a problem or issue on his or her mind including people interested in stress reduc-tion and dreams; insomniacs, of which there are over 80 million in the U.S. alone; those with relationship or parenting obstacles; therapists looking for a useful self-help program to teach their clients; creative and performing artists who can use sleep thinking to increase their cre-ativity; job hunters; substance abuse counselors; and the list goes on.

In his book, Dr. Maisel provides case-studies on how sleep thinking has helped others, and provides guidelines on how the reader can follow the program by keeping his or her own dream journal. His initial journal includes suggestions like:

1)   Only record those dreams that feel meaningful.
2)   With those dreams that feel meaningful enough to record fully, rather than ana-lyzing them in a "micro" way, trying to figure out the meaning of a skyscraper or a freight train, try instead to discern what question or life issue the dream is attempting to answer.
3)   Start to make a list of "life thread" questions or issues that emerge from your analysis of your meaningful dreams.

Sleep thinking is the best, and cheapest, self-help tool available. With this book, you can supply your audience with a huge favor—a way to help them help themselves. For further information or to schedule an interview with Dr. Maisel, please contact me directly at (781) 607-5210 or Carrielewis1@aol.com. Now get a good night's sleep tonight!

Best regards,
Carrie Lewis McGraw
Director of Publicity

MEDIA CORPORATION

August, 2001

Dear Interviewer/Reviewer:

Almost everyone knows someone—or at least has heard of someone—who is a controlling person, or is involved in a controlling relationship. Or perhaps they are the ones who have controlling personalities. Often, people don't even know when they're under the influence of controlling people but are likely to have one or more of the following illusions:

♦ They are stuck with another person's definition of them.
♦ They do not have the right to their own opinions.
♦ They can earn love and acceptance by abdicating to another person.
♦ They are "successful" if they fulfill another person's vision, even when it does not in any way support their own.
♦ They must have permission to act in matters that are their own business.

Patricia Evans is here to untangle the confusion with her latest book, **CONTROLLING PEOPLE:** *How To Recognize, Understand, And Deal With People Who Try To Control You* (January, 2002; $12.95 trade paperback; 352 pages; ISBN: 1-58062-569-X). This book takes us on a journey through a maze where we discover the words and incantations that produce a controller's spellbound behavior. And, we find out how to fend off any controller's attempts to control us.

Based on thousands of cases, **CONTROLLING PEOPLE** reveals how controllers struggle to shape the lives of others. The reader will discover the forces that compel them and why they, as if under a spell, often destroy the relationships that they want most to preserve—they usually don't realize the senselessness of their own behavior. In addition, the reader will meet some formerly spellbound controllers and find out what they have to say about their actions towards others.

In this important work, Patricia Evans provides insightful knowledge and advice on—

♦ How people become controlling.
♦ Why controllers target only certain people.
♦ Why controllers drive away the people they want to be closest to.
♦ Why controllers often get the opposite of what they want.
♦ Why most controllers appear to be nice normal people.
♦ What the controller fears most.
♦ Why controllers seem to be under the influence of a spell.
♦ How the "spell's" influence can be broken.
♦ How someone can be a spellbreaker.
♦ How someone could be under a controller's influence and not know it.
♦ What controllers say about themselves.

For anyone who is under the influence of this type of behavior, whether it be from a couple's relationship, parents, co-workers, peers, and/or friends, **CONTROLLING PEOPLE** will provide the wisdom, power and comfort they need to break through the debilitating spell.

Patricia Evans, author of *The Verbally Abusive Relationship*, is a speaker, consultant, and founder of the Evans Interpersonal Communications Institute in Alamo, CA. She conducts workshops and professional training throughout the country. She has appeared in numerous publications, including *Newsweek*, and on many television and radio shows including "Oprah".

Enclosed you'll find an advance copy of **CONTROLLING PEOPLE** for your review. Feel free to contact me directly if you need further information or would like to interview Patricia. For excerpt consideration, please contact Michael Kelly at 508-427-6716 or mjkellyamc@aol.com.

Best regards,
Carrie Lewis McGraw, Director of Publicity
508-427-6725 or Carrielewis1@aol.com

57 LITTLEFIELD STREET, AVON, MA 02322 • (508) 427-7100 • FAX: (508) 427-6790 • INTERNET: WWW.ADAMSMEDIA.COM

ADAMS
MEDIA CORPORATION

Chapel Hill author, Sol Gordon, Ph.D. wants to know...do you think you're <u>really</u> in love?

Nationally-acclaimed psychologist and author Dr. Sol Gordon can help your audience find out if they are—or aren't. His latest book, HOW CAN YOU TELL IF YOU'RE REALLY IN LOVE? (April 9, 2001; $7.95 Trade Paperback; 256 pages) provides insightful, common sense solutions, which spell out how to beat the odds and how to go about choosing the right partner.

A clinical psychologist, professor, and sex educator, Dr. Gordon has written hundreds of articles for professional journals, has authored twenty-two other books and has appeared on such national television shows as "Oprah," "Today," and "60 Minutes" to name a few.

He will be speaking about his book and signing copies at the following locations:

CHAPEL HILL

<u>Tuesday, April 10th:</u>

3:00pm-4:00pm   Bull's Head Bookshop
Talk/Q&A/Signing   UNC—Chapel Hill Campus
                                          Chapel Hill, NC 27599

RALEIGH

<u>Thursday, May 31st:</u>

7:30pm-9:00pm   Quail Ridge Books
Talk/Q&A/Signing   3522 Wade Avenue
                                         Raleigh, NC 27607

To schedule an interview with Dr. Sol Gordon, please contact: **Carrie Lewis McGraw**
                                                                   Director of Publicity
                                                                   (781) 607-5210
                                                                   Carrielewis1@aol.com

**HOW CAN YOU TELL IF YOU'RE
REALLY IN LOVE?
By Sol Gordon, Ph.D.
Publication Date: April 9, 2001
Price: $7.95 trade paperback; 256 pages
ISBN: 1-58062-472-3**

57 LITTLEFIELD STREET, AVON, MA 02322 • (508) 427-7100 • FAX: (508) 427-6790 • INTERNET: WWW.ADAMSMEDIA.COM

MEDIA CORPORATION

HOW CAN YOU TELL IF YOU'RE
REALLY IN LOVE?
by Sol Gordon, Ph.D.
Publication Date: April 9, 2001
Price: $7.95 trade paperback; 256 pages
ISBN: 1-58062-472-3

Contact: Carrie Lewis McGraw
Director of Publicity
(781) 607-5210
Carrielewis1@aol.com

Publicity Tour Schedule for
Dr. Sol Gordon

Friday, April 6 & Saturday, April 7	Portland, ME
Thursday, April 19 & Friday, April 20	Newport Beach, CA
Monday, April 23, Tuesday, April 24 & Wednesday, April 25	Los Angeles, CA
Monday, April 30	Rochester, NY
Wednesday, May 2 & Thursday, May 3	Spokane, WA
Monday, May 7	Portland, OR
Tuesday, May 15	St. Louis, MO
Thursday, May 24 & Friday, May 25	Atlanta, GA

57 LITTLEFIELD STREET, AVON, MA 02322 • (508) 427-7100 • FAX: (508) 427-6790 • INTERNET: WWW.ADAMSMEDIA.COM

Schedule as of 6/27/01:
Contact: Carrie Lewis McGraw, Director of Publicity
Tel: 781-607-5210 or Carrielewis1@aol.com

HOW CAN YOU TELL IF YOU'RE REALLY IN LOVE?
by Sol Gordon, Ph.D.
(April 9, 2001)

BOSTON, MA

Tuesday, February 13, 2001

Flight: Midway, #301; arrives into Boston at 11:54am. Joe is picking Sol up. Sol needs to call 800-298-6629 after he has claimed his baggage for car to meet him.

Sol will arrive at Adams at approximately 1pm. Company reception for Sol around 3:45pm.

Hotel: Sheraton
          100 Cabot St.
          Needham, MA
          Tel: 781-444-1110
          Confirmation#: 637111769

Wednesday, February 14, 2001

6:30am arrival   **"First Look"/NECN**
6:40am-6:45am   160 Wells Ave.
LIVE   Newton, MA 02459
                    Contact: Andrea Reese, 617-630-5000 ext. 6154; arees@necn.com
                    Host: Leslie. There will be no makeup done at the studio.

NORTH MIAMI, FL

Saturday, March 17, 2001

Flight: Midway, #864
Departs Raleigh: 5:50pm
Arrives Miami: 7:50pm

Hotel: Marriott Courtyard in Aventura

Sunday, March 18, 2000

9:30am-Noon   **Temple Sinai of North Dade** – Talk to parents about sex
                    18801 NE 22nd Ave.
                    North Miami Beach, FLL 33180
                    Contact: Rabbi James Simon, 305-932-9010

7pm-9pm   **Temple Sinai of North Dade** – Sol arranged; Michael getting 200 bks there
Singles Night   18801 NE 2nd Ave.
                    North Miami Beach, FL 33180, Rabbi James L. Simon, 305-932-9010
                    Fax: 305-932-2443

ADAMS
MEDIA CORPORATION

Tuesday, March 20, 2001

Flight:
Depart Miami: 11:45am
Arrives Raleigh: 1:45pm

Friday, March 23, 2001

10am-10:20am   **Detroit News** – Run date March 27th
Print interview   Contact: Alison Bethel, abethel@detnews.com

Wednesday, March 28, 2001

3:00pm-4:00pm   **"Love & Intimacy"/WebMD - NATIONAL**
LIVE online chat   720 SW Washington, Ste. 400
                    Portland, OR 97205-3537
                    Contact: Kate Royston, 503-943-3168, kroyston@webmd.net
Note: Kate will call you at home. You will do this interview via phone and Kate will type in your answers.
She likes longer, expansive answers as opposed to short answers. Just speak slowly so she has time to type
in your replies. You may contact her ahead of time with specific questions you want to make sure are cov-
ered. The site will actively promote the event prior to and after and will have a link to B&N.com for sales.

Wednesday, April 4, 2001

3pm-4pm   **Fort Wayne Journal-Gazette**
Print phoner   600 W. Main St.
                    Fort Wayne, IN 46802
                    Contact: Bonnie Blackburn, 219-461-8313
                    Note: Bonnie will call you at home. This piece will run
                    on or around 4/17

BANGOR, ME

Thursday, April 5, 2001

Flight:
Depart Raleigh: 11:10am
Arrive Bangor: 3:49pm

Hotel: Four Points Sheraton, 207-947-6721

Friday, April 6, 2001

9am-10am   **"Sexuality Educator of the Year" by the**
                    Margaret Vaughan Excellence Award in the State of Maine
                    Family Planning Association of Maine
                    43 Gabriel Drive
                    Augusta, ME 04330
                    Contact: Lynne Kaplowitz?, 207-622-7524

Depart Bangor: 4:05pm
Arrive Raleigh: 9:10pm

ADAMS
MEDIA CORPORATION

CHAPEL HILL, NC

Monday, April 9, 2001

9:35am-10:00am LIVE	**"Better Living Show"/WDNC-AM (620)** Contact: Moreton Neal, (H) 919-408-0567 Cel: 919-602-6266

Tuesday, April 10, 2001

2:45pm arrival 3:00pm-4:00pm Talk/Q&A/Signing	**Bull's Head Bookshop – UNC Student Store** Campus Box 1530 – Daniels Building Chapel Hill, NC 27599 Contact: Chelcy Boyer, 919-962-3450

Thursday, April 12, 2001

8:45am-9:00am LIVE phoner	**"Taylor & Rich: The Morning Mix"/KMXD-FM** Des Moines, IA Contact: Taylor Kaye, 515-242-3557 *Note: Taylor will call Sol at home.*

Monday, April 16, 2001

8:00am-8:10am LIVE phoner	**WKRH/WKRL Radio** 555 Route 31 Syracuse, NY 13030 Contact: Scorch, 315-633-0047 *Note: Scorch will call you at home.*
2:00pm-2:30pm EST Print interview via phone	**Spokesman-Review** Reporter: Dan Webster, 509-459-5483; danw@spokesman.com *Note: Dan will call you at home. This piece will run in early May when you are in Spokane.*
Print phoner	**Mademoiselle – for August issue** 268 Bush St., #3629 San Francisco, CA 94104 Contact: Mytien So, 415-860-9799; Elizabeth 212-286-8561 *Note: Mytien will call you on your cel phone.*

PALM SPRINGS, CA

Tuesday, April 17, 2001

Flight:	Southwest #699
Depart Raleigh:	8:10am
Arrive San Diego:	11:45am

Wednesday, April 18, 2001   **Speaking engagement**

57 LITTLEFIELD STREET, AVON, MA 02322 • (508) 427-7100 • FAX: (508) 427-6790 • INTERNET: WWW.ADAMSMEDIA.COM

ADAMS
MEDIA CORPORATION

NEWPORT BEACH, CA

Hotel: Sutton Place, 800-243-4141

Thursday, April 19, 2001   Open for PR

Friday, April 20, 2001   Open for PR

8:15pm-10:15pm   **"Bev Smith Show"/Nationally Syndicated**
LIVE phoner   960 Penn Ave.; Ste. 200
      Pittsburgh, PA 15222
      Contact: Richard Marshall, 412-560-4109
      Note: GREAT INTERVIEW per Sol!

Sunday, April 22, 2001   **Society for Scientific Study of Sexuality (SSSS)**

Morning   Keynote Speaker

Evening   Drive to LA – Sol at Bonnie Williams' home: 310-398-2548.

LOS ANGELES, CA

Monday, April 23, 2001

2:30pm   **Lunch Interview with writer Susan Perry**
      Early World Restaurant
      11938 San Vicente Blvd.
      Brentwood, CA
      Restaurant: 310-826-3246
      Susan: 323-667-2638

Note: This ended up happening via phone. She sells articles to United Parenting Publications (including LA Parent & 22 others), Valley Magazine, various websites. She's also researching a new book on long-term relationships. You may view her writing at www.bunnyape.com.

6:45pm arrival   **Book Star – few people**
7:00pm-8:00pm   100 N. La Cienega Blvd.
Talk/Q&A/Signing   Los Angeles, CA 90048
      Contact: Ryan McQuane, 310-289-0944

Tuesday, April 24, 2001

Booked all day   Sol is speaking at the University High School.

7:15pm arrival   **Book Star – few people**
7:30pm-8:30pm   12136 Ventura Blvd.
      Studio City, CA 91604
      Contact: Shelly Hungerford, 818-505-6914; store: 818-505-9528

57 LITTLEFIELD STREET, AVON, MA 02322 • (508) 427-7100 • FAX: (508) 427-6790 • INTERNET: WWW.ADAMSMEDIA.COM

MEDIA CORPORATION

Wednesday, April 25, 2001

6:30pm-9:30pm CANCELLED for lack Of people	**The Learning Annex** – Ramada Hotel in Culver City 11850 Wilshire Blvd., Ste. 100 Los Angeles, CA 90025 Contact: Jillian Greene, 310-478-6677

Thursday, April 26, 2001

Open for PR

Flight: Northwest
Depart Los Angeles: 10:15pm
Arrive Detroit: 5:33am

ROCHESTER, NY

Friday, April 27, 2001

Depart Detroit: 8:20am
Arrive Rochester: 9:29am

12:45pm arrival 1:00pm-2:00pm 6-7 min. segment Taping	**"Rochester in Focus"/WHEC-TV (NBC—CH. 10)** 191 East Avenue Rochester, NY 14604-2695 Host/Producer: Richard McCollough, 716-546-0708 or 546-5670

6pm   Dinner with 7th & 8th graders

8pm Guest Speaker	**Temple B'rith Kodesh – Lovenheim Lecture Series** **"Are we neglecting our friends?" – open to public** 2131 Elmwood Ave. Rochester, NY 14618 Contact: Rabbi Robert Morais, 716-244-7060 x229, tbkrabbi@usa.net

Saturday, April 28, 2001

Booked all day

Evening Dinner & Speech	**"Living Fully Now" – open to public** 40+ and 60+ Jewish Singles Temple B'rith Kodesh 2131 Elmwood Ave. Rochester, NY 14618 Contact: Carol Lykner, 716-244-7060 ext. 228

Sunday, April 29, 2001

10am-Noon Lecture	**"When Living Hurts" – open to public** Temple B'rith Kodesh – Adult Lounge 2131 Elmwood Ave. Rochester, NY 14618 Contact: Carol Lykner, 716-244-7060 ext. 228

57 LITTLEFIELD STREET, AVON, MA 02322 • (508) 427-7100 • FAX: (508) 427-6790 • INTERNET: WWW.ADAMSMEDIA.COM

Appendix B
Resource Directory

Booklist

Confessions of Shameless Self-Promoters. Debbie Allen.
   Success Showcase Publishing, 2002.
Dan Janal's Guide to Marketing on the Internet. Daniel S.
   Janal. John Wiley & Sons, 2000.
The Father of Spin. Larry Tye. Crown Publishers, Inc., 1998.
Guerrilla Marketing for Writers. Jay Conrad Levinson, Rick
   Frishman, and Michael Larsen. Writer's Digest Books,
   2001.
High-Impact Marketing on a Low-Impact Budget. John Krember
   and J. Daniel McComas. Prima Publishing, 1997.
How to Get Publicity. William Parkhurst. Harper Business, 2000.
Internet Marketing for Less than $500/Year. Marcia Yudkin.
   Maximum Press, 2000.
Multiple Streams of Internet Income. Robert G. Allen. John
   Wiley & Sons, 2001.
101 Ways to Promote Yourself. Raleigh Pinskey. Mass

Market Paperback, 1997.

Words That Sell. Richard Bayan. Caddylak Publishing, 1984.

Sell Yourself Without Selling Your Soul. Susan Harrow.
HarperCollins, 2002.

Media Directories

Bacon's Media Directors—*www.bacons.com/directories/
maindirectories.asp*

Broadcasting & Cable Yearbook—*www.bowker.com*

Burrelle's Media Directory—*www.burrelles.com/
indexmd.html*

Editor and Publisher International Yearbook—11 W. 19th
Street, New York, NY 10001, (212) 675-4380

Media Finder—*www.mediafinder.com*

MediaMap Online—*www.mediamaponeline.com*

National Directory of Magazines—*www.mediafinder.com/
secure/product1.cfm*

Online Public Relations—*www.online-pr.com*

Radio Publicity—*www.radiopublicity.com/gp*

Standard Periodical Directory—*www.mediafinder.com/
secure/product1.cfm*

Standard Rate and Data Service—*www.srds.com*

Newsletters

Guerrilla Marketing—*www.jayconradlevinson.com*

Guerrilla Publicity—*www.guerrillapublicity.com*

Internet.com—*www.channelseven.com*

InternetPRGuide—*www.internetprguide.com*

Media Map—*www.mediamap.com/webpr*

Promising Promotion—*www.promisingpromotion.com*

Radio-TV Interview Report—*www.freepublicity.com*

Ragan Communications—*www.ragan.com*

The Tip Sheet—*www.plannedtvarts.com*

Publicity Organizations

International Association of Business Communicators
One Hallidie Plaza, Suite 600
San Francisco, CA 94102-2818
Tel: (415) 544-4700, Fax: (415) 544-4747
Web Site: *www.iabc.com*
Customer Service Center e-mail:service_center@iabc.com

Public Relations Society of America
33 Irving Place
New York, NY 10003
Tel: (212) 995-2230, Fax: (212) 995-0757
Web Site: *www.prsa.org*

Public Relations Student Society of America
33 Irving Place
New York, NY 10003
Tel: (212) 460-1474, Fax: (212) 995-0757
Web Site: *www.prssa.org*

Publishers Publicity Association
299 Park Avenue
New York, NY 10017
E-mail: nlatimer@randomhouse.com

Top 100 U.S. Metropolitan Markets

(Source: Bacons Info)
1. Los Angeles-Long Beach, CA
2. New York, NY
3. Chicago, IL
4. Boston-Worcester-Lawrence-Lowell-Brockton, MA
5. Philadelphia, PA
6. Washington, DC-MD-VA-WVA
7. Detroit, MI
8. Houston, TX

9. Atlanta, GA
10. Riverside-San Bernadino, CA
11. Dallas, TX
12. Minneapolis-St. Paul, MN-WI
13. San Diego, CA
14. Nassau-Suffolk, NY
15. St. Louis, MO-IL
16. Orange County, CA
17. Baltimore, MD
18. Phoenix-Mesa, AZ
19. Pittsburgh, PA
20. Seattle-Bellevue-Everett, WA
21. Cleveland-Lorain-Elyria, OH
22. Oakland, CA
23. Tampa-St. Petersburg-Clearwater, FL
24. Miami, FL
25. Newark, NJ
26. Denver, CO
27. Portland-Vancouver, OR-WA
28. Kansas City, MO-KS
29. San Francisco, CA
30. New Haven-Bridgeport-Stamford-Waterbury-Danbury, CT
31. Cincinnati, OH
32. San Jose, CA
33. Norfolk-Virginia Beach-Newport News, VA-NC
34. Ft. Worth-Arlington, TX
35. Sacramento, CA
36. Milwaukee-Waukesha, WI
37. Indianapolis, IN
38. San Antonio, TX
39. Columbus, OH
40. Orlando, FL
41. Ft. Lauderdale, FL
42. New Orleans, LA
43. Bergen-Passaic, NJ
44. Charlotte-Gastonia-Rock Hill, NC

45. Salt Lake City-Ogden, UT
46. Buffalo-Niagara Falls, NY
47. Greensboro-Winston Salem-High Point, NC
48. Hartford, CT
49. Rochester, NY
50. Nashville, TN
51. Las Vegas, NV
52. Middlesex-Somerset-Hunterdon, NJ
53. Memphis, TN-AR-MS
54. Monmouth Ocean, NJ
55. Oklahoma City, OK
56. Louisville, KY
57. Grand Rapids-Muskegon-Holland, MI
58. West Palm Beach-Boca Raton, FL
59. Austin-San Marcos, TX
60. Raleigh-Durham-Chapel Hill, NC
61. Dayton-Springfield, OH
62. Jacksonville, FL
63. Richmond-Petersburg, VA
64. Providence-Warwick-Pawtucket, RI
65. Honolulu, HI
66. Albany-Schenectady-Troy, NY
67. Birmingham, AL
68. Greenville-Spartanburg-Anderson, SC
69. Fresno, CA
70. Syracuse, NY
71. Tulsa, OK
72. Tucson, AZ
73. Ventura, CA
74. El Paso, TX
75. Akron, OH
76. Omaha, NE-IA
77. Tacoma, WA
78. Albuquerque, NJ
79. Scranton-Wilkes Barre-Hazleton, PA
80. Knoxville, TN

81. Bakersfield, CA
82. Allentown-Bethlehem-Easton, PA
83. Gary, IN
84. Toledo, OH
85. Harrisburg-Lebanon-Carlisle, PA
86. Youngstown-Warren, OH
87. Springfield, MA
88. Baton Rouge, LA
89. Wilmington, NC
90. Charleston-North Charleston, SC
91. Jersey City, NJ
92. Little Rock-North Light Rock, AR
93. Sarasota-Bradenton, FL
94. Stockton-Lodi, CA
95. Mobile, AL
96. Wichita, KS
97. Ann Arbor, MI
98. Vallejo-Fairfield-Napa, CA
99. Columbia, SC
100. Fort Wayne, IN

Training Resources

Action Plan Marketing—*www.actionplan.com*
Tom Antion & Associates—*www.antion.com*
The Ford Group—*www.fordsisters.com*
Paul Hartunian—*www.prprofits.com*
Raleigh Pinskey's Promote Yourself—*www.promoteyourself.com*
Publicity Builder—*www.jian.com*
Joel Roberts and Associates—(310) 286-0631
Susan Harrow—*www.prsecrets.com*
Joan Stewart—*www.publicityhound.com*

The Guerrilla Marketing Hall of Fame

Besides being innovative, dedicated guerrillas, the following individuals have been constant sources of information and inspiration to other guerrillas. After blazing new trails, these pioneers have authored books that explain how other guerrillas can follow their lead. Their books stand as landmarks—testimonials to the principles of guerrilla marketing, its ease of implementation, and the results that guerrillas can achieve.

We salute and thank these guerrillas for their daring, their insights, their wisdom, and, most importantly, their generosity in graciously sharing their experiences, understanding, and knowledge with us. And, we hereby recognize them as outstanding examples of the best of guerrilla marketing:

Jay Abraham, author of *Getting Everything You Can Out of All You've Got*

Jack Canfield and Mark Victor Hansen, coauthors of the *Chicken Soup* series

Greg Godek, author of *Intimate Questions, Love: The Course They Forgot to Teach You in School, The Love Quotes Coupon Book, Romantic Essentials: Hundreds of Ways to Show Your Love,* and *Enchanted Evenings*

Seth Godin of Yahoo!, author of *Permission Marketing, Unleashing the Idea Virus, If You're Clueless About Starting Your Own Business and Want to Know More* and coauthor of *The Guerrilla Marketing Handbook*

Daniel S. Janal, author of *Dan Janal's Guide to Marketing on the Internet, The Online Marketing Handbook,* and *101 Businesses You Can Start On The Internet*

Jerrold Jenkins of the Jenkins Group, publisher of *Independent Publisher* and coauthor of *Publish to Win* and *Inside the Bestsellers*

John Kremer of Open Horizons, coauthor of *High Impact Marketing on a Low-Impact Budget,* author of *1001 Ways to Market Your Books,* and editor of *Book Marketing Update*

Harvey Mackay, CEO of Mackay Envelope, syndicated columnist and author of *Swim With the Sharks Without Being Eaten Alive, Pushing the Envelope All the Way to the Top,* and *Beware the Naked Man Who Offers You His Shirt*

Jan and Terry Nathan, executive and assistant directors of
Publishers Marketing Association, sponsor of PMA's
Publishing University.

Dan Poynter of Para Publishing, author of the *Self-Publishing
Manual*

Tom and Marilyn Ross, cofounders of the Small Publishers
Association and coauthors of the *Complete Guide to Self-
Publishing* and *Jump Start Your Book Sales*

Dottie Walters, popular speaker and coauthor of *Speak and
Grow Rich*, *The Mighty Power of Your Beliefs*, and *101
Simple Things to Grow Your Business*

Index

A

advance men, 111
advertising, xv, 31
Airborne (overnight delivery), 85
A List contacts, 62–63
Alta Vista, 204
anecdotes, 83
Annual Report Gallery, 198
answering machines, 70, 125, 126–27, 221
appeal, 95
appearances, 81
    See also special events
articles
    distribution, 35, 36
    on e-zines, 213
    and marketing plans, 37, 39
    in media kits, 81–82, 83
    samples, 271–72

Web links to, 187
assertiveness, 113–14
attachments, e-mail, 220
attitude, 97, 113–14, 149
audiences, 41–44, 94, 106

B

Bacon's Information, Inc., 200
Bacon's International, Inc., 201
Bacon's Media Directories, 43
Bacon's MediaList Online, 43, 60, 199
Belasco, David, 12
biographies, personal, 80, 241–42, 258, 262–63
Blair Witch Project, 183
B List contacts, 63
books, 285–86
    writing, 161–67

See also publications
boxes, 273
brevity, 94, 112
Broadcasting & Cable
    Yearbook, 43
brochures, 17, 38, 39, 81
budget, publicity, 34
bulleted items, 55–56
bulletin boards, online. *See*
    discussion groups, online
Burrelle's Media Directory,
    43, 60, 199
business cards, 17, 73, 82–83
business checklist, 103–4
Business 2.0 (online), 199
business schools, 199
Business Wire, 186, 189, 200,
    210
buying audiences, 42

C

calendars, 112, 201
Canadian Corporate Newsnet,
    186
CASH, 60–62
celebrities, appeal of, 96
    See also name dropping
Chambers, C. P., 45
chambers of commerce, 137
The Channel Guide, 199
chat rooms. *See* discussion
    groups, online
Clip Explorer, 200
clipping services, 200–201
C List contacts, 63
coaches, media, 121–22
cold calls, 89
community colleges, 156

company histories, 79–80
competition, 106
complementary fields, 144–45
conferences, 156, 157, 236
confidence, customer, 177–79
confirmation calls, 90
    See also following up
consultants, public relations,
    226–27, 231
contact information, 84, 188
conventions, 157, 236
Copyright Office, 198
Cortese, Richard A., 34
courtesy, 96
credibility. *See* honesty
crisis control, 177–80
customers, 107, 177–79
CyberAlert, 200

D

Deep Canyon, 201
direct mailings, 58
directories
    of directories, 199
    of e-zines, 214
    media, 199–200, 286
    of publicity resources,
        285–92
    of public relations firms, 227
Direct-PR, 201
disasters, handling, 177–80
discussion groups, online, 187,
    199, 203–8
    and market research, 204
    posting to, 205–7
    press releases on, 206, 210
    Web sites for, 204

distribution services, online, 200, 210–11

DMOZ, 197

domain names, 221–22

E

eclip.com, 201

Eichenwald, Kurt, 31

e-mail

  advantages of, 94, 151, 217–23, 236

  capital letters in, 219

  and domain names, 221–22

  following up by, 70

  initial contact by, 89

  and links to Web sites, 219–20

  on mailing list services, 214–15

  marketing by, 221

  replying to, 127, 219

  sending files through, 220

  signature files, 187, 207, 222

  subject lines, 220–21

envelopes, 84

eReleases, 189, 200

Essen, Richard, 49

eWatch, 201

experience, 95, 227

expertise, 4–6, 236

  and book-writing, 162

  and FAQs, 215–16

  and self-promotion, 19–21

  and seminars, 154

e-zines, 211, 213–14

e-zines.com, 214

eZineSearch, 214

Ezine Universe.com, 214

F

fact sheets, 215–16

  sample, 243–44

familiarity, 2–3

FAQs, 215–16

faxes, 70, 94

Federal Express, 85

Federal Web Locator, 198

FedEx, 85

financial information, 79–80, 198–99

focus, lack of, 90

folders, 84

following up, 65–75, 235

  and answering machines, 70

  and business cards, 73

  by e-mail, 70

  by fax, 70

  on media requests, 91

  persistence in, 67–72

  records, 72

  techniques, 68–74

  by telephone, 69–72

  See also confirmation calls

follow-up log, 72

food, 89

Forbes (online), 199

forms on FAQ pages, 216

frequently asked questions (FAQs), 215–16

Frishman, Rick, 45, 117

  contact information, 236

G

General Accounting Office, 198

ghostwriters, 163

gifts, 89

   See also self-promotion, materials

gimmicks, 90–91

giveaways, 83–84, 89

global reach, 182–83

goals, setting, 43–44

Good Morning America, 121

Google, 197

graphic displays, 35–36

The Guerrilla Group, 200

Guerrilla Marketing, 200, 290–92

Guerrilla Marketing Online, 214

Guerrilla Publicity website, 200, 214

guerrillas, xiii–xiv, 200

H

Haas School of Business, University of California, 199

headlines, 54–56, 129–33

honesty, 47–49, 88, 172, 234

Hoover's (Web site), 198

I

Imediafax, 210

The Info Service, 199

Internet, xv, 184–85, 236

financial information on, 198–99

global reach of, 182–83

and media lists, 60

public speaking groups on, 122

research on, 197–202

seminars on, 155, 156

and specialization, 183–84

statistics, 200

surveys, 200

trade associations on, 197–98

United States government agencies on, 198

   See also discussion groups, online; Web sites

Internet.com, 213

Internet News, 210

Internet News Bureau, 189, 200, 211

InternetPRGuide, 213

The Internet Public Library, 198

Internet Wire, 189, 200, 211

interviewers, 118, 120–21, 122, 169–74

interviews

   components of, 119–20

   conduct during, 118–22

   evaluation of performance in, 122–23

   and hiring public relations professionals, 229–30

   and introduction of product/service, 37, 38

   preparation for, 115–18, 169–74, 235–36

questions, 80–81, 119–20,
    245–48
sample, 256–57

J, K

Janal, Dan, 186
Kellogg Graduate School of
    Management, Northwestern
    University, 199
Kraft, Joan, 108

L

lectures, 6
letters, 251, 259, 264, 273–77
Levinson, Jay Conrad, 236
Library of Congress, 198
Lillo, Steve, 191, 193
links, 186, 187, 194, 219–20
Liszt, 215
literary agents, 166–67
logos, 31, 188
Lublin, Jill, 21, 27
    contact information, 236
Luce Press Clippings, 201

M

magazines, online, 199
mailing list services, online,
    203, 211, 214–15
    See also discussion
        groups, online
market area, 4
marketing, 33, 221
market research, 204
markets, top 100 U.S., 287–90

McCann, Jim, 48
media, 42–43
    directories, 199–200, 286
    dislikes, 87–91
    likes, 93–100
    and press releases, 51–56
    print, 51–53, 80–81, 200
    schedules, 45, 112
    at trade shows, 138
    See also relationships,
        building
media campaigns, 35–39, 234
    printed materials in, 37,
        38, 39
    samples, 264–67
    schedules, 111–14
    targeting, 41–44, 94, 106
    timing, 109
media centers, Web site,
    187–89
Media Finder, 43, 60, 199
media kits, 37, 77–86
    articles in, 81–82, 83
    brochures in, 81
    business cards in, 82–83
    content, 79–84
    distribution, 85, 112
    giveaways in, 83–84, 89
    packaging of, 84–85
    photographs in, 82
    press releases in, 78
    samples, 251–58, 278–80
    size of, 88–89
    suggested interview
        questions in, 80–81
    updating, 125–26
media lists, 57–63
    categorizing, 62–63
    compiling, 58–59

maintaining, 60–62, 68–74
and press releases, 210
Media Map, 201, 211, 213
MediaMap Online, 43, 60, 200
media outlets, 43
message boards, online. *See*
discussion groups, online
Messaging Online, 217
meta tags, 186
minority groups, 107–8
missions, 192–93
Murphy's Law, 174–75

N

name dropping, 90
See also celebrities,
appeal of
name recognition, 2–3
National Directory of
Magazines, 43
National Speakers
Association, 122
networks, 141–45
news, 93, 95, 125–26, 174
News Directory.com, 199
newsgroups. *See* discussion
groups, online
NewsHub, 210, 211
newsletters, 286
e-mail, 221
and media campaigns,
38, 39
online, 211–13
Newslinx, 211
newspapers, online, 199
news rooms, 187–89
New York Times (online), 199
NorthernLight, 204

O

*O'Dwyer's Directory of Public
Relations Firms,* 227
one sheets, 56, 78
See also press releases
Online Public Relations, 43,
60, 200
Oprah Winfrey Show, 45
organizations, publicity, 287
overnight delivery, 85

P

packaging of media kits,
84–85
Patent and Trademark Office,
198
perceptions, 106–7
persistence, 9, 67–69, 72,
74, 87
personal acts, 26
personal checklist, 101–2
photographs in media kits, 82
Planned Television Arts
(PTA), 126
positioning, 106–7
postcards, pre-order, 36
preparation, 88, 95, 173–74
PressAccess, 201
press conferences, 179
press kits. *See* media kits
press releases, 51–56, 235
bulleted items in, 55–56
content, 56
distribution, 36, 186–89,
209–11, 220
length, 88
in media kits, 78

on online discussion
groups, 206, 210
and print media, 51–53
on radio and television,
51, 54
samples, 238–40, 269–70
updating, 125–26
writing, 53
press rooms, 187–89
print media
media kits for, 80–81
online, 200
and press releases, 51–53
PR Newswire, 186, 189, 200,
211
producers, 54–55, 80
products
introduction, 35–39
promotion of, 2–4, 30–31,
177–80, 211, 234
ProfNet, 201
promoters, 157
promptness, 96
PRWeb, 211
publications
books, 161–67, 285–86
brochures, 17, 38, 39, 81
newsletters, 38–39, 211,
212–13, 221, 286
online, 211–16
See also articles
publicists, in-house, 227
publicity campaigns. See
media campaigns
Publicly Accessible Mailing
Lists, 215
public relations, xiv–xv
agencies, 226
consultants, 226–27, 231

directories of firms, 227
hiring professionals for,
225–31
public speaking groups, 122
publishers, 164–66
puns, 108

Q

questions
answering, 120, 171–72
on FAQ forms, 216
interview, 80–81, 119–20,
245–48
posting online, 201–2
in seminars, 158–59
quizzes, 83

R

radio, 11, 51, 54, 80
Ragan Communications, 213
Reference Desk, 199
ReferencePage.com, 199
referrals, 141, 143–45
rejection, 26, 44
and persistence, 74
using to your advantage,
66–67, 175
relationships, building, 8–9,
23–27, 94, 141–45, 147–51,
234–35
records of, 61–62
and special events, 135–40
reputations, 177–80
Resources for Economists, 200
responsibility for disasters,
178–80

Ring Surf, 208
Roberts, Joel, 121
Rule of Seven, 74

S

sales, 159–60
search engines, 204
self-promotion, 29–32
   and expertise, 19–21
   materials, 31, 83–84, 215
   as product, 2–4, 30–31,
      177–80, 211, 234
self-publication, 164–66, 211
seminars, 154–60
   at community colleges, 156
   at conferences and
      conventions, 157
   and the Internet, 155, 156
   organizing, 154–55
   for promoters, 157
   questions in, 158–59
   sales at, 159–60
   for service clubs, 155–56
   teaching, 154–58
service clubs, 155–56
services, introduction of, 35–39
75/25, 212
signature files, 187, 207, 222
small talk, 88
solutions, 120
sound bites, 11–17
   content, 12–14
   customizing, 16–17
   delivering, 16, 22
   for radio, 11
   samples, 259–63
   for television, 11
   writing, 15–16

spam, 194, 222
special events, 135–40
specialization, 183–84
speeches, 6
staff, 22
   See also public relations,
      hiring professionals
Standard Periodical Directory,
   43
Stanford Graduate School of
   Business, 199
statistics, Internet, 200
strategies, online publicity,
   209–16
subject lines, e-mail, 220–21
surveys, Internet, 200

T

talks, 6
teaching, 120, 154–58
telephone, 69–72
television, 11, 51, 54, 80
The Tenagra Apogee, 214
testimonials, 7
   and media campaigns, 39
   and positioning, 106
   samples, 252–53
Tile.Net/Lists, 215
Toastmasters International, 122
tour date schedules, 268, 279–84
trade associations, 197–98
trade shows, 137–39, 236
training resources, 290
translations, foreign, 200
trivia, 83

U

uniqueness, 99–109
  capitalizing on, 105–9, 113
  identifying, 101–4
United Parcel Service, 85
United States Census Bureau, 198
United States government agencies, 198
United States Postal Service, 85
United States Securities and Exchange Commission, 198

V

The Virtual Reference Desk, 200
Virtual Sites, 199
viruses, 222
visual aids, 96
visualization, 95–96
voice mail, 221

W

Wall Street Journal (online), 199
Webclipping.com, 201
Web Digest for Marketers, 214
Web rings, 207–8
Web sites
  advantages of, 181–84
  contact information on, 188
  content, 188, 191, 194–95
  design, 185–87, 190–94

for discussion groups, 204
downloadable files on, 220
FAQs on, 215
links, 186, 187, 194, 219–20
and media campaigns, 39
media centers on, 187–89
newsletters on, 212
press releases on, 186–87, 209–10
reflection of mission on, 192–93
registration, 186, 189
reviews of, 191
and seminars, 155
sensitive information on, 188
testimonials on, 7
traffic on, 187–90, 193–94, 200, 207–8
updating, 125, 126, 194
  See also Internet
Wharton School of the University of Pennsylvania, 199
Wired (online), 199
writing. *See* publications

Y

Yahoo, 198
Yahoo Web Ring, 208
"Year-End 2000 Mailbox Report," 217

Jay Conrad Levinson

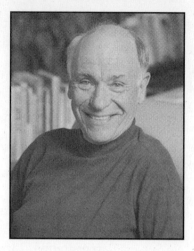

J ay Conrad Levinson is the author of the best-selling marketing series in history, *Guerrilla Marketing,* plus twenty-eight other business books. His "Guerrilla" concepts have influenced marketing so much that today, his books appear in thirty-seven languages and are required reading in many MBA programs worldwide.

Jay taught Guerrilla marketing for ten years at the extension division of the University of California in Berkeley. He was also a practitioner of it in the United States, as Senior Vice President at J. Walter Thompson, and in Europe, as Creative Director and Board Member at Leo Burnett Advertising.

He has written a monthly column for *Entrepreneur Magazine*, articles for *Inc. Magazine,* and online columns published monthly on the Microsoft Web site, in addition to occasional columns in the *San Francisco Examiner*. He also writes online columns for several Internet Web sites, including Netscape, America Online, and *Fortune* Small Business.

Jay is the chairman of Guerrilla Marketing International, a marketing partner of Adobe and Apple. He has served on the Microsoft Small Business Council and the 3Com Small Business Advisory Board. His *Guerrilla Marketing* is series of books, audiotapes, videotapes, an award-winning CD-ROM, a newsletter, a consulting organization, a Web site, and a way for you to spend less, get more, and achieve substantial profits.

Jay can be reached at:
www.jayconradlevinson.com
or (800) 748-6444

Rick Frishman

Rick Frishman, president of Planned Television Arts since 1982, is the driving force behind PTA's exceptional growth. In 1993, PTA merged with Ruder*Finn and Rick now serves as an executive vice president at Ruder*Finn. While supervising PTA's success, he has remained one of the most powerful and energetic publicists in the media industry.

Rick continues to work with many of the top editors, agents, and publishers in America, including Simon & Schuster, Random House, Harper Collins, Pocket Books, Penguin Putnam, and Hyperion Books. Some of the authors he has worked with include: Bill Moyers, Richard Preston, Mark Victor Hansen, Hugh Downs, Henry Kissinger, Jack Canfield, Alan Deshowitz, Arnold Palmer, and Harvey Mackay.

Rick joined the company in 1976 after working as a producer at WOR-AM in New York City. He has a B.F.A. in acting and directing and a B.S. from Ithaca College School of Communications. Rick is a sought-after lecturer on publishing and public relations and is a member of PRSA and the National Speakers Association. He and his wife Robbi live in Long Island with their three children, Adam, Rachel and Stephanie, and a cockapoo named Rusty.

Rick is the coauthor of *Guerrilla Marketing for Writers: 100 Weapons for Selling Your Work* with Jay Conrad Levinson and literary agent Michael Larsen (Writer's Digest Books).

Rick can be reached at:
Planned Television Arts
1110 Second Avenue, New York, NY 10022
Phone: (212) 593-5845
E-mail: Frishmanr@plannedtvarts.cm
Web site: *www.plannedtvarts.com*

Jill Lublin

Since 1985, Jill Lublin has been CEO of the public relations strategic consulting firm Promising Promotion. She is a dynamic, sought-after international speaker on public relations and marketing.

Working with ABC, NBC, CBS, CNN, and other national media has given her great insight into what gets results in the media. She works with diverse clientele—from financial institutions and technology companies to national and international seminar leaders, nonprofit organizations, authors, entertainment professionals, and entrepreneurs. Her clients have been featured in major newspapers and national magazines including *The Wall Street Journal, USA Today, Fast Company, Entrepreneur, Inc.,* and *Fortune Small Business* as well as television shows such as *The Today Show, Live with Regis and Kelly,* and *Good Morning America.*

Jill is the host of the nationally syndicated radio program, "Do the Dream," on which she interviews celebrities, CEOs, and extraordinary people who are achieving their dreams. Her guests have included Deepak Chopra and the author of *The Four Agreements,* Don Miguel Ruiz. "Do the Dream" is a joint venture between GoodNews Media Inc. and PCBroadcast.com.

Jill is also a member of the National Speakers Association and the National Association of Women Business Owners, and founder of GoodNews Media, Inc., a media production and distribution company dedicated to positive news and information. Jill has authored several audio programs including "7 Key Points to Powerful Publicity" and "Insider's Edge to Powerful Publicity" as well as a PR workbook, *Insider's Edge to Powerful Publicity.*

Jill can be reached at:
Promising Promotion
PO Box 5428, Novato, CA 94948
Phone: 415-883-5455; e-mail: info@promisingpromotion.com
Web site: *www.promisingpromotion.com*